OSGATH

PARISH REGISTERS & BISHOP'S TRANSCRIPTS 1583 – 1891

NEIL ROE

WEST GOSCOTE PRESS

Published by West Goscote Press, 2002
6 Ashbrook, Stapenhill, Burton on Trent, Staffs. DE15 9FS.
Further copies are available from the author at the above address.

ISBN 0 9543442 0 0

Cover illustration: Osgathorpe Church (S.E.) 1795 from an original print, watermarked 1811 in the ownership of the author, from J. Nichols, '*The History & Antiquities of the County of Leicester*', (4 vols, 1795–1811)

ACKNOWLEDGEMENTS
Many thanks to The Record Office for
Leicestershire, Leicester & Rutland,
Long Street, Wigston Magna, for allowing access to the
original registers, bishop's transcripts &
marriage licence allegations & bonds.
Also to the
Parochial Church Council of St Mary the Blessed Virgin Osgathorpe,
for their permission to publish this transcript.
Miss Lesley Hale, Swannington
Mr Robert Owen Jones, Osgathorpe
Mr Andrew William & Mrs Deborah Christine Roe, Netherseal

Printed in the UK by Parchment (Oxford) Ltd, Crescent Road, Cowley.

OSGATHORPE

PARISH REGISTERS & BISHOP'S TRANSCRIPTS 1583 – 1891

CONTENTS

ILLUSTRATIONS

Large Illustrations

Small Illustrations

Figures

MANUSCRIPT SOURCES

OSGATHORPE PARISH REGISTERS
Leics. Record Office. DE 1668/1 – 8. & DE 3967/1 – 2.
OSGATHORPE BISHOP'S TRANSCRIPTS
Leics. Record Office. 1D41/3 or Microfilm 384.
MARRIAGE LICENCE ALLEGATIONS & BONDS
Leics. Record Office. 1D 41/38 +year.

'Wherever anything lives, there is, open somewhere, a register in which time is being inscribed'

(Henri Bergson, *Creative Evolution*. Ch. 1.)

ABBREVIATIONS

b.	= Born	BT	= Bishop's Transcript
s./	= Son of	d./	= Daughter of
w./	= Wife of	b./	= both of
pa.	= Parish	JAN	= January (*etc*)
Bs	= Marriage by Banns	Lic	= Marriage by Licence
ofa	= of full age (21 & over)	c./ p.	= Consent of Parents

[ ] = Info added from another source / abbr. expanded

\- = No further information recorded

-/ = Sex of child not stated

P.[B]. = Private Baptism

MI = Monumental Inscription (erected)

* = Will or Letters of Administration (known to exist)

b./ this pa. & of this pa. = Osgathorpe (in all instances)

LATIN NAMES & WORDS

Latin names & words have been included as they appear in the original records, but are *italicised.* A translation for the more difficult entries is provided in the footnotes. Most names, although prone to the usual errors in spelling, employ only an extension such as 'us', 'es', 'i' & 'a'.

FRANCISCI / FFRANNCE	= FRANCIS / FRANCES
GULIELMS / GULI[H]ELMI / WILLYEMI	= WILLIAM
JACOB	= JAMES / JACOB
JOHANNES / JHONNES / JHON	= JOHN
MARIA	= MARY
SARA	= SARAH
THOM[A]E	= THOMAS

INTRODUCTION

This book is a transcript & index of the parish registers for the ancient parish of Osgathorpe, situated in West Goscote Hundred in N.W. Leicestershire. It also includes entries from the bishop's transcripts, which in the case of Osgathorpe have survived prior to the oldest surviving register. Additional information has also been included from marriage licence allegations & bonds, which frequently between 1683 & 1753 gave information that was not recorded in either the registers or bishop's transcripts. (See chapter 3, Marriage at Osgathorpe)

Doubtful Entries

The entries have been extracted from the original registers & bishop's transcripts, which are deposited in the Record Office for Leicestershire, Leicester & Rutland. The condition of these records and the clarity of the entries are excellent. However, where an entry was doubtful then a '?' has been used immediately preceding the word in question, without a space. (e.g. ?Riate)

Cross-checking

All the register entries have been cross-checked against all of the surviving bishop's transcripts and those entries that differed significantly are indicated in the footnotes. Marriages have additionally been cross-checked against the banns registers and marriage licence allegations & bonds, with any additional information being incorporated. One can consider the entries to be an amalgamation of all the information from the registers, bishop's transcripts and marriage licence allegations & bonds.

Spellings

All names and words have been transcribed exactly as spelt; consequently the reader should look under all variants. Where a particular spelling differed in the register, bishop's transcript or marriage allegation & bond, then the most common spelling has been used and any major differences placed in the footnotes.

Dates

All dates, although abbreviated & occasionally translated from Latin, are as written and have not been altered to account for calendar changes. Prior to 1752, the year started on Lady Day the 25 March with January, February & March being the 10, 11 & 12 months of each year. However, Chesterfield's Act of Parliament stated that from 1752 the year should begin on 1 January.

Accuracy

Great effort has been taken to verify names & places for accuracy by cross-checking them against other primary source material, including the censuses for England & Wales 1841–1901; parish chest records for Osgathorpe & other parishes; taxation records; wills & administrations; marriage licence allegations & bonds; maps & other geographical material. While great care has been taken to avoid any errors, a few may still exist, and it is recommended that the reader consult the original primary source for verification.

Baptism, Burial & Marriage Sections

Baptism, Burial, & Marriage entries have been separated into three sections, which also include the appropriate entries from the bishop's transcripts that pre-date the oldest surviving register.

Additional Information

This transcript also includes additional information, such as the witnesses to marriages and the names & occupations of the bride's & groom's fathers. It also indicates if wills, letters of administration or monumental inscriptions are known to exist for those being buried. Further details regarding the latter three are available at the Record Office for Leicestershire, Leicester & Rutland, Long Street, Wigston Magna, Leicester, LE18 2AH.

FOREWORD

In 1991, I began to take an interest in local & family history that I had started in a limited sense as a boy. Shortly after this resurgence of interest, I discovered my family's connection with the parish of Osgathorpe. This connection now dates back to at least the reign of Henry VIII and to a number of local families. My Roe ancestors first came to the village in 1739 but ended with the death, in 1889, of John Roe whose gravestone can be seen in St Mary's churchyard.

It was during the research into my Osgathorpe ancestors that I started to transcribe parts of the registers, which then grew into the labour of love you see here. At this point I became aware of the interest being shown, in Osgathorpe's history, from other members of the local community and from others both nationally & internationally. With this in mind, I approached the church authorities for their permission to publish this book.

Due to the interest shown it is hoped that in the future a complete history of the church & village will be published. If anyone has any information regarding the village I would be grateful if he or she would get in touch, as the history of this beautiful & characteristic English village deserves to be recorded.

In all, we should not forget the human factor within these registers. Our concern must be with the lives of these ordinary individuals, which had meaning and dignity. We can only imagine what life must have been like at the time of these events.

Neil Roe,
Stapenhill,
Michaelmas 2002.

THOMAS CROMWELL, EARL OF ESSEX (c.1485–1540)
The Instigator of Parish Registers 1538

A Painting after Hans Holbein the Younger c.1533–1534
By courtesy of the National Portrait Gallery London

1. A SHORT HISTORY OF PARISH REGISTERS

Parish registers are the primary source for family history before civil registration began in 1837. Before this date people had no birth or marriage certificates as we know them today. The only source available to them to prove their identity and the parish to which they belonged was the parish register.

The beginnings of parish registers date from the time of Henry VIII who appointed Thomas Cromwell as Vicar-General in July 1535.[1] Cromwell planned the registration project early on in his administration, although it was not until September 1538 that he issued royal injunctions to the clergy of every parish to keep registers of baptisms, marriages and burials.

However, there was some resistance to the project among the clergy as many resented the additional duties. Furthermore, there was a fear by the public of a tax being imposed on them for every baptism, marriage or burial. This hostility resulted in the injunctions having to be repeated on several occasions during the reigns of Edward VI, Philip & Mary and Elizabeth I.

Eventually in 1597, the injunctions were reinforced by the issue of the Provincial Constitutions of Canterbury and approved by Elizabeth I in the following year. One of the requirements being that the existing paper registers or loose sheets be copied into more hardwearing parchment registers, especially those entries from the beginning of her reign in 1558. Consequently few of the original paper registers have survived and many of the 'copy registers' only

---

[1] It was Cromwell who suggested to Henry VIII, that the king make himself head of the Church of England to facilitate his divorce from Catherine of Aragon. Cromwell was later imprisoned in the tower and executed in 1540 for treason.

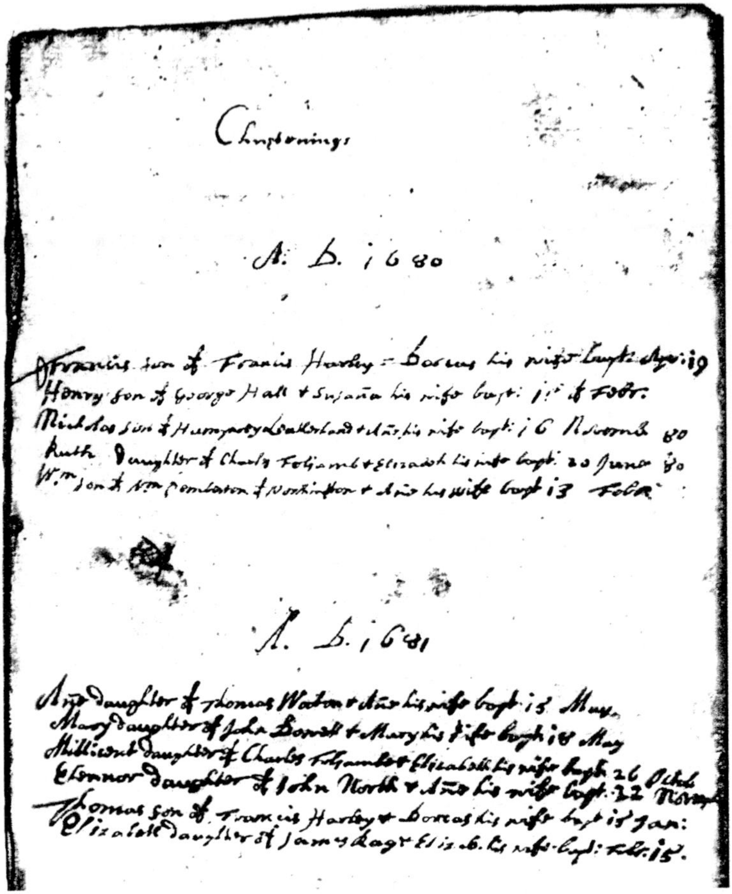
Christenings

A: D. 1680

Francis son of Francis Harley & Dorcas his wife bapt: Apr: 19
Henry son of George Hall & Susanna his wife bapt: 1st of Febr:
Nicholas son of Humphrey Leatherland & Ann his wife bapt: 16 Novemb 80
Ruth daughter of Charles Foljambe & Elizabeth his wife bapt: 20 June 80
Wm son of Wm Pemberton of Worthington & Ann his wife bapt 13 Febr

A: D. 1681

Ann daughter of Thomas Watson & Ann his wife bapt 13 May
Mary daughter of John Barrett & Mary his wife bapt 18 May
Millicent daughter of Charles Foljambe & Elizabeth his wife bapt 26 Octob
Elenor daughter of John North & Ann his wife bapt 22 Nov
Thomas son of Francis Harley & Dorcas his wife bapt 13 Jan:
Elizabeth daughter of James [illegible] & Elizab. his wife bapt: Febr: 15

The Christening Section of Osgathorpe's Oldest Surviving Register

Early registers were often separated into sections for Marriages, Baptisms & Burials. They recorded only the briefest of details, with any additional information added at the discretion of the incumbent.

start from the first year of her reign. Finally, in 1603, these orders were reinforced again by a similar directive, which had the added weight of being embodied into the 70th canon (Church law).

Early Registers

Early parish registers only recorded the briefest of details. Events were recorded in chronological order, although some parishes separated the baptisms, marriages and burials into different sections.[2] Any additional information was at the discretion of the incumbent, who sometimes included such details as the names of the parents of a child or whether marriages were by banns or licence.[3] Also early registers often contained entries written in Latin, which was in general use before English officially replaced it in 1733.

Bishop's Transcripts

The 1597 & 1603 directives also required that the bishop receive an annual copy of the previous year's entries, from Lady Day to Lady Day (25 March), for preservation. These copies, known as bishop's transcripts, are invaluable where the original register has not survived or where there are gaps or entries that are difficult to read.

Some transcripts survive for dates earlier than the 1597 directive and would appear to be returns made from the numerous injunctions sent out previously. Few transcripts were made during the Civil War and Commonwealth period (1642–1660). However, they soon recommenced after the restoration of the monarchy, in 1660 and continued in use until the practice was discontinued in the middle of the 19th century.[4]

---

[2] Osgathorpe also divided its register in this way.

[3] During the period 1683–1730, Osgathorpe's register only occasionally recorded if a marriage was by banns or licence.

[4] The bishop's transcripts (BTs) for Osgathorpe ceased in 1863.

The Commonwealth Period 1645 – 1660

From 1645 parliament ordered that parish registers were also to record dates of birth & death. However, from 1653 an Act denied ministers the custody of registers and removed their power to solemnize marriages. The responsibility for keeping them was transferred to an elected official known as the Parish Register.[5] In practice this was often the parish clerk or incumbent, who sometimes carried on using the old register. Some new 'civil registers' were also begun, which in some cases continued to be used as parish registers after 1660. Between 1653 & 1657, the state only recognized civil marriages conducted by Justices of the Peace. Few parish registers contain details of these, although they were occasionally entered retrospectively after the restoration.

In all, the widespread disruption during the Civil War and Commonwealth caused considerable irregularities in the registers. Many are incomplete and some were undoubtedly lost when many clergy were removed from their livings during these turbulent years.

Marriage Registers

The first change in the recording of marriages took place with Lord Hardwicke's Marriage Act, of 1753. Until then the law regarding marriage was lax and often abused by 'irregular' and 'clandestine' marriages.[6] From April 1754, the act required that a separate register be used to record marriages and that a precise form of wording should be used.[7]

The new registers had to be signed by both bride & groom and by at least two witnesses. Both parties were also required to state the parish in which they resided, with the marriage having to take place in one of them. Furthermore, a marriage would only be valid if banns were read prior to the ceremony or a licence was obtained.

---

[5] Register is the correct term, not registrar.

[6] These irregular & clandestine marriages often took place without a licence, the reading of banns or the consent of the parents of a minor.

[7] Most parishes adopted printed registers, although this was not a specific condition.

Standardization of Registers

From 1538 to 1812, the arrangement of baptism and burial registers remained generally unchanged.[8] However, George Rose's Act of 1812 required the mandatory introduction of separate standardized printed registers from January 1813.[9] These registers recorded extra details, such as the abode & occupation of the father of a baptised child, or the age & abode of the person being buried. It is these two types of register that continue to be used to the present day, but with the addition of dates of birth & death.

Introduction of Civil Registration

In July 1837, the introduction of civil registration changed the format of marriage registers to the system we have today. These registers were also required to record the ages, occupations & abodes of the bride & groom and the names and occupations of their fathers. A duplicate register had also to be kept for the Local Superintendent Registrar who retained it when full. Furthermore, a copy of the entries was to be sent every three months to their offices for passing onto the General Register Office for indexing. It is these indexes that can be searched today and a certificate purchased.

Summary

Despite some shortcomings & omissions, parish registers provide us with an unequalled wealth of information about our ancestors' lives. Careful study can reveal details such as population trends; occupational development; family size; health & longevity; infant mortality; marital status; average age at marriage and much more. Indeed the family & local historian would be much the poorer without the great resource that is '*the parish register*'.

[8] A few parishes had previously used printed registers from 1783, after the imposition of Stamp Duty, which included the dates of birth of those being baptised and the age & parish of the deceased.

[9] This also applied to the marriage registers, which continued to follow the wording specified in the Hardwicke Act albeit now printed.

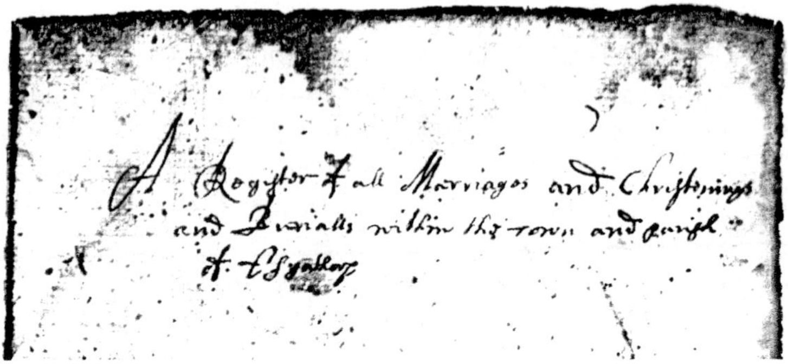

The page heading of the 1680 Osgathorpe Parish Register

'A Register of all Marriages and Christenings
and Burialls within the town and parish
of Osgathorp' [*sic*]

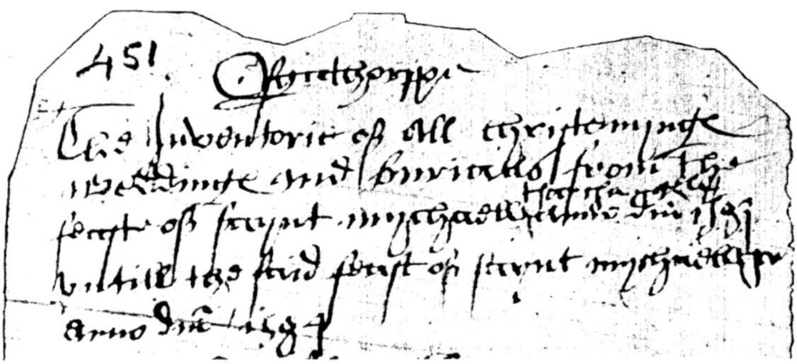

The heading of the 1583–84 Bishop's Transcript

'Osgathorpe'
'The Inventorie of all christenyngs
weddings and burialls from the
feast of saynt mychaell tharchangell anno Dni 1583
untill the said feast of saynt mychaell thar
anno dni 1584' [*sic*]
[i.e. Feast of St. Michael the archangel = Michaelmas/29 September]

2. OSGATHORPE'S EARLIEST REGISTERS

The oldest register that has survived for Osgathorpe was started in 1680 by the then new rector, the Rev. Cadwallader Vaughan (B.A., M.A.).[10] However, this begs the question as to what happened to the previous registers that possibly dated back to 1538. During the research for this book, some evidence of Osgathorpe's earliest registers has come to light. Fragmentary though this evidence is, the interpretation presented is a sound and reasonable one.

In the period immediately prior to the 1680 register (1669–1679), bishop's transcripts were regularly being sent to the diocesan registry for preservation, having resumed a few years after the restoration of the monarchy (1660). This implies that a register must also have been kept during this time. *For how could you send a transcript of a non existent register?*

During the Commonwealth (1645–1660), a period of turbulent change and disruption, the keeping of parish registers became haphazard and little is known of Osgathorpe's register. Some of the old parish registers were used to record the new civil registrations of births & deaths, but there is no way of telling if this took place at Osgathorpe.

However, prior to the Civil War & Commonwealth, bishop's transcripts have survived for the period 1604–1639 and as such we can assume that there was a register. If we take the view that one register was in use, however incomplete, throughout the period 1604–1679 we should consider when its start date was.

---

[10] Was vicar of Belton from 1671–1679 and rector of Osgathorpe from the 21 September 1679.

The 1597 directive to begin new parchment registers was only partially successful. It had to be reinforced by a similar directive in 1603, which was later embodied into church law. This directive again stated that existing paper registers should be copied into more hardwearing parchment registers, 'especially since the beginning of the reign of the late Queen' (1558). Furthermore, it was again stated that transcripts were to be sent annually to the bishop.

Our best evidence lies in this last point, for the '*main sequence*' of bishop's transcripts for Osgathorpe start immediately after this directive in 1604, as they do for many Leicestershire parishes. This suggests that the 1603 directive met with a better response and was more successful in finally achieving compliance. This being the case it would be reasonable to assume that the rest of the directive was carried out and a new parchment register begun. As a result of the 1597 & 1603 directives, many of the new parchment registers were only backdated to 1558 and many of the original paper registers lost.[11] On balance this probably happened to the Osgathorpe registers, with the new volume being backdated and the original being discarded.

Osgathorpe's First Register

When Osgathorpe originally commenced the keeping of a register is a matter of conjecture. However, the fact that a sole surviving 16th century bishop's transcript has survived for the parish, dated 1583–84, indicates that a register was then in use.[12] Other odd transcripts, that pre-date the directives of 1597 & 1603, exist for most Leicestershire parishes and are probably returns made from the injunctions sent out previously. Many of these transcripts date from or soon after an injunction in 1561/2. This was the case with Ashby de la Zouch & Breedon on the Hill, whose earliest surviving

[11] A number of Leicestershire parish registers date from 1558, while others not backdated start between 1601–1604.

[12] This BT has previously been incorrectly given as 1584, when it actually covers the last 6 months of 1583 and the first 6 months of 1584 (Michaelmas 29 September 1583 to Michaelmas 1584).

registers also date from that time. Neighbouring Belton & Shepshed have register start dates in 1538, with Castle Donnington starting in 1539. This suggests that Osgathorpe's register began, either at the commencement of parish registers in 1538/9 or after the 1561/2 injunction.

Conclusion

It seems clear that from at least (Michaelmas) 29 September 1583 Osgathorpe had a parish register. A register that was almost certainly replaced by a new parchment register in 1603/4, which probably included backdated entries to 1558. This register was then probably used through to the death of the Rev. John Rosse in 1679,[13] followed, in 1680, by the register begun by the Rev. Cadwallader Vaughan. As to what became of the pre 1680 register, we shall probably never know. Was it later destroyed? Or did it remain in the possession of the Rev. John Rosse's family?

List of Osgathorpe's Lost Registers

c.1538 / c.1561	–	*1603*	*Baptisms, Marriages & Burials.*
c.1603/4	–	*1679*	*Baptisms, Marriages & Burials.*

List of Surviving Registers (no longer in use)

1680	–	1779	Baptisms & Burials: Marriages to 1753.
1754	–	1812	Marriages.
1780	–	1812	Baptisms & Burials.
1813	–	1888	Baptisms.
1813	–	1979	Burials.
1813	–	1837	Marriages.
1837	–	1929	Marriages.
1930	–	1956	Marriages.
1776	–	1793	Banns.
1831	–	1945	Banns.

[13] The Rev. John Rosse, rector of Osgathorpe c.1642–1679. Walker, p.442, in his study of the clergy during the Civil War notes 'Mr Ross, by the interest of some friends, was saved from a formal sequestration; but was miserably harassed for many years and often forced to abscond. He was a man of good life and learning'.

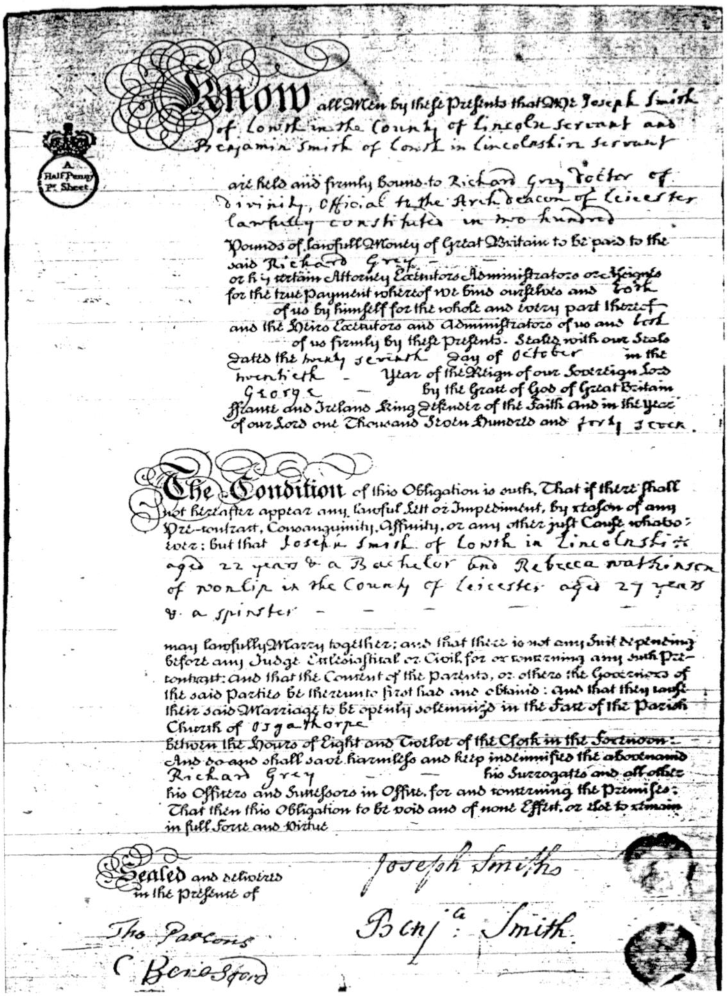
A Half Penny P.r Sheet

Know all Men by these Presents that We Joseph Smith of Lowth in the County of Lincoln servant and Benjamin Smith of Lowth in Lincolnshire servant

are held and firmly bound to Richard Grey Doctor of Divinity, Official to the Archdeacon of Leicester lawfully constituted in two hundred Pounds of lawfull Money of Great Britain to be paid to the said Richard Grey or his certain Attorney Executors Administrators or Assigns for the true Payment whereof We bind ourselves and both of us by himself for the whole and every part thereof and the Heirs Executors and Administrators of us and both of us firmly by these Presents. Sealed with our Seals Dated the twenty seventh Day of October in the twentieth Year of the Reign of our Sovereign Lord George by the Grace of God of Great Britain France and Ireland King Defender of the Faith And in the Year of our Lord one Thousand Seven Hundred and forty seven.

The Condition of this Obligation is such, That if there shall not hereafter appear any lawful Lett or Impediment, by reason of any Pre-contract, Consanguinity, Affinity, or any other just Cause whatsoever: but that Joseph Smith of Lowth in Lincolnshire aged 22 years & a Bachelor and Rebecca Watkinson of Wonlip in the County of Leicester aged 27 years & a spinster

may lawfully Marry together; and that there is not any Suit depending before any Judge Ecclesiastical or Civil for or concerning any such Pre-contract: And that the Consent of the Parents, or others the Governors of the said Parties be thereunto first had and obtained: And that they cause their said Marriage to be openly solemnized in the Face of the Parish Church of Osgathorpe Between the Hours of Eight and Twelve of the Clock in the Forenoon: And do and shall save harmless and keep indemnified the abovenamed Richard Grey his Surrogates and all other his Officers and Successors in Office, for and concerning the Premises; That then this Obligation to be void and of none Effect, or else to remain in full Force and Virtue.

Sealed and delivered in the Presence of

Joseph Smith

Benja: Smith

Tho. Parsons

C Beresford

The Marriage Licence Bond for Joseph Smith & Rebecca Watkinson

Issued at Osgathorpe on the day of the wedding

Note the two Osgathorpe residents, Tho. Parsons & C. Beresford, witnessing the document and Benja[min] Smith as the bound surety.

3. MARRIAGE AT OSGATHORPE

Before 1837 & the introduction of register office ceremonies, marriages were either by banns or licence. Banns had been read out in church since time-immemorial and licence marriages had taken place regularly since the reign of Henry VIII.

Marriage by Licence

Licences were speedier than the reading of banns, but had to be purchased from the bishop or his surrogate.[14] They were usually granted a few days before the marriage or on the day itself. They were also private, being favoured by the gentry, Nonconformists and undoubtedly some couples who found it convenient to marry quickly and without too many questions being asked.

The issuing of licences at Osgathorpe was commonplace and especially so during the period 1718–1748, when 166 marriages out of 205 were by licence (See Fig. 1, p. 13). This represents 8 out of 10 marriages, an extremely high figure, which in periods before and after this had only been 1 in 10. Osgathorpe's rector issued the vast majority of these licences, 82 percent, on the same day as the marriage.[15] A position that implies that he had to be available at short notice and which kept him rather tied to the village.

The reason for the large number of licences was probably due to the rector increasing his earnings, by specialising in licence marriages. His income increased significantly, compared to his earnings from the small number of marriages performed involving an Osgathorpe resident. However, this may only be a partial

---

[14] Leicestershire had an archdeacon who was the head of the archdeaconry, a division of the diocese of Lincoln until 1839.

[15] During this period, two rectors served Osgathorpe the Rev. Cadwallader Vaughan (1679–1728) & the Rev. Samuel Holbrooke (1729–1748) whose signatures appeared, as surrogates of the archdeacon, on almost all of the licence allegations.

explanation, as other small neighbouring parishes do *not* show similar high instances of licence marriages, as one might expect.

It is conceivable that the archdeacon may have requested licence marriages to take place in specified parishes in particular areas. This is further supported by the fact that 91 percent of all licence marriages at Osgathorpe had no party with an apparent connection with the village, but had at least one party from a parish within N.W. Leicestershire. This clearly suggests that Osgathorpe was a preferred place for the performance of licence marriages, whether by request of the archdeacon or through the incumbents increasing their incomes.

Allegations & Bonds

When obtaining a marriage licence, the groom gave a statement (allegation) on oath that there was no just impediment by way of a former existing marriage or other lawful hindrance to prevent the marriage taking place at the specified church or churches.[16] These allegations, many of which have survived, frequently gave information that was not recorded in either Osgathorpe's registers or bishop's transcripts. This included the abodes of the two parties and their present marital status (single or widowed). Their ages were also included, but often only approximately as it was only necessary to prove that they were over the age of 21 or if a minor that they had their parent's consent. The occupation of the groom was also recorded and may now be the only surviving documentation giving his trade.

Allegations were often accompanied by a bond that gave the name, abode & occupation of the person who acted as bound surety for the truth of the allegations, usually a relative or friend. However, some local tradesman & farmers undoubtedly specialised as bonds-man, for an appropriate fee.

---

[16] It was possible to state more than one church venue.

Marriage by Banns

Banns of marriage are the proclamations in church of an intended wedding, in order that those who know of any impediment may object. They are usually read out in the parish churches of both the bride & groom, on the 3 Sundays preceding the marriage.

The 1753 Marriage Act required that banns were to be recorded either in the marriage register itself or in a separate banns register. As a result Osgathorpe adopted a new printed marriage register, although occasionally between 1776 & 1793 a separate banns register recorded the banns of 19 marriages. A more complete banns register was begun in 1832, which included those banns, which were read at Osgathorpe, but whose marriages were performed elsewhere. It also recorded the banns of those marriages that were withdrawn at the last minute and did *not* take place.

The 1832 register was probably begun due to the 1823 Marriage Act, which revived the registering of banns after a long period of decline. This Act required the keeping of a separate banns register, which has remained so to the present day.

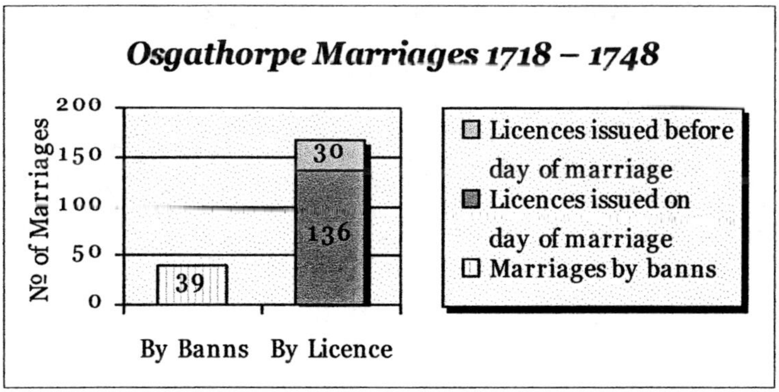

Fig. 1; Showing the high numbers of licence marriages at Osgathorpe during the period 1718–1748
Most licences were issued by the rector on the day of the wedding and undoubtedly helped to increase his income.

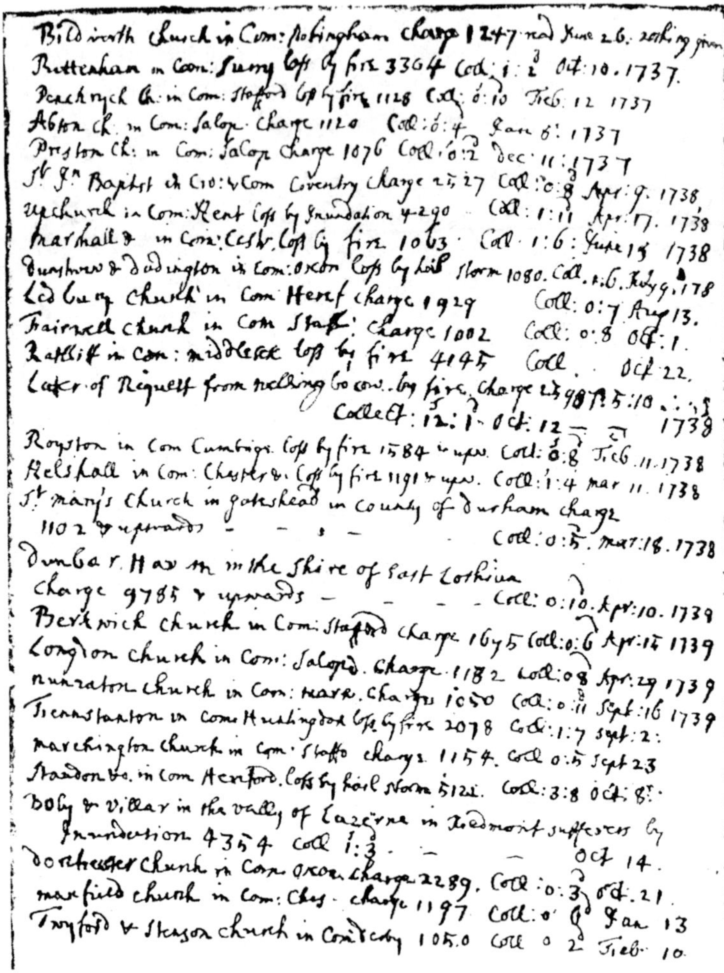

Bildworth Church in Com: Notingham Charge 1247 nad June 26. nothing given
Ritteahan in Com: Surry loss by fire 3364 Coll: 1: 2d Oct: 10. 1737.
Peachwych Ch: in Com: Stafford loss by fire 1128 Coll: 0: 10 Feb. 12 1737
Abton Ch: in Com: Salop Charge 1120 Coll: 0: 4 Jan 6: 1737
Preston Ch: in Com: Salop Charge 1076 Coll: 0: 2 dec 11: 1737
St Jn Baptist Ch Cit: & Com Coventry Charge 2527 Coll: 0: 8d Apr: 9. 1738
Upchurch in Com: Kent loss by Inundation 4290 Coll: 1: 11 Apr: 17. 1738
Marshall & in Com: Cestr. loss by fire 1063 Coll 1: 6: June 15 1738
Dunstrew & Deddington in Com: Oxon loss by hail Storm 1080. Coll. 1: 6. July 9. 1738
Ledbury Church in Com Heref Charge 1929 Coll: 0: 7 Aug 13.
Fairwell Church in Com Staff: Charge 1002 Coll: 0: 8 Oct: 1.
Ratcliff in Com: Middlesex loss by fire 4145 Coll. Oct 22.
Letter of Request from Welling bo com. by fire, Charge 2598 ... 5: 10
Collect: 12: 1. Oct: 12 1738
Royston in Com Cambrigs. loss by fire 1584 & upw. Coll: 0: 8 Feb 11. 1738
Helshall in Com: Chester &c. loss by fire 1191 & upw. Coll: 1: 4 Mar 11. 1738
St Mary's Church in Gateshead in County of Durham Charge 1102 & upwards - - - Coll: 0: 5. Mar: 18. 1738
Dunbar Har in the Shire of East Lothian Charge 9785 & upwards - - - Coll: 0: 10. Apr: 10. 1739
Berkwick Church in Com: Stafford Charge 1675 Coll: 0: 6 Apr: 15 1739
Longdon Church in Com: Salop. Charge 1182 Coll: 0 8 Apr: 29 1739
Nunraton Church in Com: Warw. Charge 1050 Coll: 0: 11 Sept: 16 1739
Fennstanton in Com Huntingdon loss by fire 2078 Coll: 1: 7 Sept: 2:
Marchington Church in Com: Staffo Charge 1154. Coll 0: 5 Sept 23
Standon &c. in Com Hertford. loss by hail Storm 5121. Coll: 3: 8 Oct: 8:
Boly & Villar in the valley of Lazerne in Piedmont sufferers by Inundation 4354 Coll 1: 3. - - Oct 14.
Dorchester Church in Com Oxon Charge 2289. Coll: 0: 3 Oct: 21.
Marfield church in Com: Ches. Charge 1197 Coll: 0: 6d Jan 13
Twyford & Stenson church in Com Derby 1050 Coll 0 2d Feb 10.

Church Briefs 1737–1739

Note the bottom entry 'Twyford & Stenson church in Co. Derby 1050 Coll: 0 2 d Feb 10' [1739]

4. CHURCH BRIEFS

Church or King's Briefs were royal mandates authorizing nationwide parish collections, towards a deserving cause such as church repairs or losses by severe weather conditions. The details of these briefs were sometimes recorded in the parish registers. This was the case with Osgathorpe, which has in the front of the 1680 register 224 recorded, dating from 11 June 1727 to 1 October 1747.[17]

The briefs were read from the pulpit and at the end of the service the clerk reminded the leaving congregation 'to remember the brief'. The funds were then passed on to the appropriate authorities and when totalled often amounted to a decent sum. In 1828, the collections were finally abolished after a long period of decline through the latter part of the 18th century.

Samples of the type of entries recorded in Osgathorpe's register are given below. The few entries that occur for Leicestershire have been included; unfortunately the reasons for their appeals were not recorded. The national brief number or charge appears in brackets.

		£:s:d –	Collected
Sibson ch, Co. Leic.	-	0:1:7	09 Jul 1727
Tamworth church, Co. War/Stafford (3219)		0:0:9	21 Sep 1727
St Johns Wapping, Co. Mid.	Loss by fire	0:4:4	17 Jul 1728
Protestants at Copenhagen in Denm.	Lost by fire a great loss	0:1:0	15 Dec 1729
Waltham in ye Wolds church, Co. Leicest (1736)		0:1:3	24 Oct 1736
?Measham church, Co. Darby (1059)	-	0:0:2	24 Sep 1737
Upchurch, Co. Kent (4290)	Loss by Inundation	0:1:11	17 Apr 1738
Stauton Vc, Co. Hereford (5121)	Loss by Hail Storm	0:3:8	08 Oct 1739
Twyford & Stenson church, Co. Derby (1050)		0:0:2	10 Feb 1739
Pristwould church, Co. Leicest (1292)	-	0:1:0	12 Apr 1741
Melverley, Co. Salop (1333)	Loss by Floods	0:1:0	06 Nov 1743
Weston Turville, Co. Bucks. (1214)	Loss by Fire	0:0:10	17 Aug 1746

---

[17] Osgathorpe's briefs are on paper and appear to have been incorporated with the parchment pages of the register when it was rebound.

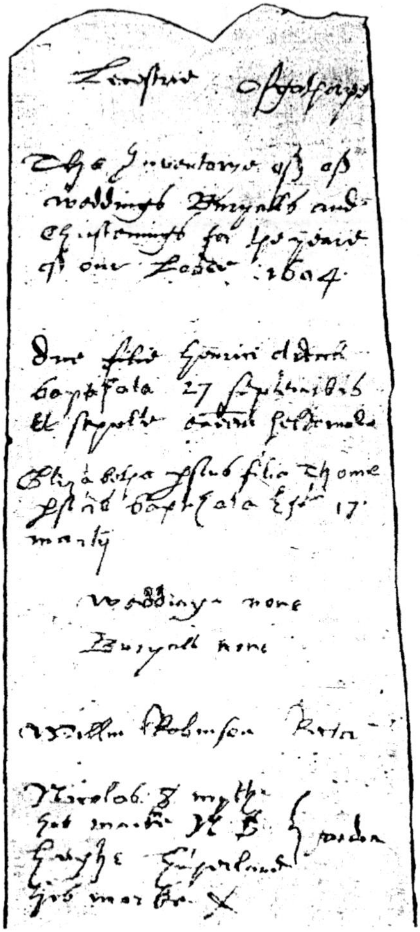

The 1604 Bishop's Transcript
Recording the baptism of Elizabeth
the daughter of Thomas Parsons
Note the entry was in Latin & the abbreviations used
'Elizabetha P[ar]sons filia Thom[a]e P[ar]sons baptzata est 17 marti[u]s'
Elizabeth Parsons daughter of Thomas Parsons baptised she 17 March

5. BAPTISMS 1583 – 1888

The entries for the period 1583 to 1679 have been transcribed from the bishop's transcripts that pre-date the oldest surviving register. The reader should note that some of the following entries were written in Latin (See Latin names & words) and that until 1752 the first day of the year was Lady Day, 25 March. (See introduction: Dates)

16	JAN	1583	ESTER	PALMER	-
16	FEB	1583	GARTERETH	SNENETH	-
22	FEB	1583	AGNES	TOMLYNSON	-
23	MAR	1583	ANNE	HURST	-
29	MAR	1584	ANNE	LETHERLAND	-
	1585–1603		[No BTs]		
27	SEP	1604	*?duo filie*	ADCOCK	d./ *HENRIRI et sepult eadem ?postemodo*[1]
17	MAR	1604	*ELIZABETHA*	P[AR]SONS	d./ *THOM[A]E*
		1605	[No BT]		
11	APR	1606	MARGEREY	ROBYNS	d./ WILLM
23	NOV	1606	JOAN	PARSONS	d./ THOMAS
01	JAN	1606	THOMAS	KIDDYER	s./ NICHOLAS
03	JAN	1606	JHON	FFRANNCE	s./ JHON
20	JUN	1607	ROBERT	FAYRFEILD	s./ WILLIAM
16	AUG	1607	MARY	GREENE	d./ JHON
16	AUG	1607	ELIZABETH	GREENE	d./ JHON
15	NOV	1607	JANE	SMYTHE	d./ NICHOLAS
20	DEC	1607	NICHOLAS	NORTHE	s./ JULIAN
30	OCT	1608	AN	GREENE	d./ JHON
12	MAR	1608	WILLIAM	ROBYNS	s./ WILLIAM
19	NOV	1609	*ELENA*	KIDDIER	d./ NICOLAS
24	DEC	1609	*SARA*	PARSONS	d./ THOMAS
01	APR	1609	*JHOANNES*	MARSHALL	s./ *JACOB*[2]
	1610–1611		[No BTs]		
03	MAY	1612	*ELIZABETHA*	ROBYNS	d./ *WILLYEMI*
24	JAN	1612	*WILLYELMS*	ADCOCK	s./ *ROGERI*
07	MAR	1612	*HENRICUS*	WRIGHT	s./ *SAMUELIS*
21	MAR	1612	*NYCHOLAS*	KIDDIER	s./ NICHOLAS
		1613	[No BT]		

[1] *?duo filie* = ?two daughters: *et sepult eadem ?postemodo* = and buried the same afterwards.

[2] The Latin *JACOB* in this instance means JAMES, who was named as such at his wife's burial in December 1636. (e.g. 'The *Jacobites*' / followers of James II's heirs)

22	MAY	1614	JHON	ROBYNS	s./ WILLIAM	
18	SEP	1614	ANN	NORTHE	d./ JULIAN[1]	
04	DEC	1614	ANN	KIDDIER	d./ HAMLETT	
		1615–1616	[No BTs]			
15	MAR	1617	WILLIAM	HARLEY	s./ FRANCIS	
07	APR	1617	RICHARD	NORTH	s./ *JULIANAS*	
		1618–1620	[No BTs]			
08	JUN	1621	THOMAS	NORTH	-	

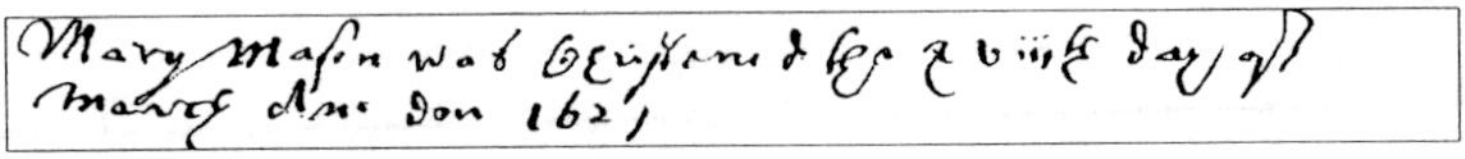

18	MAR	1621	MARY	MASON	-	
		1622–1624	[No BTs]			
20	NOV	1625	FFRANCIS	DAWSON	s./ FFRANCIS	
05	MAR	1625	SARAH	PARSONS	d./ ROBERT	
05	MAR	1625	NICHOLAS	HALL	s./ ZACHARIE	
		1626	No Baptisms			
06	MAY	1627	JANE	ROBINS	d./ WILLIAM	
09	MAR	1628	THOMAS	DAWSON	s./ FFRANNCIS[2]	
29	MAR	1628	THOMAS	DAWSON	s./ *THOM[A]E*	
27	APR	1628	THOMAS	PARSONS	s./ *ROBERTI*	
27	AUG	1628	ELIZABETH	HUTCHINSON	d./ ZACHARIE	
28	SEP	1628	*RICHARDUS*	FFRANCIS	s./ *JOHANNES junioris*	
20	JUL	1629	JOHN	DAWSON	s./ FFRANCIS	
14	MAR	1629	MARY	KIDDIER	d./ *GULIELMI*	
20	MAR	1629	FFRANCIS	ROBINS	s./ *GULIHELLMI*	
09	OCT	1630	MARY	DAWSON	d./ FFRANCIS	
27	MAR	1630	THOMAS	HODGKINSON	s./ *ZACHARIAS*	
		1631	[No BT]			
16	SEP[3]	1632	NICHOLAS	KIDDIER	s./ *GULIELMI*	
17	NOV	1633	FFRANCIS	NORTH	s./ *JOHANNES*	
11	JAN	1633	FFRANCIS	HODGKINSON	s./ *ZACHARIS*	
07	SEP	1634	THOMAS	PARSONS	s./ *THOM[A]E*	
16	JAN	1634	MARGERIE	DAWSON	d./ *FRANCISCI*	
20	JAN	1634	*GULIELMS*	MASON alias BALIE	-	
16	FEB	1634	*GULIELMS*	KIDDIER	s./ *GULIELMI*	
		1635	[No BT]			
07	NOV	1636	GEORGE	HODGKINSON	s./ ZACHARIE & MARIA	Labourer
04	DEC	1636	NICHOLAS	PARSONS	s./ THOMAS & MARGERIE	Husbandman
06	APR	1637	THOMAS	SALISBURIE	s./ HUMFRIE & JANE	Husbandman
17	SEP	1637	THOMAS	KIDDIER	s./ WILL & ELIZAB	Husbandman

[1] Register gave 'baptized the 18 September & buried 24'.

[2] This baptism was the last entry on the 1627 BT, which gave the date as 9 March *1628*, (not 1627). Although 1628 did not begin until 25 March (Lady Day).

[3] A second BT gave 1633 instead of 1632.

15	OCT	1637	JOHN	NORTH	s./ JOHN & ALICE	Husbandman
15	OCT	1637	MARY	PARSONS	d./ EDWD & JANE	Husbandman
10	DEC	1637	JOHN	ADCOCKE	s./ WILL & JANE	Husbandman
02	SEP	1638	ANNE	SUTTON	d./ JOHN & ISABELL	Smith
21	OCT	1638	ANNE	ALLALIE	d./ WILLIAM & SARAH	Tailor
17	JAN	1638	JOHN	SALISBURIE	s./ HUMFRIE & JANE	Yeoman
28	JAN	1638	ANNE	PARSONS	d./ THOMAS & MARGERIE	Yeoman
06	OCT	1639	ANNE	NORTHE	d./ JOHN & ALICE	-
17	NOV	1639	FFRANCIS	HARLIE	s./ FFRANCIS & *SARA*	-
09	FEB	1639	JOHN	COLTON	s./ GEORGE & ELIZ	Yeoman
08	MAR	1639	ISSABELL	SUTTON	d./ JOHN & ISABELL	Smith
	[1640–1668]		[No BTs for the Civil War & Commonwealth period]			
03	SEP	1669	JOHN	JERUAS alias KIDDIER	s./ GEORGE	
17	SEP	1669	MARY	PARSO[N]S	d./ THOMAS & KATHERINE	
06	JAN[1]	+1670	ANNE	PALMER	d./ EDWARD & MARGARET	
12	JAN	+1670	ELIANOR	GREENE	d./ THOMAS & KATHARINE	
28	MAR	+1670	ELIZABETH	KIDDIER	d./ NICHOLAS & ALICE	
06	APR	1670	THOMAS	SHAW	s./ JOHN & RUTH	
19	APR	1670	JOHN	HALL	s./ GEORGE & SUSANNA	
12	SEP	1671	MARGET	BODLE	-	
27	OCT	1671	NATHANIELL	PARSONS	-	
24	FEB	1671	WILLIAM	SMITH	-	
04	MAR	1671	EDWARD	NORTH	-	
17	APR	1672	WILL	SHAW	-	
20	MAR	+1673	WILLIAM	HATHAWAY	s./ EDWARD & ABIA	
23	NOV	1673	THOMAS	GREENE	-	
26	NOV	1673	WILLIAM	SHAW	-	
21	FEB	+1674	BRIGET	LITHERLAND	d./ HUMPHREY & ANNE	
27	FEB	+1674	THOMAS	CLARKE	-	
14	MAR	+1674	NICHOLAS	KIDDIER	s./ NICHOLAS & ALICE	
22	MAR	+1674	JANE	WHITE	d./ HENRY & JANE	
20	OCT	1674	JANE	NORTH	d./ JOHN & ANNE	
21	MAR	+1675	THOMAS	SMITH	s./ JOHN & ANNE	
20	APR	1675	ELIZABETH	GILBERT	d./ SAMUEL & ELIZABETH	
06	MAY	1675	RICHARD	BAYLEY	s./ JOHN & MARGARET	
10	JUN	1675	MILLICENT	FULGIUM	d./ CHARLES & ELIZABETH	
26	JUN	1675	HENRY	BROWET	-	
07	NOV	1675	KATHARINE	GREENE	-	
02[2]	FEB	+1676	HENRY	FULGIUM	s./ CHARLES & ELIZABETH	
03[3]	FEB	+1676	THOMAS	GILBERT	s./ SAMUEL & ELIZABETH	

[1] The following 12 entries marked with a plus sign+, appear to be dated using the 1 January as the beginning of the year and not Lady Day (25 March). This undoubtedly persisted from the Commonwealth period, when 1 January was the official start of the year.

[2] A second BT gave 1 February.

[3] A second BT gave 2 February.

20	FEB	[+]1676	SARAH	HALL	d./ GEORGE & SUSANNA
05	MAY	1676	MARY	WHITE	d./ HENRY & JANE[1]
18	DEC	1676	DOROTHY	ROBINS	d./ WILLIAM & DOROTHY
19	APR	1677	CHARLES	FULGIAM	s./ CHARLES & ELIZABETH
19	APR	1677	ELIZ	FULGIAM	d./ CHARLES & ELIZABETH
08	MAY	1677	MARY	NORTH	d./ JOHN & ANN
14	MAY	1677	EDWARD	BELTON	s./ EDWARD & ANN
21	DEC	1677	ELEANOR	HALL	d./ GEORGE & SUSANNA
09	APR	1678	MARY	GILBERT	d./ SAMUEL & ELIZABETH
22	APR	1678	PETER	BELTON	s./ EDWARD & ANNE
06	MAY	1678	MARY	LITHERLAND	d./ HUMPHREY & ANNE
08	MAY	1678	JOSEPH	WHITE	s./ HENERY & JANE
14	JUL	1678	ELIZABETH	JERUAS	d./ GEORGE & ELIZABETH
22	OCT	1678	WILLIAM	ROBINS	s./ WILLIAM & DOROTHY
20	NOV	1678	THOMAS	WOTTON	s./ THOMAS & ANNE
17	DEC	1678	ANNE	FULGIAM	d./ CHARLES & ELIZABETH
11	JUN	1679	HUMPHREY	LITHERLAND	s./ HUMPHREY & ANE
28	SEP	1679	THOMAS	GREENE	s./ THOMAS & ANE
24	NOV	1679	RICHARD	BAYLY	s./ RICHARD & SUSANA
13	JAN	1679	ANE	BELTON	d./ EDWARD & ANE
27	JAN	1679	EDWARD	BELTON	s./ WM & MARY
			[The oldest surviving register starts in 1680]		
19	APR	1680	FRANCIS	HARLEY	s./ FRANCIS & DORCAS
01	FEB[2]	1680	HENRY	HALL	s./ GEORGE & SUSANA
16	NOV	1680	NICHOLAS	LEATHERLAND	s./ HUMPHREY & ANE
20	JUN[3]	1680	RUTH	FOLIAMBE	d./ CHARLES & ELIZABETH
13	FEB	1680	WM	PEMBERTON	s./ WILLM & ANE of Worthington
15	MAY	1681	ANE	WOOTON	d./ THOMAS & ANE
18	MAY	1681	MARY	BOWETT	d./ JOHN & MARY
26	OCT	1681	MILLICENT	FOLIAMBE	d./ CHARLES & ELIZABETH
22	NOV	1681	ELENNOR	NORTH	d./ JOHN & ANE
15	JAN	1681	THOMAS	HARLEY	s./ FRANCIS & DORCAS
15	FEB	1681	ELIZABETH	RAG	d./ JAMES & ELIZAB
28	MAY	1682	MARY	BAREFOOT	d./ HENRY & ELIZABETH of Breedon
18	JUN	1682	MARY	WILLMSON	d./ RICHARD & ELIZABETH of Breedon
20	AUG	1682	SAMUEL	WHITE	s./ HENRY & JANE
04	SEP	1682	JOSEPH	SHAW	s./ JOHN & MARGARET
31	JAN	1682	MARY	HARLEY	d./ FRANCIS & DORCAS
17	MAR	1682	MARY	CLARK	d./ THOMAS & SARAH
18	MAR	1682	EDWARD	FOLIAMB	s./ CHARLES & ELIZABETH
20	MAR	1682	ELIZABETH	BELTON	d./ EDWARD & ANE
28	MAY	1683	JOHN	WILLOWS	s./ JAMES & ELIZABETH

[1] A second BT gave 6 May 1676.

[2] Out of chronological order in register.

[3] Out of chronological order in register.

08	JUN	1683	SAMUEL	GILBERT	s./ SAMUEL & ELIZABETH
06	DEC	1683	ANA	VAUGHAN	d./ CADWALLADER Rev & ANA
23	JAN	1683	RACHEL	BELTON	d./ WILLM & MARY
23	JAN	1683	LEAH	BELTON	d./ WILLM & MARY
09	MAR	1683	SARAH	HARLEY	d./ FRANCIS & DORCAS
02	APR	1684	SARAH	NORTH	d./ JOHN & ANE
06	APR	1684	MARY	WOOTTON	d./ THOMAS & ANE
12	JUL	1684	JOHN	FOLIAMB	s./ CHARLES & ELIZABETH

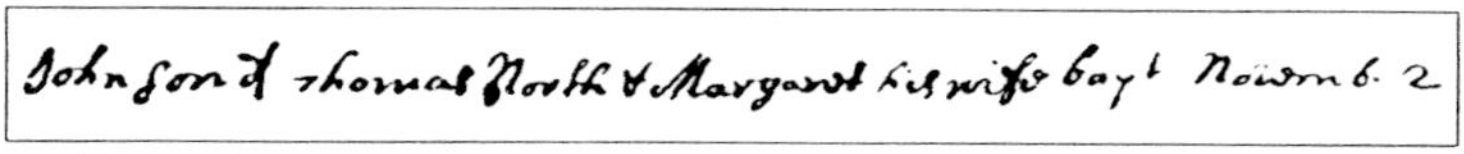
John son of Thomas North & Margaret his wife bapt Novem 6. 2

02	NOV	1684	JOHN	NORTH	s./ THOMAS & MARGARET
13	NOV	1684	JOHN	VAUGHAN	s./ CADWALLADER Rev & ANA
05	DEC	1684	MARY	BELTON	d./ EDWARD & ANE
15	APR	1685	WILLIAM	BELTON	s./ WILLM & MARY
20	APR	1685	FRANCIS	HARLEY	s./ FRANCIS & DORCAS
21	JUL	1685	JAMES	RAGGE	s./ JAMES & ELIZABETH
02	AUG	1685	JOHN	ROBINS	s./ WM & DOROTHY
13	OCT	1685	ABIA	GILBERT	d./ SAMUEL & ELIZABETH
24	NOV	1685	THOMAS	STINSON	s./ THOMAS & DOROTHY
13	DEC	1685	JAMES	GYLES	s./ JAMES & SARAH
01	MAR	1685	THOMAS	BELTON	s./ EDWARD & ANE
04	MAY	1686	CADWALLADER	VAUGHAN	s./ CADWALLADER & ANA
10	JUN	1686	JANE	RAGGE	d./ FRANCIS & JANE his wife ?yn also buried[1]
25	JUL	1686	SUSANA	HALL	d./ GEORGE & ANE
30	AUG	1686	JAMES	WILLOWES	s./ JAMES & ELIZABETH
05	SEP	1686	ELIZABETH	WOOTTON	d./ THOMAS & ANE
26	SEP	1686	CATHERINE	NORTH	d./ JOHN & ANE
26	DEC	1686	BRIDGETT	SHEEYHEARD	d./ THOMAS & ELIZABETH of Breedon
21	FEB	1686	ELIZABETH	HEARTLEY	d./ JOSEPH & MARY of Breedon
15	JUL	1687	FRANCES	NEEDHAM	d./ MAURICE & LETTIS
07	AUG	1687	GEORGE	HALL	s./ GEORGE & ANE
04	JUN	1688	JOSEPH	STINSON	s./ THOMAS & DOROTHY
19	JUN	1688	WILLM	MONTENAY	s./ WM & ANE
-[2]	AUG	1688	JOHN HATHAWAY	SMITH	s./ JOHN & ABIAH
04	DEC	1688	ELIZABETH	VAUGHAN	d./ CADWALLADER & ANA
08	FEB	1688	ELIZABETH	HARLEY	d./ FRANCIS & DORCAS
21	APR	1689	SARAH	WOOTTON	d./ THOMAS & ANE
05	MAY	1689	RICHARD	BELTON	s./ WILLIAM & MARY
21	JUN	1689	SARAH	BOWETT	d./ JOHN & MARY
21	JUL	1689	MARY	BACON	d./ WILLM & MARY of Breedon
29	JUL	1689	THOMAS	WILLOWS	s./ JAMES & ELIZABETH

[1] Burial note probably refers to the mother, as the burial entry of the same day did not state that the deceased was an infant.

[2] Day of the month was left blank. The BT for this year has not survived.

30	JUL	1689	THOMAS	GREEN	s./ THOMAS & ANE
22	OCT	1689	EDWARD	BELTON	s./ EDWARD & ANE
13	JAN	1689	THOMAS	VAUGHAN	s./ CADWALLADER & ANA
05	MAR	1689	EDWARD	HALL	s./ GEORGE & ANE
18	MAR	1689	WILLIAM	STINSON	s./ THOMAS & DOROTHY
20	JUN	1690	RICHARD	HEATHERLEY	s./ WILLM & ANE
08	JUL	1690	THOMAS	BROWNE	s./ JOHN & ELIZABETH
16	JUL	1690	MARTHA	WOOD	d./ THOMAS & HANAH

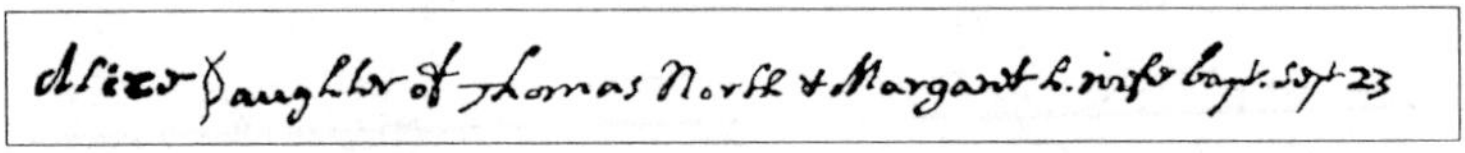
Alice daughter of Thomas North & Margarett h. wife bapt. Sept 23

23	SEP	1690	ALICE	NORTH	d./ THOMAS & MARGARET
18	NOV	1690	MARY	HALL	d./ JAMES & BARBARA
06	MAY	1691	HANAH	NORTH	d./ JOHN & ANE
02	SEP	1691	SARAH	BELTON	d./ WILLM & MARY
03	NOV	1691	DAVID	VAUGHAN	s./ CADWALLADER & ANA
22	JUN	1691	JOHN	WOOTTON	s./ THOMAS & ANE
02	MAR	1691	THOMAS	HALL	s./ GEORGE & ANE
03	MAR	1691	WILLM	HEATHERLEY	s./ WILLM & ANE
12	DEC	1692	ELIZABETH	WILLOWS	d./ JAMES & ELIZABETH
26	DEC	1692	JOHN	HALL	s./ JAMES & BARBARA
21	FEB	1692	WINIFFRID	VAUGHAN	d./ CADWALLADER & ANNA
01	JAN	1693	CATHERINE	BELTON	d./ WILLM & MARY
28	JAN	1693	JOHN	BROWN	s./ JOHN & ELIZABETH
29	JUN	1694	MARY	BARRODEL	d./ WM & SARAH
06	JUL	1694	THOMAS	NORTH	s./ THOMAS & MARGARET
10	OCT	1694	WILLIAM	WOOTTON	s./ THOMAS & ANNE
09	DEC	1694	WILLIAM	AVERY	s./ THOMAS & DOROTHY
03	AUG	1695	ELIZABETH	HALL	d./ JAMES & BARBARA
06	OCT	1695	MARY	BAILY	d./ EDWARD & SARAH of Coleorton
28	NOV	1695	GEORGE	VAUGHAN	s./ CADW & ANA
03	JAN	1695	WILLM	BROWN	s./ JOHN & ELIZABETH
07	JAN	1695	JOHN	HALL	s./ GEORGE & ANE
19	JAN	1695	MARY	ROYLEY	d./ RALPH & ANE of Breedon
10	FEB	1695	MARY	AVERY	d./ THOMAS & DOROTHY
06	APR	1696	FRANCES	POXON	d./ WM & SARAH of Worthington
09	MAY	1696	ELIZABETH	COULTON	d./ GEORGE & MARY
03	JUL	1696	MARY	SYMKIN	d./ THOMAS & MARY
03	OCT	1696	CHARNELL	WILLSON	s./ EDWARD & ELIZABETH born 2 Oct
01	DEC	1696	TIMOTHY	JOYNES	s./ TIMOTHY & HANNAH
10	FEB	1696	ELIZABETH	LEATHERLAND	d./ WILLM & ELIZABETH born[1]
11	JUL	1697	SUSANA	HALL	d./ JAMES & BARBARA
10	AUG	1697	MARY	COULTON	d./ GEORGE & MARY
29	AUG	1697	JOHN	SWAINE	s./ JOHN & BRIDGET

[1] Entry recorded on a separate page of the register, immediately prior to the start of the Marriages.

17	SEP	1697	JAMES	WHITE	s./ THOMAS & ELIZABETH
29	OCT	1697	WILLIAM	BOULTBY	s./ WILLIAM & RUTH
15	MAR	1697	HARRY alias HENRY	KNIGHT	s./ JOHN & ELIZABETH
25	MAR	1698	JOHN	WILLSON	s./ EDWARD & ELIZABETH born & bapt
14	MAY	1698	JOHN	SHAW	s./ THOMAS & ELLEN
22	MAY	1698	JANE	WOOTTON	d./ THOMAS & ANE
30	JUN	1698	SARAH	BROWN	d./ JOHN & ELIZABETH
05	DEC	1698	-	LEATHERLAND	man child of WM & ELIZABETH borne[1]
15	DEC	1698	MARY	GILLET	d./ JAMES & MARY
15	DEC	1698	MARY	SWAINE	d./ JOHN & BRIDGET
24	FEB	1698	NICHOLAS	KIDDIER	s./ WM & DOROTHY
15	MAY	1699	ELIZABETH	BOULTBY	d./ WILLM & RUTH
20	OCT	1699	WILLIAM	SHAW	s./ THOMAS & ELLEN
08	NOV	1699	THOMAS	MORLEY	s./ WALTER & ANNE of Whitwick
02	JAN	1699	JAMES	HALL	s./ JAMES & BARBARA
12	MAR	1699	JOHN	CLARK	s./ THOMAS & ELIZABETH
10	APR	1700	ELIZABETH	JOYNES	d./ JOHN & MARY
29	APR	1700	FRANCES	VAUGHAN	d./ CADWALLADER & ANNA
[Blank]		1700	SARA	TOMLINSON	d./ WM & MARGARET
15	DEC	1700	THOMAS	SHAW	s./ THOMAS & ELLEN
04	FEB	1700	ELIZABETH	SWAINE	d./ JOHN & BRIDGET
18	FEB	1700	ANN	BOULTBY	d./ WM & RUTH
07	JUN	1701	THOMAS	PARSONS/HODGKINSON	s./ THOMAS PARSONS & ELIZABETH HODGKINSON
16	DEC	1701	ELIZABETH	COULTON	d./ GEORGE & ELIZABETH
11	FEB	1701	THOMAS	RICE	s./ JOHN & CATHERINE of Breedon
13	FEB	1701	JOHN	JOYNES	s./ JOHN & MARY
24	MAY	1702	SARAH	HALL	d./ JAMES & BARBARA
21	SEP	1702	JOHN	TOMLISON	s./ GEORGE & ANN
26	OCT	1702	BRIDGET	SWANE	d./ JOHN & BRIDGET
05	JAN	1702	JOHN	BOULTBY	s./ WILLM & RUTH
25	MAY	1703	ELIZABETH	BOULTBY	d./ THOMAS & MARY of Storton
12	SEP	1703	FRANCIS	MORLEY	s./ ROBERT & MARGARET
07	JAN	1703	JOHN	HORSEPOOL	s./ JOHN a pooreman & SARAH[2]
13	FEB	1703	JOHN	BROWN	s./ HENRY & ANE
10	MAR	1703	JOSEPH	SHAW	s./ TH. a pooreman & ELLEN
30	JUL	1704	THOMAS	JOYNES	s./ JOHN & ELIZABETH
01	SEP	1704	ANNE	SWAINE	d./ JOHN & BRIDGET
17	OCT	1704	MARY	HARDY	d./ THOMAS & MARGARET of Whitwick
13	DEC	1704	GEORGE	HALL	s./ JAMES & BARBARA
06	FEB	1704	SARAH	REED	d./ HENERY & ALICE of Thringston

[1] Entry recorded on a separate page of the register, immediately prior to the start of the Marriages; 'A man child of WM LEATHERLAND & ELIZABETH his wife borne December 5. The same child departed this life December ii [11]'.

[2] Register also gave 'by settlement of ye parish of Southwell in ye county of Notingham'.

09	JUN	1705	WM	LEATHERLAND	s./ WILLM & ELIZABETH
02	APR	1705	ANE	BOULTBY	d./ WILLIAM & RUTH
23	OCT	1705	SARAH	BOULTBY	d./ THOMAS & MARY of Storton
09	DEC	1705	TIMOTHY	JOYNES	s./ JOHN & ELIZABETH
11	DEC	1705	JOSEPH	MORLEY	s./ ROBERT & MARGARET
01	JAN	1705	DANIEL	HAROLD	s./ ROBERT & MARY
05	FEB	1705	WILLIAM	SHAW	s./ THOMAS & ELLEN
15	MAR	1705	WILLIAM	SWAINE	s./ JOHN & BRIDGET
07	APR	1706	JOSEPH	THOMLISON	s./ GEORGE & ANE
05	NOV	1706	THOMAS	BAILY	s./ JOSHUA & CATHERINE
04	DEC	1706	EDWARD	BELTON	s./ PETER & MARY
28	JAN	1706	GEORGE	HORSEPOOL	s./ JOHN & SARAH
15	JUN	1707	MARY	JOYNES	d./ JOHN & ELIZABETH
23	AUG	1707	JOHN	HAROLD	s./ ROBERT & MARY
30	SEP	1707	MARY	MORLEY	d./ ROBERT & MARGARET
22	NOV	1707	MARY	HUSKINSON	d./ JOHN & MARY
30	DEC	1707	JUDETH	ILLSLEY	d./ GILBERT & JANE
21	JAN	1707	HUMPHREY	SWAIN	s./ JOHN & BRIDGET
26	APR	1708	JOSEPH	BOULTBEE	s./ WILLM & RUTH
11	NOV	1708	ANA	BOULTBEE	d./ THOMAS & MARY
10	JAN	1708	THOMAS	THOMLISON	s./ GEORGE & ANN
11	MAR	1708	ELIZABETH	MORLEY	d./ ROBERT & MARGARET
02	AUG	1709	JOHN	ILLSLEY	s./ GILBERT & JANE
12	AUG	1709	JOSEPH	SHAW	s./ THOMAS & ELLEN
25	NOV	1709	ELIZABETH	VALE	d./ HENRY & ELIZABETH
18	JAN	1709	SARAH	HAROLD	d./ ROBERT & MARY
21	JAN	1709	ELIZABETH	HUSKINSON	d./ JOHN & ELIZABETH
25	JAN	1709	MARY	HEMSLEY	d./ JOHN & ELIZABETH
12	MAR	1709	ELIZABETH	SMITH	d./ RICHARD & DOROTHY
17	MAR	1709	JOSHUA	BAILY	s./ JOSHUA & CATHARINE
28	MAY	1710	SARAH	BALL	d./ ROBERT & ANNE
01	OCT	1710	GEORGE	JOYNES	s./ JOHN & ELIZABETH
21	NOV	1710	ANNA	SWANE	d./ JOHN & BRIDGET
18	APR	1711	MARY	PEGG	d./ THOS & ANN
30	MAR[1]	1711	BARBARA	ALLEN	d./ WILLM & CHRISTIAN
30	APR	1711	ROBERT	CHURCHILL	s./ TIMOTHY & ELIZABETH
18	MAY	1711	JOHN	STINSON	s./ JOHN & DOROTHY
22	SEP	1711	THOMAS	MORLEY	s./ ROBERT & MARGARET
11	DEC	1711	JAMES	?HAMLETON	s./ unknown parents
06	FEB	1711	FRANCES	BOULTBEE	d./ THO & MARY
21	APR	1712	ELIZABETH	MORE	d./ THO & ALICE
25	JUN	1712	MARY	HAYS	d./ THOMAS & ANNE
13	SEP	1712	HANNAH	BELTON	d./ THOMAS & MARY
15	OCT	1712	JOHN	NORTH	s./ CATHERINE

[1] Out of chronological order in register. Two BTs gave 13 & 30 March respectively.

14 NOV 1712 RUTH MORLEY d./ ROBERT & MARGARET
10 MAY 1713 ELIZABETH FIELDING d./ THOMAS & MARY
17 MAY 1713 ELIZABETH THOMLISON d./ GEORGE & ANNE
04 JUL 1713 CHRISTIAN ALLEN d./ WILLIAM & CHRISTIAN
19 AUG 1713 MARY HUSKINS d./ JOHN & MARY
08 NOV 1713 SARAH FLETCHER d./ JOHN & ELIZABETH
07 JAN 1713 HUGH STINSON s./ JOHN & DOROTHY
12 JAN 1713 WILLIAM HAYS s./ THO & ANN

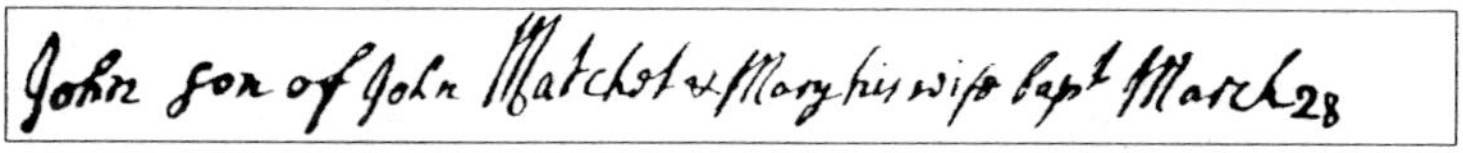
John son of John Matchet & Mary his wife bapt March 28

28 MAR 1714 JOHN MATCHET s./ JOHN & MARY
06 SEP 1714 GEORGE ILLSLEY s./ GILBERT & JANE
31 OCT 1714 MARY SIMPSON d./ WM & ELIZ
28 NOV 1714 THOMAS MORE s./ THOM & ALICE
18 APR 1715 FRANCES JOYNES d./ JOHN & ELIZ
07 MAY 1715 REBECAH FIELDING d./ THOMAS & MARY
28 JUL 1715 ELIZABETH RIGHT d./ RICHARD & ELIZ
08 JUN 1716 ANE PALMER d./ WM & RUTH
27 FEB 1716 DOROTHY STINSON d./ JOHN & DOROTHY
20 APR 1717 JOHN TATENALL s./ JOHN & SUSANNA
22 APR 1717 MARY BELTON d./ THOMAS & MARY
10 SEP 1717 JANE HAYS d./ THOMAS & ANE
08 JAN 1717 WILLIAM MATCHET s./ JOHN & MARY
22 JAN 1717 THOMAS WOOTTON s./ RICHARD & HANNAH
21 FEB 1717 ELLEN FIELDING d./ THO & MARY
04 MAY 1718 ELIZABETH WILLIAMSON d./ MELBOURN & SARAH
11 MAY 1718 FRANCES WRIGHT d./ RICHARD & ELIZ
15 JUN 1718 SAMUEL BAILEY s./ JOSUHA & CATHARINE
07 SEP 1718 SARAH JOYNES d./ JOHN & ELIZABETH
24 SEP 1718 WILLIAM PALMER s./ HENRY & ELIZ
18 NOV 1718 ROBERT TATENAL s./ JOHN & SUSANNAH
26 DEC 1718 ELIZABETH HAYS d./ THOMAS & ANE
14 APR 1719 RICHARD WOOTTON s./ RICHARD & HANNAH
31 MAY 1719 THOMAS BROWN s./ THO & MARY
06 OCT 1719 CATHERINE CLERKE d./ CHARLES & ELIZ. Schoolmaster
09 OCT 1719 CHRISTOPHER SOARS base s./ ELIZABETH
16 OCT 1719 ROBERT BRADFORD s./ ROBERT & MARY
08 JAN 1719 JANE WILLIAMSON d./ MELBOURN & SARAH
12 JAN 1719 SARAH BELTON d./ THOMAS & MARY
04 FEB 1719 NATHANIEL JOYNES s./ JOHN & ELIZ
29 MAR 1720 WILLIAM PEAT s./ WM & ALICE
23 MAY 1720 HANNAH WOOTTON d./ RICHARD & HANNAH
21 JUL 1720 GILBERT ILLSLEY s./ GILBERT & JANE
11 AUG 1720 THOMAS TATENAL s./ JOHN & SUSANNA
17 AUG 1720 ANE MATCHET d./ JOHN & MARY

06	NOV	1720	REBECKAH	BALL	d./ JAMES & MARY
11	DEC	1720	MARY	STINSON	d./ JOHN & DOROTHY
11	DEC	1720	SARAH	FLETCHER	d./ JOHN & ELIZ
27	DEC	1720	MARY	FREEMAN	d./ GEORGE & JANE
17	MAR	1720	RICHARD	WRIGHT	s./ RICHARD & ELIZ
07	JUL	1721	ELIZABETH	HEMSLEY	d./ JOHN & ABIA
23	JUL	1721	ANE	BRADFORD	d./ ROBERT & MARY
19	NOV	1721	ELIZABETH	BROWN	d./ THOMAS & MARY

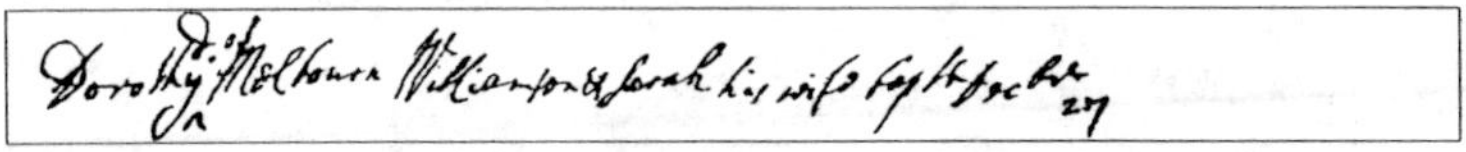
Dorothy d. of Melbourn Williamson & Sarah his wife Baptized December 27

27	DEC	1721	DOROTHY	WILLIAMSON	d./ MELBOURN & SARAH
13	MAR	1721	MARY	CLERKE	d./ CHARLES & ELIZ. Schoolmaster
27	APR	1722	JAMES	TATENAL	s./ JOHN & SUSANNAH
07	MAY	1722	ANE	BELTON	d./ THOMAS & MARY
01	JUN	1722	ELIZABETH	WOOTTON	d./ RICHARD & ALICE
27	JAN	1722	THOMAS	BONSER	s./ THOMAS & MARY
26	FEB	1722	JOHN	STINSON	s./ JOHN & DOROTHY
29	MAR	1723	SAMUEL	GILBERT	s./ SAMUEL & ELLEN
03	JUN	1723	ELIZABETH	MATCHET	d./ JOHN & MARY
19	JUN	1723	ANNA	VAUGHAN	d./ JOHN Mr & ELIZABETH
08	OCT	1723	SAMUEL	BROWN	s./ THOMAS & MARY
10	DEC	1723	SARAH	WILLIAMSON	d./ MELBOURN & SARAH
14	MAR	1723	JOSHUA	SENYOR	s./ JOSHUA & MARTHA[1]
12	JUL	1724	ROGER	UPTON	s./ WILLM & REBECCAH
24	JUL	1724	ELIZ	PARSONS	d./ THOMAS & ELIZ
07	SEP	1724	ELIZABETH	BELTON	d./ THOMAS & MARY
30	OCT	1724	ABIA	HEMSLEY	d./ JOHN & ABIA
11	DEC	1724	JAMES	GILBERT	s./ SAMUEL & ELLEN
05	OCT	1725	HARLEY	VAUGHAN	s./ JOHN & ELIZ
15	OCT	1725	SARAH	WILLOWS	d./ JAMES & ANNE
23	JAN	1725	JOHN	BROWN	s./ THOMAS & MARY
09	FEB	1725	SARAH	PARSONS	d./ THOMAS & ELIZ
23	MAR	1725	DANIEL	HEMSLEY	s./ JOHN & ABIA
04	MAY	1726	ANNE	TOMLINSON	d./ JOHN & ELIZ
04	NOV	1726	ELIZABETH	HARDY	d./ FRANCIS & ELIZ
16	DEC	1726	MARY	WITE	d./ JOHN & ANNE
16	DEC	1726	SARAH	BRADFORD	d./ ROBERT & MARY
04	JAN	1726	ELIZABETH	CLERK	d./ CHARLES & ELIZ. Schoolmaster
05	JAN	1726	SAMUEL	MATCHET	s./ JOHN & MARY
02	APR	1727	JAMES	WILLOWS	s./ JAMES & ANNE
25	JUN	1727	SARAH	HARDY	natural d./ MARY
13	AUG	1727	SAMUEL	TATENAL	s./ JOHN & SUSANNAH
26	SEP	1727	DORCAS	VAUGHAN	d./ JOHN & ELIZ

[1] The register also gave 'of the parish of Fellchurch near Wakefield, Yorkshire. Travellers'.

06	OCT	1727	THOMAS	PARSONS	s./ THOMAS & ELIZ
03	DEC	1727	THOMAS	TOMLINSON	s./ JOHN & ELIZ
		1728	No Baptisms		
29	AUG	1729	MARY	TATENAL	d./ JOHN
14	NOV	1729	ANN	PARSONS	d./ THOMAS
18	MAR	1729	JOHN	MEMORY	s./ THOMAS
28	JUN	1730	JOHN	TOMLINSON	s./ JOHN
02	AUG	1730	ANN	WILLOWS	d./ JAMES
14	MAR	1730	JOHN	JOYNES	base s./ MARY
09	APR	1731	WILLIAM	GIBSON	s./ WILL
26	SEP	1731	JOHN	PARSONS	s./ THO
27	JUN	1732	JOHN	FORD	s./ HENRY
26	JUL	1732	JOHN	RICHARDS	s./ SIMON
26	JUL	1732	MARY	BRADLY	d./ JOHN
11	FEB	1732	THO	MEMORY	s./ THO
23	FEB	1732	JOHN	GIBSON	s./ WILL
14	APR	1733	MARY	PARSONS	d./ THO
09	SEP	1733	ROBERT	WILLOWS	s./ JAMES deceased
19	NOV	1733	JOHN	BRADLY	s./ JOHN
27	DEC	1733	THO	BOTHOMER	s./ JOHN
17	FEB	1733	JOSEPH	MATCHET	s./ JOHN
03	MAR	1733	MARY	GOODARD	d./ THO
15	APR	1734	JAMES	GIBSON	s./ WILL
16	AUG	1734	WILL	SMITH	s./ JOHN
08	SEP	1734	ANN	HUCKNAL	posthumous d./ [Blank] HUCKNAL
22	SEP	1734	JOHN	SHAW	s./ JOHN
04	MAR	1734	ANN	PAYNE	d./ JOSEPH
10	MAR	1734	THOMAS	CLERKE	s./ JOHN born & bapt
09	APR	1735	JOHN	ROPER	s./ RICHARD
11	APR	1735	MARY	TOMLINSON	d./ GEORGE
20	APR	1735	GEORGE	HALL	s./ GEORGE
01	MAY	1735	MARY	RICHARDS	d./ SIMON
06	JUN	1735	HANNAH	PARSONS	d./ THO
07	SEP	1735	JOHN	ROSE	s./ JOHN
10	FEB	1735	JOHN	SMITH	s./ JOHN
08	APR	1736	HENRY	COOK	s./ RICHARD
15	JUL	1736	MARY	FREEMAN	d./ ISAAC
11	AUG	1736	HENRY	TUGBY	s./ JOHN
05	NOV	1736	ELIZ	PAYNE	d./ JOS
27	NOV	1736	WILL	ROSE	s./ JOHN
27	DEC	1736	ANN	HALL	d./ EDWARD
22	JAN	1736	GEORGE	ILLSY	s./ GEORGE
11	FEB	1736	JAMES	FORD	s./ HENRY
27	FEB	1736	JOHN	PARSONS	s./ THO
12	APR	1737	ELLEN	HARRIS	d./ WILL
29	OCT	1737	THO	SMITH	s./ JOHN

13	NOV	1737	WILL	ROPER	s./ RICHD
20	NOV	1737	SARAH	COOK	d./ RICHD
16	DEC	1737	ELIZ	PAYNE	d./ JOS
18	DEC	1737	ELLEN	GODDARD	d./ THO
30	APR	1738	WILLIAM	RICHARDS	s./ SIMON
19	JUN	1738	SARAH	FREEMAN	d./ ISAAC
21	JAN	1738	JOHN	TUGBY	s./ JOHN
22	JAN	1738	TRIPHENA	BRADLY	d./ JOHN
20	APR	1739	EDWARD	HALL	s./ EDW
22	APR	1739	JOANNA	TOMLINSON	d./ JOHN
27	APR	1739	WILL	ILLSLY	s./ GEORGE
10	JUN	1739	HANNAH	PARSONS	d./ THO
09	JUL	1739	ROBERT	ROSE	s./ JOHN
09	SEP	1739	WILL	HARRIS	s./ WILL
05	OCT	1739	JOSEPH	SMITH	s./ JOS
26	DEC	1739	RICHARD	DURANT	s./ GEORGE
02	MAR	1739	[Blank]	RICHARDS	-/ of SIM
06	APR	1740	JOHN	MATCHET	s./ JOHN
06	APR	1740	RICHARD	ROPER	s./ RICHARD
25	MAY	1740	EDW	HALL	s./ EDW
30	MAY	1740	WILL	MATCHET	s./ WILL
30	MAY	1740	SARAH	ROE	d./ WM[1]
22	JUN	1740	ROB	EARP	s./ ROB
05	OCT	1740	GEORGE	FREEMAN	s./ ISAAC
06	JAN	1740	TRYPHENA	BRADLY	d./ JOHN
30	JAN	1740	THO	GODDARD	s./ THO
13	APR	1741	WILLIAM	MATCHET	s./ WILLIAM
24	MAY	1741	DIANA	TUGBY	d./ JOHN
08	JUL	1741	THOMAS	HUNT/MATCHET	base child of SARAH HUNT & J. MATCHET
09	AUG	1741	SARAH	HALL	d./ EDW
02	OCT	1741	JOS	PEG	s./ JOSEPH
13	NOV	1741	JOHN	GIBSON	s./ WILL
19	NOV	1741	JOHN	SMITH	s./ JOSEPH
05	FEB	1741	WILL	ASHER	s./ WILLIAM
12	MAR	1741	WILL	ROE	s./ WILL
18	APR	1742	[Blank]	ROSE	s./ JOHN
18	JUN	1742	HENRY	INSLY	s./ GEORGE
20	JUN	1742	JOSEPH	SMITH	s./ JOHN
10	DEC	1742	JOHN	ASHAR	s./ THO
11	FEB	1742	CATHERINE	BAILY	base d./ MARY
16	FEB	1742	SUSANNA	SHEPHARD	base d./ SUSAN
17	FEB	1742	WILLIAM	MORLY	s./ JOS
20	FEB	1742	SIMON	RICHARDS	s./ SIMON
08	MAY	1743	[Blank]	ROPER	-/ RICH

[1] This entry was written vertically in the right-hand margin of the register.

17	JUL	1743	CHRISTIAN	ROSE	d./ JOHN
12	SEP	1743	ELIZABETH	PEG	d./ JOHN
22	DEC	1743	SARAH	BRADLY	d./ JOHN
22	MAR	1743	ELIZABETH	HALL	d./ GEORGE
09	SEP	1744	WILL	BROWNE	s./ SAM
26	OCT	1744	HANNAH	HUSKINSON	d./ JOHN
25	NOV	1744	ELIZ	ASHUR	d./ THOMAS
02	DEC	1744	JANE	ROE	d./ WILL

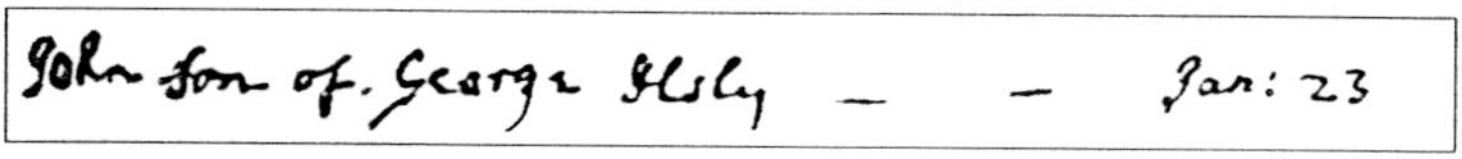
John son of George Ilsly — — Jan: 23

23	JAN	1744	JOHN	ILSLY	s./ GEORGE
23	JAN	1744	MARY	TATENAL	d./ ROB
11	JAN	1745	MARY	PEG	d./ JOHN
24	JAN	1745	ANN	MATCHET	d./ WILL
24	JAN	1745	BARBARA	ROSE	d./ JOHN
30	MAR	1746	JOSEPH	WARD	s./ [Blank] [THOMAS & JANE[1]]
18	MAY	1746	CATHERINE	HALL	d./ EDWARD
19	MAY	1746	MARY	BROWNE	d./ SAM
08	SEP	1746	JAMES	ASHUR	s./ WILL
14[2]	DEC	1746	JANE	ASHUR	d./ THO
22	FEB	1746	ANN	GODDARD	d./ THO
24	FEB	1746	MARY	ASHUR	d./ SAM
01	MAY	1747	ELIZ	TUGBY	d./ JOHN
26	MAY	1747	CHARLES	BERISFORD	s./ CHARLES
26	FEB	1747	ELIZABETH	MATCHET	d./ WILL
15	APR	1748	GILBERT	INSLEY	s./ GEORGE & HANNAH
28	MAY	1748	THOMAS	WARD	s./ THOMAS & JANE
28	JUN	1748	JAMES	HALL	s./ EDWARD & ANN
05	SEP	1748	SARAH	ASHER	d./ THOMAS & MARY
05	SEP	1748	MARTHA	JOYNS	d./ TIMOTHY & ELIZABETH
25	DEC	1748	SARAH	BERISFORD	d./ CHARLES & RACHEL
01	JAN	1748	MARY	ROPER	d./ RICHARD & JANE
10	FEB	1748	RICHARD	DANE	s./ RICHARD & JANE
16	JUL	1749	MARTHA	BROWNE	d./ SAMUEL & ELIZABETH
26	NOV	1749	THOMAS	PLANT	s./ ROBT & SARAH
05	DEC	1749	MARY	YOUNGE	d./ MOSES & SARAH
06	JAN	1749	MARY	MATCHET	d./ WM & CATHARINE
02	MAR	1749	MARY	MATCHET	d./ SAML & REBECCA
04	MAR	1749	THOMAS	BROWNE	s./ JOHN & REBECCA
13	MAY	1750	MARY	SMALLEY	d./ HENRY & MARY of Grace Dieu
15	MAY	1750	JOHN	HAYFIELD	s./ JOHN & ELIZABETH
04	JUN	1750	HEMSLEY JOHN	GLOVER	s./ WILLIAM & ABIA

[1] Names of parents from child's burial in 1750.

[2] BT gave 18 December.

07	SEP	1750	MARY	DANE	d./ RICHARD & JANE
09	SEP	1750	ANNE	WARD	d./ THOMAS & JANE
21	DEC	1750	JANE	INSLEY	d./ GEORGE & HANNAH
25	DEC	1750	THOMAS	ASHER	s./ THOMAS & MARY
29	MAR	1751	SAMUEL	BROWNE	s./ SAML & ELIZTH private bapt
28	APR	1751	CATHARINE	YOUNG	d./ MOSES & SARAH
27	MAY	1751	NATHANAEL	JOHNSON	s./ JOHN & SARAH of Whitwick
30	MAY	1751	GEORGE	TOON	s./ THOMAS & SARAH of Whitwick

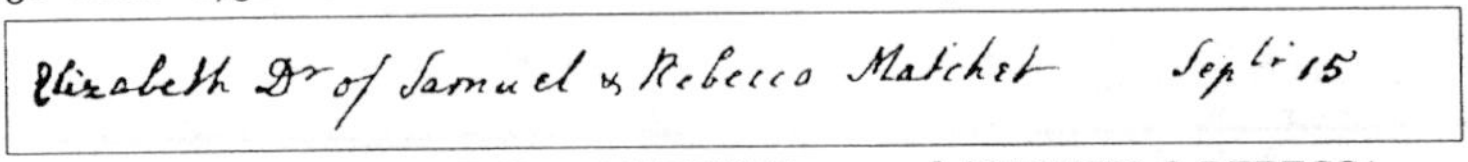
Elizabeth Dr of Samuel & Rebecca Matchet Septr 15

15	SEP	1751	ELIZABETH	MATCHET	d./ SAMUEL & REBECCA
26	DEC	1751	JANE	ROPER	d./ RICHARD & JANE
27	OCT[1]	1751	LUCY	BOULTBEE	d./ THO Mr & JANE of Stordon
			'NB. ys year begins Janry ye 1st by act of Parliamt'[*sic*]		
11	FEB	1752	ANNE	BROWNE	d./ JOHN & REBECCA
18	FEB	1752	MARY	ROSE	d./ JOHN & BARBARA
12	FEB[2]	1752	ROBERT	TATNELL	s./ ROBERT & SARAH private bapt
29	MAR	1752	ELIZABETH	ROW	d./ WM & ANNE
10	MAY	1752	JOSEPH	ROW	s./ WM & ANNE
22	JUN	1752	JOHN	HUSKISSON	s./ JOHN & MARY
12	JUL	1752	JAMES	YOUNG	s./ MOSES & SARAH
25	DEC	1752	ELIZABETH	BROWNE	d./ SAMUEL & ELIZA
16	APR	1753	HENRY	WHITBY	s./ [Blank] & ELIZABETH
23	APR	1753	HANNAH	SMALLEY	d./ HENRY & MARY of Grace Dieu
06	MAY	1753	ANN	GLOVER	d./ WILLIAM & SARAH
18	MAY	1753	DOROTHY	HALL	d./ EDWARD & ANN
04	JUN	1753	JOHN	BOULTBEE	s./ THOS & JANE of Stordon
04	JUN	1753	THOMAS	BOULTBEE	s./ THOS & JANE of Stordon
11	JUN	1753	THOMAS	HAYWOOD	s./ MATTHEW & MARY of Worthington
16	SEP	1753	SAMUEL	ASHER	s./ THOS & MARY
16	NOV	1753	HANNAH	INSLEY	d./ GEORGE & HANNAH
09	DEC	1753	DAWSON	BERISFORD	s./ CHARLES & RACHAL
17	FEB	1754	ANN	BAILEY alias DUDLEY	d./ JOHN & MARY of Worthington
14	APR	1754	DANIEL	HARWOOD	s./ JOHN & MARY of Worthington
14	APR	1754	MARY	HICKLIN	d./ WILLIAM & MARY
19	APR	1754	SARAH	BENNET	d./ JOHN & SARAH
19	APR	1754	ELIZABETH	HUSKISSON	d./ THOS & SARAH
28	APR	1754	WILLIAM	BALL	s./ WM & MARY of Worthington
28	APR	1754	SARAH	BARFOOT	d./ JOHN & SARAH of Worthington
19	MAY	1754	JOHN	MATCHET	s./ SAMUEL & REBECCAH
26	MAY	1754	JOHN	BONSER	s./ JOSEPH & ELIZA' of Worthington
28	JUL	1754	MARY	PLANT	d./ ROBERT & SARAH

1 Out of chronological order in register.

2 Out of chronological order in both register & BT.

22	SEP	1754	SAMUEL	BROWNE	s./ JOHN & REBECCAH
13	OCT	1754	HANNAH	SYLVESTER	d./ WILLIAM & ELIZABETH of Worthington
24	JAN	1755	JOHN	HICKLIN	s./ JOHN & SARAH of Breedon
07	FEB	1755	HANNAH	GLOVER	d./ WILLIAM & SARAH
20	APR	1755	BRIAN	PEGG	s./ JOSEPH & ANNE
21	MAY	1755	ELIZABETH	BOULTBEE	d./ THOS Mr & JANE of Stordons
28	MAY	1755	SAMUEL	SMITH	s./ SAMUEL & CATHARINE of Swannington
06	JUN	1755	SAMUEL	GILBERT	s./ SAMUEL & ELIZABETH
01	SEP	1755	ELIZABETH	MASSEY	d./ GEORGE & MARY of Whitwick
21	SEP	1755	ROBERT	YOUNG	s./ MOSES & SARAH
25	NOV	1755	SARAH	NEWBALD	d./ THOMAS & ANNE
30	NOV	1755	MARY	BALL	d./ RICHARD & MARY of Worthington
07	DEC	1755	WILLIAM	HICKLIN	s./ WILLIAM & MARY
14	DEC	1755	MARY	HODGES	d./ THOMAS & ANNE of Breedon
06	JAN	1756	ELIZABETH	BAILEY	d./ EDWARD & SARAH
13	FEB	1756	ELIZABETH	TIVEY	d./ EDWARD & ELIZABETH
09	MAR	1756	JANE	BOWLEY	d./ THOMAS & ELIZABETH
19	APR	1756	MARY	PLATT	d./ HUGH Mr & CATHARINE
01	JUN	1756	ROBERT	CORBET	s./ ROBERT & MILLICENT
07	JUN	1756	THOMAS	KENDRICK	s./ THOS & CATHARINE
13	AUG	1756	JAMES[1]	GILBERT	s./ SAMUEL & ELIZABETH
12	JAN	1757	WILLIAM	ASHER	s./ THOS & MARY
14	FEB	1757	HANNAH	NEWBALD	d./ THOS & ANN
11	MAR	1757	SARAH	EARP	d./ JOHN & MARY
22	APR	1757	ELIZABETH	ILLSLEY	d./ GEORGE & HANNAH
01	MAY	1757	JAMES	DANIELS	d./ HENRY & JANE
08	MAY	1757	SARAH	HUSKISSON	d./ THOMAS & SARAH
29	MAY	1757	ROBERT	CORBET	s./ ROBERT & MILLICENT
12	JUN	1757	WILLIAM	SMALLEY	s./ HENRY & MARY of Grace Dieu
01	JUL	1757	GEORGE	ROW	s./ WILLIAM & ANN
08	AUG	1757	MARY	BOULTBEE	d./ THOMAS Mr & JANE of Stordons
18	SEP	1757	MARY	BROWNE	d./ JOHN & REBECCA
26[2]	DEC	1757	HANNAH	KENDRICK	d./ THOMAS & CATHARINE
27	DEC	1757	THOMAS	BOWLEY	an adult
31	MAR	1758	ELIZABETH	GLOVER	d./ WILLIAM & SARAH
02	APR	1758	SARAH	BAILEY	d./ EDWARD & SARAH
23	JUL	1758	ELLEN	GILBERT	d./ SAMUEL & ELIZABETH
20	AUG	1758	THOMAS	HEAPE	s./ THOS & ESTHER
05	OCT	1758	MARY	EVERARD	d./ FRANCIS & HANNAH
31	OCT	1758	ANN	EARP	d./ JOHN & MARY
01	NOV	1758	ELIZABETH	BILLSON	d./ JOHN & MARY
17	DEC	1758	JANE	NEWBALD	d./ THOMAS & ANN
01	JAN	1759	ANNE	PERKINS	d./ ELIZABETH of Thringstone

[1] BT gave SAMUEL.

[2] BT gave 6 December.

04	JAN	1759	JOSEPH	BOULTBEE	s./ THOMAS Mr & JANE of Stordons
09	JAN	1759	MARY	HUSKISSON	d./ JOHN & MARY
26	JAN	1759	SARAH	HOLT	d./ THOMAS & SARAH of Thringstone
28	JAN	1759	ELIZABETH	CHAPLIN	d./ JAMES & ELIZABETH
05	MAR	1759	ROBERT	WILLOWS	d./ ROBERT & HANNAH
04	JUN	1759	JOHN	PLATT	s./ HUGH Mr & CATHARINE
23	JUN	1759	MARY	BARRET	d./ RICHARD & SARAH
22	JUL	1759	SAMUEL	BROWN	s./ SAMUEL & ELIZABETH
18	SEP	1759	JOSEPH	UNDERWOOD	s./ JOSEPH & ELIZABETH of Dyseworth
19	SEP	1759	ANNE	BOWLEY	d./ THOMAS & ELIZABETH
27	DEC	1759	JOHN	PEGG	s./ JOSEPH & ANNE
08	FEB	1760	GEORGE	TIVY	s./ EDWARD & ELIZABETH
06	APR	1760	ANNE	CHAPLIN	d./ JAMES & ELIZABETH of Griffy Dam
16	APR	1760	CATHARINE	KENDRICK	d./ THOMAS & CATHARINE
03	AUG	1760	MARY	HEAPE	d./ THOMAS & ESTHER
21	SEP	1760	MILLICENT	CORBET	d./ ROBERT & MILLICENT
22	SEP	1760	JOSEPH	FARMER	s./ JOHN & ELIZABETH
31	OCT	1760	HENRY	ILLSLEY	s./ GEORGE & HANNAH
10	NOV	1760	THOMAS	LAYKIN	s./ THOMAS & SARAH
05	JAN	1761	LYDIA	PEGG	an adult
13	JAN	1761	THOMAS	EARP	s./ JOHN & MARY
28	JAN	1761	WILLIAM	GLOVER	s./ WILLIAM & SARAH
31	JAN	1761	WILLIAM	BOULTBEE	s./ THOMAS Mr & JANE of Stordons
25	FEB	1761	SARAH	BARRAT	d./ RICHARD & SARAH
03	APR	1761	HANNAH	MATCHET	d./ SAMUEL & REBECCAH
19	APR	1761	EDWARD	BAILEY	s./ EDWARD & SARAH
07	JUN	1761	MARY	TUGBY	d./ HOSEA & MARY of the Brand
16	AUG	1761	ANN	WILLOWS	d./ ROBERT & HANNAH
22	SEP	1761	MOSES	YOUNG	s./ MOSES & SARAH
24	NOV	1761	JAMES	CHAPLIN	s./ JAMES & ELIZABETH
06	DEC	1761	MARY	SWAN	d./ THOMAS & ANN
06	DEC	1761	WILLIAM	ROSE	s./ JNO & ELIZABETH
01	JAN	1762	WILLIAM	NEWBALD	s./ THOMAS & ANN
01	JAN	1762	JOSEPH	SHARP	s./ JOHN & ANN of Griffy Dam
23	JAN	1762	SARAH	BROWNE	d./ SAMUEL & ELIZABETH
05	FEB	1762	FANNY	BOWLEY	d./ THOMAS & ELIZABETH
28[1]	MAR	1762	JANE	WRIGHT	d./ WILLIAM & [Blank] of Griffy Dam
11	APR	1762	ELIZABETH	CORBET	d./ ROBERT & MILLICENT
10	JUN	1762	JOHN	HEAP	s./ THOMAS & ESTHER
06	JUL	1762	WILLIAM	ADCOCK	s./ JOHN & MARGARET of Worthington
10	AUG	1762	JAMES	LAKINS	s./ THOMAS & SARAH
20	SEP	1762	CHARLES	FARMER	s./ JOHN & ELIZABETH
08	NOV	1762	ELIZABETH	ROBINSON	d./ JOHN & ELIZABETH
29	DEC	1762	JOSEPH	WRAGG	s./ JOHN & MARY of Thringstone

1 BT gave 8 March.

02	JAN	1763	ELIZABETH	BURGSS	d./ WILLIAM & ELIZABETH of Worthington
16	JAN	1763	MARY	CHAPLIN	d./ JAMES & ELIZABETH of Breedon
02	MAR	1763	MARY	ROSE	d./ JOHN & ELIZABETH
03	APR	1763	THOMAS	NEWBALD	s./ THOMAS & ANN
25	MAY	1763	ROBERT	BOULTBEE	s./ THOS Mr & JANE of Stordon Grange
05	JUN	1763	WILLIAM	GLOVER	s./ WILLIAM & SARAH
12	JUN	1763	MARY	TIVY	d./ EDWARD & ELIZABETH
18	SEP	1763	ELIZABETH	SWAN	d./ THOMAS & ANN

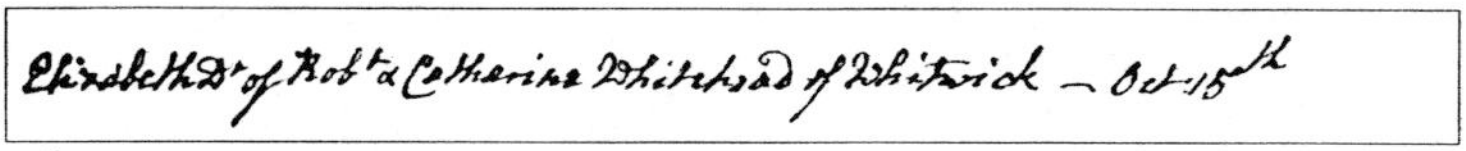
Elizabeth Dr of Robt & Catharine Whitehead of Whitwick – Oct 15th

15[1]	OCT	1763	ELIZABETH	WHITEHEAD	d./ ROBT & CATHARINE of Whitwick
31	OCT	1763	JOSEPH	BARRAT	s./ RICHARD & SARAH
04	NOV	1763	FRANCIS	HUFFON	s./ HUGH & MARTHA of Whitwick
09	MAR	1764	SARAH	HEAP	d./ THOS & ESTHER
15	APR	1764	JOHN	CORBET	s./ ROBT & MILLICENT
06	MAY	1764	WILLIAM	BRADLEY	s./ WM & DEB
15	MAY	1764	ELIZ	WILKINS	d./ WM & MARY of Whitwick
10	JUN	1764	MARY	HUSKISSON	d./ THOS & SARAH
17	JUN	1764	JAMES	WILLERS	s./ ROBT & HANNAH
16	SEP	1764	JOHN	ROBINSON	s./ JOHN & ANN
10	DEC	1764	HANNAH	BROWN	d./ SAML & ELIZ
18	JAN	1765	MARY	TATNELL	d./ SARAH of Thringstone
01	FEB	1765	JOHN	ROSE	s./ JOHN & ELIZ
02	FEB	1765	ANN	SWAN	d./ THOS & ANN
10	FEB	1765	MARY	GODDARD	d./ THOS & ELIZ
21	APR	1765	THOS	WHITEHEAD	s./ THOS & CATHARINE of Whitwick
05	SEP	1765	JANE	BOULTBEE	d./ THOS & JANE of Stordon Grange
22	SEP	1765	JAMES	CHAPLIN	s./ JAMES & ELIZ
22	SEP	1765	THOS	NEWBALD	s./ THOS & ANN
22	SEP	1765	MARY	BAILEY	d./ EDWD & SARAH
26	JAN	1766	ELIZ	LAKINS	d./ THOS & SARAH
18	MAY	1766	WILLIAM	YOUNG	s./ MOSES & SARAH
18	MAY	1766	ANN	CORBET	d./ ROBT & MILICENT
27	JUL	1766	JOSEPH	MATCHET	s./ JOSEPH & ANN
03	AUG	1766	THOMAS	TIVY	s./ EDWD & ELIZ
24	AUG	1766	JAMES	FORD	s./ JAMES & JANE
14	SEP	1766	SARAH	ROSE	d./ ROBT & ANN
26	DEC	1766	ANN	HUSKISSON	d./ THOS & SARAH
28	DEC	1766	ELIZ	BRADLEY	d./ WM & DEBORAH
15	FEB	1767	WILLIAM	ROPER	s./ RICHD & SARAH
29	MAR	1767	SARAH	SWAN	d./ THOS & ANN
31	MAY	1767	WILLIAM	BROWN	s./ SAML & ELIZ
19	JUN	1767	JOHN	SLEATH	s./ WM & MILCT

[1] BT gave 5 October.

07	AUG	1767	WILLIAM WILSON	ROSE	s./ JOHN & ELIZ
20	SEP	1767	WILLIAM	HARRIS	s./ WM & MARY
18	OCT	1767	WILLIAM	HEAP	s./ THOS & ESTHER
24	NOV	1767	FRANCES	BOULTBEE	d./ THOS & JANE of Stordons Grange
11	DEC	1767	MARY	ROSE	d./ ROBT & ANN
22	JAN	1768	SARAH	MATCHET	d./ JOSEPH & ANN
31	JAN	1768	THOS	STINSON	s./ WM & ANN
13	MAR	1768	JANE	CHAPLIN	d./ JAMES & ELIZABETH

Sarah D. of Moses & Sarah Young -- Apr.c 16th

16	APR	1768	SARAH	YOUNG	d./ MOSES & SARAH
17	APR	1768	MARY	CORBET	d./ ROBT & MILLECT
19	APR	1768	JOHN	WILLERS	s./ ROBT & HANNAH
21	MAY	1768	THOS	BARRAT	s./ RICHD & SARAH
03	JUL	1768	MARY	DARBY	d./ WM & ELIZ
10	JUL	1768	THOS	GODDARD	s./ THOS & ELIZ
22	JUL	1768	SARAH	BURTON	d./ GEORGE & MARY
28	SEP	1768	ANN	FORD	d./ JAMES & JANE
25	DEC	1768	HENRY	FORD	s./ THOS & ELIZ
10	MAR	1769	ELIZ	ROSE	d./ JOHN & ELIZ
24	MAR	1769	ROSE WARDLE	MATCHET	natural d./ MARY
23	APR	1769	JAMES	SLEATH	s./ WM & MILLECT
14	MAY	1769	MARY	CORBET	d./ ROBERT & MILLECT
21	MAY	1769	SARAH	LAKINS	d./ THOS & SARAH
18	JUN	1769	ROBT	ROSE	s./ ROBT & ANN
16	JUL	1769	DOROTHY	SWAN	d./ of THOS & ANN
21	AUG	1769	MARY	HARRIS	twin d./ WM & MARY
21	AUG	1769	HELLEN	HARRIS	twin d./ WM & MARY
17	SEP	1769	ANN	BAILEY	d./ EDWD & SARAH
09	NOV	1769	THOS	WOODWARD	s./ THOS & SARAH
21	DEC	1769	SARAH	DEXTER	d./ GEORGE & ELIZ
24	DEC	1769	CHARLES	MATCHET	s./ JOSEPH & ANN
28	DEC	1769	SARAH	BOULTBEE	d./ THOS & SARAH
23	FEB	1770	STARKEY	MARLER	s./ STARKEY & MARY
16	SEP	1770	JOHN	BURTON	s./ GEORGE & MARY
29	OCT	1770	JOHN	HARRIS	s./ WILLIAM & MARY
30	OCT	1770	WILLIAM	ROE	s./ WILLIAM & MARY
20	JAN	1771	WILLIAM	BALEY	s./ JOHN & ELIZ
27	JAN	1771	ELIZABETH	GODDARD	d./ THOS & ELIZ
28	JAN	1771	JAMES	ROSE	s./ ROBT & ANN
15	MAR	1771	GEORGE	BARRAT	s./ RICHD & SARAH
07	APR	1771	MARY	DEXTER	d./ GEORGE & ELIZ
28	APR	1771	ELIZABETH	FORD	d./ THOS & ELIZ
05	MAY	1771	WILLIAM	LAKIN	s./ THOS & SARAH
02	JUN	1771	SAMUEL	ROSE	s./ JOHN & ELIZ

30	JUN	1771	HANNAH	WILLERS	d./ ROBT & HANNAH
05	JUL	1771	JOSEPH	DARBY	s./ WM & ELIZ
28	JUL	1771	REBECCA	SWAN	d./ THOS & ANN
11	SEP	1771	ANN	MARLER	d./ STARKEY & MARY
22	SEP	1771	THOMAS	BRADLEY	s./ WM & DEBORAH
22	SEP	1771	ANN	STINSON	d./ WM & ANN
22	SEP	1771	SARAH	POTTS	d./ THOS & ELIZ
27	DEC	1771	CATHERINE	CORBET	d./ ROBT & MILISCENT
10	MAY	1772	MARY PRINGLE	YOUNG	natural d./ CATHARINE
19	JUN	1772	STARKEY	BAILEY	s./ JOHN & MARY
01	JUL	1772	JOSEPH CHEATLE	BAILEY	s./ EDWD & REBECCA
04	DEC	1772	THOMAS	PALMER	natural s./ ANN
09	JAN	1773	THOMAS TAYOR	KELLEY	natural s./ SARAH
27	JAN	1773	GEORGE	ROSE	s./ ROBT & ANN
05	FEB	1773	THOMAS	GILBERT	s./ SAML & ELIZ
10	FEB	1773	THOMAS MATON	HARRIS	s./ WILLIAM & MARY
19	FEB	1773	ANN	ROE	d./ WILLIAM & MARY
31	MAY	1773	JOHN	BARRAT	s./ RICHD & SARAH
02	JUN	1773	WILLIAM	MARLER	s./ STARKEY & MARY
06	JUL	1773	CHARLES	LAKIN	s./ THOS & SARAH
20	SEP	1773	SARAH	ROSE	d./ JOHN & ELIZ
14	NOV	1773	JAMES	GODDARD	s./ THOS & ELIZABETH
03	JAN	1774	ELIZABETH	POXSON	d./ JOHN & ANN
23	JAN	1774	THOMAS	BRADLEY	s./ WM & DEBORAH
22	APR	1774	WM	STINSON	s./ WM & ANN
09	JUN	1774	JOSEPH	BLADON	s./ WM & ANN
01	JUL	1774	JOHN	MARLER	s./ STARKEY & MARY
01	JUL	1774	THOS	SWAN	s./ THOS & ANN
01	AUG	1774	MARY	FORD	d./ THOS & ELIZ
09	OCT	1774	SARAH	WILLIERS	d./ ROBT & HANNAH
29	DEC	1774	JANE	ASHER	d./ WM & MARY
30	DEC	1774	HANNAH	GIBSON	d./ JOHN & HANNAH
16	APR	1775	SARAH	BAGNEL	d./ SAML & ANN
17	APR	1775	MARY	ROSE	d./ JOHN & ELIZ
22	APR	1775	GEORGE	ROE	s./ WM & MARY
09	MAY	1775	CHRISTIAN	ROSE	d./ ROBT & ANN
20	AUG	1775	JANE	DARBY	d./ WM & ELIZ
17	SEP	1775	CHARLES	HARRIS	s./ WM & MARY
17	SEP	1775	WILLIAM	MEEKIN	s./ WM & HANNAH
25	DEC	1775	JANE	YOUNG	d./ JAMES & ANN
01	JAN	1776	JOSEPH	KELLEY	natural s./ SARAH
03	MAR	1776	WILLIAM	RICHARDS	s./ WM & ELIZ
10	APR	1776	HANNAH	ASHER	d./ WM & MARY
21	JUL	1776	WILLIAM	BLADEN	s./ WM & ANN
08	AUG	1776	ELI	MARLER	s./ STARKEY & MARY

25	OCT	1776	WILLIAM	SWAN	s./ WM & ANN[1]
08	DEC	1776	HANNAH	SMITH	natural d./ [Blank] SMITH
11	JAN	1777	RICHARD	BARRAT	s./ RICHD & SARAH
02	MAR	1777	SARAH	CROSS	natural d./ MARY
30	MAR	1777	JOSEPH	LAKIN	s./ THOMAS & SARAH
04	APR	1777	ANN	YOUNG	d./ ROBERT & SARAH
15	MAY	1777	ELIZABETH	POTS	d./ THOMAS & ELIZABETH
19	MAY	1777	THOMAS	BAGNEL	s./ SAML & ANN
07	SEP	1777	WILLIAM	YOUNG	s./ JAMES & ANN
21	SEP	1777	WILLIAM	WILLERS	s./ ROBT & HANNAH
21	SEP	1777	JOSEPH	CROWSON	s./ JOSEPH & JANE
03	NOV	1777	THOMAS	MEEKIN	s./ WILLIAM & HANNAH
09	NOV	1777	ELIZABETH	MOUNTNEY	d./ ROBT & MARY
17	NOV	1777	JANE	BRALESFORD	of riper years. d./ ROBERT & ROSE
26	DEC	1777	JANE	CHARLESWORTH	d./ STEPHEN & SARAH
19	JAN	1778	JOSEPH	MARLER	s./ STARKEY & MARY
08	MAR	1778	JOHN	GIBSON	s./ JOHN & HANNAH
29	MAR	1778	ELIZABETH	DARBY	d./ WM & ELIZ
03	MAY	1778	RACHEL	YOUNG	d./ ROBERT & SARAH
21	JUN	1778	WILLIAM	ASHER	s./ WM & MARY
21	JUN	1778	MARY	HARRIS	d./ JAMES & MARY
20	SEP	1778	JOHN	GODDARD	s./ THOMAS & ELIZ
21	SEP	1778	ELIZABETH	BALL	d./ THOMAS & JANE
21	SEP	1778	SAMUEL	MATCHET	s./ JOHN & ELIZ
28	SEP	1778	SARAH	ROE	d./ WM & MARY
08	OCT	1778	ROWLSON	BEER	s./ THOMAS & SARAH
27	DEC	1778	ELIZABETH	CROWSON	d./ JOSEPH & JANE
24	JAN	1779	FRANCIS	SWAN	s./ THOMAS & ANN
31	JAN	1779	GEORGE	MEEKIN	s./ WM & HANNAH
21	FEB	1779	SARAH	LAKIN	d./ THOS & SARAH
25	APR	1779	ELIZABETH	YOUNG	d./ JAMES & ANN
23	MAY	1779	THEOPHILUS	ROPER	s./ RICHARD & SARAH
09	AUG	1779	ELI	MARLER	s./ STARKEY & MARY
19	SEP	1779	HANNAH	POTTS	d./ THO & ELIZABETH
07	DEC	1779	SARAH	HARRIS	d./ JAMES & MARY
30	DEC	1779	JOSEPH	BAILEY	s./ ELIZABETH
26	MAR	1780	HENRY	ROE	s./ WILLM & MARY
25[2]	MAY	1780	JOHN	EARP	s./ JOHN & ANN
29	MAY	1780	DAWSON BERRISFORD	YONGE	s./ ROBERT & SARAH
17	SEP	1780	JANE	BAGNALLE	d./ SAMUEL & ANN
17	SEP	1780	ELIZABETH	MATCHETT	d./ JOHN & ELIZABETH
27	OCT	1780	ELIZABETH	PEGG	natural d./ MARY
20	DEC	1780	MARY	MARLER	d./ STARKEY & MARY

[1] BT gave THOS & ANN.

[2] BT gave 5 May.

31[1] DEC 1780 JENNEY YONGE d./ JAMES & ANN
'A copy of this register is given in at the visitation by the year'
24 JUN 1781 SAMUEL HARRISE s./ WILLIAM & MARY
22 JUL 1781 ELIZABETH RAGG d./ CHARLES & ELIZABETH of Worthington
29 JUL 1781 MARY CROSON d./ JOSEPH & JANE
21 SEP 1781 THOMAS BRADLEY s./ THOMAS & ELLEN
01 FEB 1782 JOHN MEE s./ JOHN & HANNAH in the church of Breedon
20 MAY 1782 JAMES ASHER s./ WILLIAM & MARY

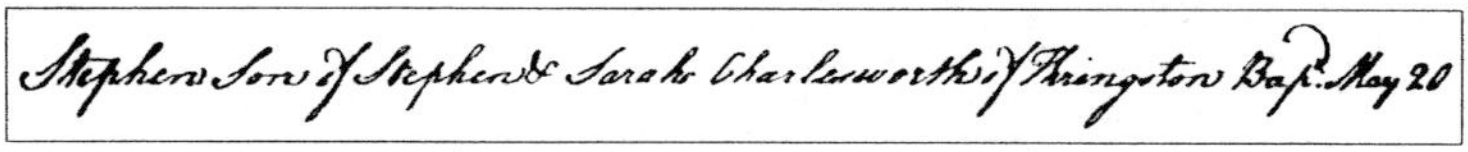
Stephen Son of Stephen & Sarah Charlesworth of Thringston Bapd. May 20

20 MAY 1782 STEPHEN CHARLESWORTH s./ STEPHEN & SARAH of Thringston
22 MAY 1782 ANN HARRISE d./ JAMES & MARY
02 JUN 1782 CHARLES YONGE s./ ROBERT & SARAH
14 JUN 1782 HANNAH MATCHETT d./ JOHN & ELIZABETH
22 SEP 1782 DIANAH BAGNALL d./ SAMUEL & ANN
22 SEP 1782 ELIZABETH PEAT d./ GEORGE & MARY
22 OCT 1782 JANE WILLIAMSON d./ THO & ANN
19 JAN 1783 JAMES YONGE s./ JAMES & ANN
24 JAN 1783 NORRIS MARLER s./ STARKEY & MARY
16 FEB 1783 JOHN MEEKIN s./ WILLIAM & HANNAH
20 APR 1783 ANN BLADON d./ WILLIAM & ANN
25 APR 1783 THOMAS KING s./ THOMAS & SARAH
10 JUL 1783 WILLIAM KENDRICK base s./ CATHERINE
18 JUL 1783 ELIZABETH DARBY d./ JOHN & ELIZABETH
31 AUG 1783 ELIZABETH VICKERS d./ JOSEPH & MARY
26 DEC 1783 MARY YONGE d./ ROBERT & SARAH
08 FEB 1784 HANNAH GLOVER d./ WILLIAM & FANNY
10 APR 1784 GEORGE FOX of riper years
30 MAY 1784 ELIZABETH GIBSON d./ JOHN & HANNAH
31 MAY 1784 JOSEPH HARRISE s./ JAMES & MARY
19 SEP 1784 WILLIAM GERMAN s./ GEORGE & ANN
19 SEP 1784 JOHN ASHER s./ WILLIAM & MARY
19 SEP 1784 JOHN BRADLEY s./ THOMAS & ELLEN
19 SEP 1784 SAMUEL PEAT s./ GEORGE & MARY
16 OCT 1784 MARGARET SMITH d./ JOHN & MARY
01 NOV 1784 JOSEPH BROWN s./ JOSEPH & SARAH
30 NOV 1784 ELIZABETH HOWARD d./ SARAH privately baptized
31 DEC 1784 SARAH WOODCOCK d./ DANIEL & MARTHA[2]
31 DEC 1784 THOMAS DARBY s./ JOHN & ELIZABETH
02 MAR 1785 JOHN CORBETT base s./ MILLICENT poor
30 MAY 1785 SARAH YONGE d./ JAMES & ANN
11 NOV 1785 SAMUEL KING s./ THO & SARAH poor

---

[1] BT gave 30 December.
[2] BT gave d./ DANIEL & MARY.

23	DEC	1785	JOHN	MATCHETT	s./ JOHN & ELIZABETH poor
25	DEC	1785	DEXTER	RICHARDS	s./ GEORGE & SARAH
06	JAN	1786	HENRY	NEWAM	s./ JOHN & ANN of Merril Grange
06	FEB	1786	THOMAS	YONGE	s./ ROBERT & SARAH
12	MAR	1786	HENRY	PEAT	s./ GEORGE & MARY
30	APR	1786	SARAH	JONES	d./ THOMAS & MARY of Thringstone
07	MAY	1786	ELIZABETH	SIDDON	d./ JOHN & KATHERINE
18	JUN	1786	ELEANOR	HARRISE	d./ JAMES & MARY

John Son of William and Mary Moseley Baptiz'd June 23rd 1786

23	JUN	1786	JOHN	MOSELEY	s./ WILLIAM & MARY
25[1]	JUN	1786	MARIA	MARLER	d./ STARKEY & MARY
28	JUL	1786	ANN	GODDARD	base d./ MARY
28	JUL	1786	JACOB JOHNSON	MATCHETT	base s./ HANNAH
03	NOV	1786	SARAH	GLOVER	d./ WILLIAM & FANNY
05	NOV	1786	THOMAS	WOODCOCK	s./ DANIEL & MARTHA
12	JAN	1787	HANNAH	DARBY	d./ JOHN & ELIZABETH
16	MAR	1787	THOMAS	YOUNGE	s./ JAMES & ANN p.[Poor]
16	MAR	1787	SARAH	CHARLESWORTH	d./ STEPHEN & SARAH
23	MAR	1787	SARAH	MATCHETT	d./ JOHN & ELIZABETH poor
30	MAR	1787	CHARLES	MOUNTNEY	s./ ROBERT & SARAH poor
16	SEP	1787	GEORGE	PEAT	s./ GEORGE & ELIZABETH
15	FEB	1788	THOMAS	JOHNSON	s./ JACOB & MARY
15	FEB	1788	ALICE	HARRISE	d./ JAMES & MARY
26	MAY	1788	JOSEPH	SIDDON	s./ JOHN & CATHERINE
15	JUN	1788	ELIZABETH	KING	d./ THO & SARAH pr[Poor]
12	SEP	1788	ANN	GLOVER	d./ WILLIAM & FANNY pr[Poor]
19	SEP	1788	NICHOLIS KIDDIER	DARBY	s./ JOHN & ELIZABETH[2]
21	SEP	1788	THOMAS JOHNSON	CORBETT	s./ MARY
21	SEP	1788	JAMES	WILLOWS	s./ ANN
03	OCT	1788	RUTH	CROSON	d./ JOSEPH & JANE p.[Poor]
19	DEC	1788	WILLIAM	MATCHETT	s./ JOHN & ELIZABETH p.[Poor]
01	FEB	1789	CHRISTOPHER	YOUNG	s./ JAMES & ANN poor
04	MAR	1789	THOMAS	BOULTBEE	s./ ROBERT & SARAH of Stordon Grange
22	MAR	1789	SARAH	WOODCOCK	d./ DANIEL & MARTHA
22	MAY	1789	JOHN	YOUNGE	s./ ROBERT & SARAH
26	JUN	1789	ELEANOR	MOUNTNEY	d./ ROBERT & SARAH poor
21	SEP	1789	ANN	BAGGALEY	d./ SAMUEL & ANN poor
04	DEC	1789	MARY	FARMER	d./ FRANCIS & ANN
29	JAN	1790	JOHN	WHITE	s./ MATTHEW & HANNAH
15[3]	JAN	1790	HANNAH	PEAT	d./ GEORGE & MARY

1 BT gave 23 June.

2 BT gave WILLM instead of JOHN and appeared to be an error by the incumbent.

3 BT gave 29 January.

29	JAN	1790	MARGARET	JOHNSON	d./ JACOB & MARY
26	MAR	1790	SAMUEL	HARRISE	s./ JAMES & MARY poor
20	JUN	1790	THOMAS	BAXTER	s./ THOMAS & HANNAH
26	SEP	1790	WILLIAM	BROWN	s./ WILLIAM & URSULA
27	JUN	1791	MARY	YOUNG	d./ JAMES & ANN
27	JUN	1791	ANN	MATCHETT	d./ JOHN & ELIZABETH
15	AUG	1791	SARAH	BOULTBEE	d./ ROBERT & SARAH
21	AUG	1791	WILLIAM	MARTIN	s./ JOSEPH & ELIZABETH
18	SEP	1791	ELIZABETH	HANDFORD	d./ THOS & SARAH
19	SEP	1791	MARY	KING	d./ THOMAS & SARAH
16	OCT	1791	SARAH	FARMER	d./ FRANCIS & ANN
17	OCT	1791	WILLIAM	BAILEY	s./ WILLIAM & ANN
08	JAN	1792	RICHARD	CORBET	base s./ CATHERINE
05	FEB	1792	WILLIAM	HARVEY	s./ FRANCIS & CATHERINE
04	MAR	1792	SARAH	BRADLEY	d./ WILLIAM & SARAH
11	JUN	1792	NATHANIEL LAKIN	NICHOLS	s./ JOHN & HANNAH
11	JUN	1792	ROBERT	YOUNG	s./ ROBERT & SARAH
17	JUN	1792	CATHERINE	EALLING	d./ JOHN & ANN
16	SEP	1792	HANNAH	WHITE	d./ MATTHEW & HANNAH
09	DEC	1792	JAMES	EDWARDS	s./ RICHARD & ROSE
19	APR	1793	ELIZABETH	MARTIN	d./ JOSEPH & ELIZABETH
03	JUN	1793	JOHN	NICHOLS	s./ JOHN & HANNAH
03	JUN	1793	ANN	YOUNG	d./ JAMES & ANN
20	SEP	1793	ANN	GRIMLEY	d./ JOHN & MARTHA
22	SEP	1793	ROBERT	HARRIS	s./ JAMES & MARY
27	SEP	1793	JOSEPH	WOODCOCK	s./ JOSEPH & SARAH
27	OCT	1793	HANNAH	COOPER	d./ THOMAS & SARAH
15	DEC	1793	WILLIAM	FARMER	s./ FRANCIS & ANN
29	DEC	1793	SARAH	JONES	d./ WILLIAM & JANE
14	FEB	1794	SAMUEL	BROWN	s./ WILLIAM & URSULA p.[Poor]
09	MAY	1794	WILLIAM	PICKARD	of riper years
18	MAY	1794	WILLIAM	KING	s./ THOMAS & SARAH p.[Poor]
30	MAY	1794	ROBERT	COX	s./ ROBERT & MARY
27	JUN	1794	ANN	EDWARDS	d./ RICHARD & ROSE
03	AUG	1794	REBECCA	MATCHET	d./ JOHN & ELIZABETH p.[Poor]
21	SEP	1794	THOMAS	WHITE	s./ MATTHEW & HANNAH
28	SEP	1794	JAMES	NICHOLS	s./ JOHN & HANNAH
23	OCT	1794	WILLIAM	BRADLEY	s./ THOMAS & ANN
25	DEC	1794	DANIEL	WOODCOCK	s./ JOSEPH & SARAH
25	DEC	1794	THOMAS SMITH	GRIMLEY	s./ JOHN & MARTHA
18	JAN	1795	ANN	HURST	d./ THOMAS & HANNAH
01	JUN	1795	ANN	DEXTER	d./ STEPHEN & LATITIA
14	JUN	1795	JOHN	PARE	natural s./ MARY
20	SEP	1795	JOHN	WALDRUM	s./ JAMES & MARY
20	SEP	1795	WILLIAM	BRADLEY	s./ WILLIAM & SARAH
03	JAN	1796	JAMES	BULL	s./ THOMAS & ANN

22	JAN	1796	ELEANOR	GILBERT	d./ THOMAS & ANN
02	FEB	1796	ANN	FARMER	d./ FRANCIS & ANN
19	JUN	1796	JOHN	HURST	s./ THOMAS & HANNAH
11	SEP	1796	ROBERT MATTHEW	NICHOLS	s./ JOHN & HANNAH
18	SEP	1796	JANE	MATCHET	d./ JOHN & ELIZABETH
18	SEP	1796	ELIZABETH	BROWN	d./ WILLIAM & URSULA
18	SEP	1796	HANNAH	DARLINGTON	d./ WILLIAM & ELIZABETH
18	SEP	1796	MARY	WHITE	d./ MATTHEW & HANNAH
18	SEP	1796	REBEKAH	BEALEY	d./ WILLIAM & ANN
18	SEP	1796	ELEANOR	HARRIS	d./ CHARLES & ANN
02	OCT	1796	MARY	EDWARDS	d./ RICHARD & ROSE
08	FEB	1797	JOHN	JONES	s./ THOMAS & MARY
12	FEB	1797	THOMAS	YOUNG	s./ JAMES & ANN
19	MAR	1797	JAMES	WALDRAM	s./ JAMES & MARY
09	MAY	1797	THEOPHILUS HENRY HASTINGS	KELK	s./ Revd WM & ELIZABETH CATHERINE
24	MAY	1797	SAMUEL	HARDY	s./ WM & SARAH
18	JUN	1797	THOMAS	SWAN	s./ THOS & CATHERINE
06	AUG	1797	JOHN	KING	s./ THOS & SARAH
13	AUG	1797	ANN	STINSON	d./ WILLM & MILLISENT
17	SEP	1797	JOSEPH	KING	s./ JOSEPH & MARY
10	NOV	1797	ELIZABETH	KING	d./ JOSPH & ELIANOR
12	NOV	1797	JOHN	DEXTER	s./ JOHN & LATTIA
09	DEC	1797	ELIZABETH	BURTON	d./ WM & ELIZABETH
14	JAN	1798	ELIZABETH	MITCHIL	d./ JAS & MARY
23	APR	1798	ELIZABETH	GILBERT	d./ THOS & ANN
18	MAY	1798	THOMAS	MARTIN	s./ JOSEPH & ELIZABETH
27	MAY	1798	WILLIAM	WILLIAMSON	s./ WM & ALICE MEAKIN
08	JUL	1798	JOSEPH	HURST	s./ THOMAS & HANNAH
15	JUL	1798	JOHN	HARDY	s./ WILLIAM & MARY
15	JUL	1798	SARAH	EDWARDS[1]	d./ RICHARD & ROSE
15	JUL	1798	CHARLES	HARRIS	s./ CHARLES & ANN
12	AUG	1798	MARY WILSON	NICHOLS	d./ JOHN & HANNAH
15	JUL[2]	1798	JAMES	DARRINGTON	s./ WILLIAM & ELIZ
16	SEP	1798	WILLIAM	DEXTER	s./ STEPHEN & LATITIA
16	SEP	1798	CHARLES	FARMER	s./ FRANCIS & RACHEL
25	NOV	1798	THOMAS	WALDRAM	s./ JAMES & MARY
23	DEC	1798	RICHARD	ALLEN	s./ RICHARD & MARY
30	DEC	1798	STEPHEN LEEDHAM	BEALEY	s./ WILLM & ANN[3]
31	MAR	1799	JOSEPH	KNIGHT	s./ WILLIAM & MARY of Thringstone
03	MAY	1799	MARY	MATCHETT	d./ JOHN & ELIZABETH
26	MAY	1799	JOHN	WHITE	s./ MATTHEW & HANNAH
21	JUL	1799	MARY	HARVEY	d./ FRANCIS & CATHERINE

[1] BT gave DEXTER instead of EDWARDS.

[2] Out of chronological order in both register & BT.

[3] BEALEY was commonly used for BAILEY, in the register & BTs during this period.

18	AUG	1799	ANN	GILBERT	d./ THOMAS & ANN
08	SEP	1799	THOS	STINSON	s./ WILLM & MILLICENT
08	SEP	1799	WILLM	?OSZIHINK	s./ WILLM & REBECCA
10	NOV	1799	SARAH	MOUNTAINE	d./ GEORGE & ELIZABETH
13	APR	1800	MARY	WALDRAM	d./ JAMES & MARY
13	APR	1800	JAMES	MAKAY	s./ JOHN & ANN
11	MAY	1800	WILLIAM	DARINGTON	s./ WILLM & ELIZABETH
15	JUN	1800	WILLM	KING	s./ JOSEPH & MARY

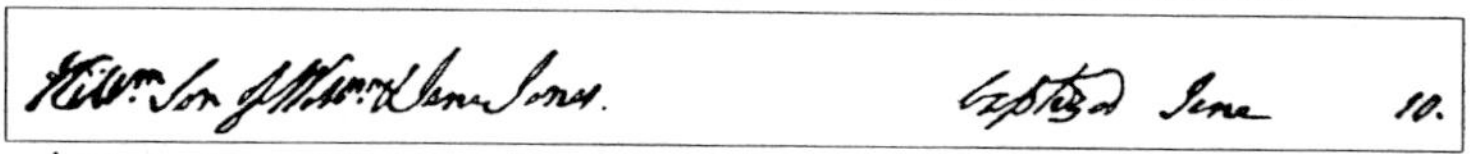
Willm Son of Willm & Jane Jones. Baptized June 10.

10[1]	JUN	1800	WILLM	JONES	s./ WILLM & JANE
03	AUG	1800	ANN	BAGERLEY	d./ JANE
15	MAR	1801	JAMES	KING	s./ THOMAS & SARAH
12	JUL	1801	CHARLOTTE	EDWARDS	d./ RICHARD & ROSE
16	AUG	1801	JAMES	KNIGHT	s./ WILLIAM & SARAH
20	SEP	1801	JOSEPH	WOODCOCK	s./ JOSEPH & SARAH
20[2]	SEP	1801	SARAH	NICHOLLS	d./ JOHN & HANNAH
20	SEP	1801	WILLIAM	HURST	s./ THOMAS & HANNAH
27	SEP	1801	WILLIAM	WARD	s./ FARMER & CATHERINE[3]
04	OCT	1801	SARAH	MARTIN	d./ JOSEPH & ELIZABETH
25	OCT	1801	RICHARD	BAILEY	s./ WILLIAM & ANN
08	NOV	1801	JOHN	DARBY	s./ WILLIAM & ELIZABETH
31	JAN	1802	SAMUEL	STINSON	s./ WILLIAM & MILLICENT
07	MAR	1802	JOHN	PICKARD	s./ WILLIAM & ANN
12	MAR	1802	WILLIAM	WALDRAM	s./ JAMES & MARY
25	APR	1802	WILLIAM	BLADON	s./ JOSEPH & ELIZABETH
22	AUG	1802	WILLIAM	NORMAN	s./ THOMAS & MARY
22	AUG	1802	HELEN[4]	WHITE	d./ MATTHEW & HANNAH
07	NOV	1802	ROBERT	KING	s./ JOSEPH & MARY
24	APR	1803	JAMES	CARLINE	s./ THOMAS & ANN
05	JUN	1803	ROBERT	MARTIN	s./ JOSEPH & ELIZABETH
03	JUL	1803	MARY ANN	NORMAN	d./ THOMAS & MARY
18	SEP	1803	WILLIAM	BLADON	s./ WILLM & ANN
18	SEP	1803	ANN	DARBY	d./ MARY
02	OCT	1803	JAMES	ROE	s./ GEORGE & HANNAH
06	NOV	1803	WILLIAM	KNIGHT	s./ WILLM & MARY
04	DEC	1803	MARY	FARMER	d./ FRANCIS & MARY
19	FEB	1804	MARY	STINSON	d./ WILLIAM & MILLICENT
22	APR	1804	WILLIAM WILSON	WOODCOCK	s./ JOSEPH & SARAH

1 Out of chronological order in both register & BT.

2 BT gave 21 September.

3 Farmer is correct; he married Catherine Hinsley, 24 February 1801, at Shepshed. Farmer & Catherine Ward should not be confused with Benjamin & Catherine Ward, who also appear in the registers.

4 BT gave ELLEN.

06	MAY	1804	BENJAMIN	WALDRAM	s./ JAMES & MARY
23	JUL	1804	CHARLES	NORMAN	s./ THOMAS & MARY
16	SEP	1804	HANNAH	ASHER	d./ JAMES & SARAH
16	SEP	1804	HANNAH	BAILEY	d./ WILLIAM & ANN
16	SEP	1804	ANN	ALLEN	d./ RICHARD & MARY
14	APR	1805	JOHN	WOODCOCK	s./ JOSEPH & SARAH
16	JUN	1805	THOMAS	GILBERT	s./ THOMAS & ANN
19	JUN	1805	BENJAMIN	JOHNSON	s./ THOMAS & ELIZABETH

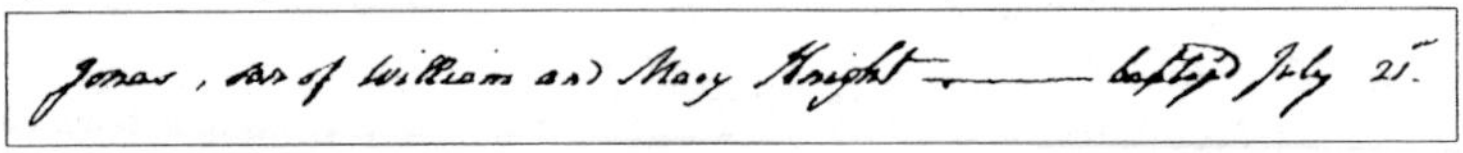
Jonas, son of William and Mary Knight — baptiz'd July 21st.

21	JUL	1805	JONAS	KNIGHT	s./ WILLIAM & MARY
04	AUG	1805	ANN	WALDRAM	d./ JAMES & MARY
08	DEC	1805	JOSEPH	ROE	s./ WILLIAM & MARY
25	DEC	1805	EDWARD	KING	s./ JOSEPH & MARY
26	JAN	1806	MATILDA	SMEDLEY	d./ JOHN & ANN
16	FEB	1806	JOHN	SWANN	s./ THOMAS & CATHERINE
16	FEB	1806	MARY	SWANN	d./ THOMAS & CATHARINE
02	MAR	1806	JOSEPH	MOSELEY	s./ WILLIAM & ELIZABETH
08	JUN	1806	BENJAMIN	WARD	s./ BENJAMIN & CATHERINE
15	JUN	1806	ELIZABETH	DEXTER	d./ STEPHEN & LATITIA
17	AUG	1806	ANN	FARMER	d./ FRANCIS & MARY
27	AUG	1806	THOMAS	KING	s./ SAMUEL & MARY
27	AUG	1806	DANIEL	HARDY	s./ WILLIAM & SARAH
27	AUG	1806	HANNAH	HARDY	d./ WILLIAM & SARAH
21	SEP	1806	MARY	ROE	d./ GEORGE & HANNAH
21	SEP	1806	MARY	DARBY	d./ WILLIAM & ELIZABETH
21	SEP	1806	JOHN	ASHER	s./ JAMES & SARAH
19	OCT	1806	SAMUEL	INGRAM	s./ SAMUEL & SARAH of Breedon
16	NOV	1806	MARY	PICKARD	d./ WILLIAM & ANN
16	NOV	1806	THOMAS	PICKARD	s./ WILLIAM & ANN
25	JAN	1807	ELIZABETH	HURST	d./ THOMAS & HANNAH
25	JAN	1807	HANNAH	HURST	d./ THOMAS & HANNAH
31	MAY	1807	WM	BROWN	s./ WM & URSULA
31	MAY	1807	LEAR	BROWN	d./ WM & URSULA
31	MAY	1807	RACHEL	BROWN	d./ WM & URSULA
31	MAY	1807	SAMUEL	BROWN	s./ WM & URSULA
31	MAY	1807	BEMJANIN	STINSON	s./ WM & MILICENT
21	JUN	1807	WILLIAM	ROE	s./ WM & MARY
28	JUN	1807	MARTHA	BAILEY	d./ WM & ANN
21	AUG	1807	ANN	JOHNSON	d./ JACOB & MARY
21[1]	AUG	1807	MARY	WOODCOCK	d./ JOSEPH & SARAH
20	SEP	1807	ELIZTH	MOSELEY	d./ WM & ELIZTH
20	SEP	1807	THOS	TOPLEY	s./ JAMES & JANE

[1] BT gave 20 September.

11	OCT	1807	JOSEPH	WALDRAM	s./ JAMES & MARY
31	DEC	1807	WM	WARD	s./ BENJAMIN & CATHERINE
10	JAN	1808	MATTHEW	WHITE	s./ MATTHEW & HANNAH
19	JUN	1808	JOHN	FARMER	s./ FRANCIS & MARY
18	SEP	1808	JOSEPH	ASHER	s./ JAMES & SARAH
18	SEP	1808	WILLIAM	TOW	s./ WM & SARAH
18	SEP	1808	ANN	KING	d./ SAMUEL & MARY
23	SEP	1808	FRANCIS	SWAN	s./ THOS & CATHERINE
30	OCT	1808	JOHN	DARBY	s./ WM & ANN
04	DEC	1808	ANN	KNIGHT	d./ WM & MARY
23	APR	1809	MARTHA	GILBERT	d./ THOS & ANN
14	MAY	1809	SARAH	ROE	d./ WM & MARY
16	JUL	1809	JOHN	WEBSTER	s./ JOHN & HANNAH
15	SEP	1809	GEORGE	MOSELEY	s./ WM & ELIZTH
10	DEC	1809	DRUSILLA[1]	BALEY	d./ WILLIAM & ANN
03	JAN	1810	HANNAH	PICKARD	d./ WILLIAM & ANN
15	JAN	1810	CATHERINE ANN	JOHNSON	d./ THOS & ELIZABETH
16[2]	JAN	1810	HANNAH	MEAKIN	d./ JOHN & SARAH
15	APR	1810	JOSEPH	SIDAN	s./ ELIZABETH
22	APR	1810	HENRY	MOUNTNEY	s./ WILLIAM & ABIGAL
22	APR	1810	THOS	MOUNTNEY	s./ WILLIAM & ABIGAL
17	SEP	1810	FRANCIS	FARMER	s./ FRANCIS & MARY
13	JAN	1811	ROBERT	WALDRAM	s./ JAMES & MARY
13	JAN	1811	MARY	BRADLEY	base born d./ SARAH
31	MAR	1811	SARAH	WALLIS	d./ ABRAHAM & ELIZABETH
21	MAY	1811	SARAH	SWAN	d./ FRANCIS & MARY
16	JUN	1811	HANNAH	MOSELEY	d./ WM & ELIZTH
21	SEP	1811	WILLIAM	WOODCOCK	s./ JOSEPH & SARAH
22	SEP	1811	WILLIAM	DARBY	s./ WM & ANN
22	SEP	1811	SAMUEL	DARBY	s./ JOHN & HANNAH
22	SEP	1811	JOHN	KING	s./ SAML & MARY
22	SEP	1811	ANN	TOW	d./ WM & SARAH
05	FEB	1812	MARY	BAILEY	d./ WM & ANN
07	FEB	1812	SAMUEL	GILBERT	s./ THOS & ANN
31	MAY	1812	MARY ANN	ASHER	d./ JAMES & SARAH
09	JUN	1812	BENJAMIN	JOHNSON	of riper years
09	JUN	1812	MARY	JOHNSON	of riper years
09	JUN	1812	WILLIAM	JOHNSON	s./ JACOB & MARY
28	JUN	1812	SARAH	FARMER	d./ FRANCIS & MARY
20	SEP	1812	WILLIAM	MOSELEY	s./ WM & ELIZTH
04	OCT	1812	WILLIAM	SMALWOOD	s./ THOS & PHEBY
23	OCT	1812	ELIZTH	WALDRAM	d./ JAMES & MARY

1 BT gave TREWSILLER. Drusilla - from a word of Greek origin, meaning soft-eyed.

2 BT gave 16 February.

From 1813, all the baptism entries included each family's place of abode. However, due to the limitations of space & for clarity Osgathorpe has been omitted. All other places of abode have been included. The initials (P.) or (P.B.) denote a private baptism, performed either at church or at a private residence. In some cases it has been necessary to abbreviate 'Framework Knitter to F.W.K.

14	NOV	1813	JAMES	ROE	s./ WM & MARY	Farmer
14	NOV	1813	JOHN	ROE	s./ WM & MARY	Farmer
09	MAR	1814	FREDERICK	WARD	s./ BENJAMIN & CATHARINE	Farmer
09	MAR	1814	JOSEPH	WARD	s./ BENJAMIN & CATHARINE	Farmer
23	MAR	1814	JOSEPH WM MUGLISTON	BOSTOCK	s./ JOSEPH & ANN	Farmer
22	APR	1814	ANN	WALLIS	d./ ABRAHAM & ELIZ	Shoe Maker
03	JUL	1814	JOHN	FARMER	s./ JOSEPH & MARY	Farmer
03	JUL	1814	MARY ANN[1]	GOODMAN	d./ JOHN & SARAH	Wool-comber
03	JUL	1814	CARALINE	GOODMAN	d./ JOHN & SARAH	Wool-comber
03	JUL	1814	HENRY	GOODMAN	s./ JOHN & SARAH	Wool-comber
07	JUL	1814	SARAH ANN	TOWLE	d./ WM & SARAH	Wool-comber
21[2]	AUG	1814	SARAH	WALDRAM	d./ JAMES & MARY	Laborer
18	SEP	1814	ANN	SWAN	d./ THOS & CATHARINE	Wool-comber
18	SEP	1814	MARY	MOORSELEY	d./ WM & ELIZTH	Farmer
02	OCT	1814	FRANCIS WILLIAM	HARVEY	s./ ANN	Spinster
06	AUG	1815	THOS	SMITH	s./ WM & HANNAH	Spinster[3]
06	AUG	1815	CATHARINE	SMITH	d./ WM & HANNAH	Laborer
17	SEP	1815	THOS	DARBY	s./ WM & ANN	Laborer
17	SEP	1815	HANNAH	TOWE	d./ WM & SARAH	Wool-comber
08	OCT	1815	HANNAH	ROE	d./ WM & MARY	Farmer
19	MAY	1816	WILLIAM JOHN	BRANSON	s./ WM & SARAH	Wheelwright
30	JUN	1816	JOSEPH	FARMER	s./ JOSEPH & MARY	Farmer
28	JUL	1816	ELIZABETH	WARD	d./ BENJAMIN & CATHARINE	Farmer
03	NOV	1816	WILLIAM	MARSHALL	s./ JOHN & MARY	Stockin Weavers
03	NOV	1816	SAMUEL	MARSHALL	s./ JOHN & MARY	Stockin Weaver
01	DEC	1816	JOSEPH	SMALLWOOD	s./ THOS & PHEBY	Stockin Weaver
01	DEC	1816	BENJAMIN	SMALLWOOD	s./ THOS & PHEBY	Stockin Weaver
21	SEP	1817	MARY	GILBERT	d./ THOMAS & MARTHA	Hosier
21	SEP	1817	JAMES	TOW	s./ WILLIAM & SARAH	Wool-comber
21	SEP	1817	JOHN	MOSELEY	s./ WILLIAM & ELIZATH of Belton	Farmer
02	NOV	1817	ELIZATH	FARMER	d./ WILLIAM & FRANCES	Hosier
18	JAN	1818	JOHANNA	GOODMAN	d./ JOHN & SARAH	Wool-comber
18	JAN	1818	HARRIET	GOODMAN	d./ JOHN & SARAH	Wool-comber
18	JAN	1818	MARY	YOUNGE	d./ CHRISTOPHER & HANNAH	Laborer

[1] BT gave JOHN instead of MARY ANN.

[2] BT gave 22 August.

[3] BT & register both gave spinster, as the occupation for this entry & the one above.

18	JAN	1818	SARAH	YOUNGE	d./ CHRISTOPHER & HANNAH	Laborer
18	JAN	1818	JAMES	YOUNGE	s./ CHRISTOPHER & HANNAH	Laborer
18	JAN	1818	JOHN	SMITH	s./ WILLIAM & ANN	Laborer
25	JAN	1818	ELIZTH	KING	d./ WILLIAM & ANN	Wool-comber
14	AUG	1818	JAMES	GILBERT	s./ THOS & ANN	Shoemaker
14	AUG	1818	JOSIAH	GILBERT	s./ THOS & ANN	Shoemaker
14	AUG	1818	WILLIAM	GILBERT	s./ THOS & ANN	Shoemaker
20	SEP	1818	SARAH	BRANSON	d./ WILLIAM & SARAH	Wheelwright

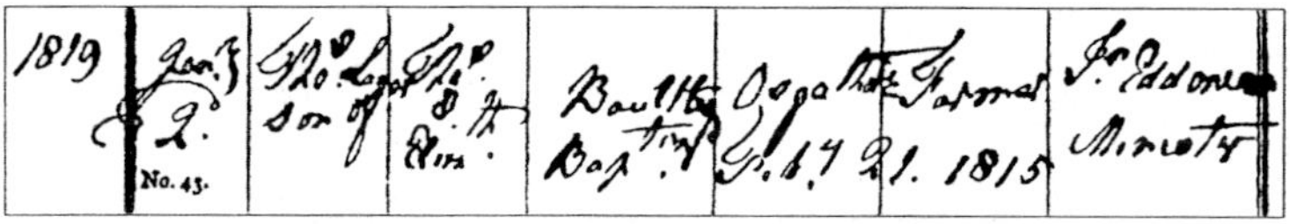
1819 | Jan 2 | No. 43 | Thos Lager son of | Thos & Eliz | Boultby Bap 21 Feb 1815 | Osgathorpe | Farmer | J. Eddowes Minister

02	JAN	1819	THOS LAGER	BOULTBY	s./ THOS & ELIZTH bap 21 Feb 1815[1]	Farmer
28	MAR	1819	ANN	WILLIAMSON	d./ ELIZTH	Spinster
28	MAR	1819	MARY	FARMER	d./ WILLIAM & FRANCES	F.W.K.
04	APR	1819	ANN	BAILEY	d./ WILLIAM & ANN	Blacksmith
15	JUN	1819	BENJAMIN JOHNSON	GILBERT	s./ THOMAS & MARTHA	Hosier
29	AUG	1819	CHATHARINE	OSBOURN	-/ GEORGE & ELIZABETH	Laborer
19	SEP	1819	CHATHARINE	WARD	-/ BENJAMIN & CHATHARINE	Farmer
31	OCT	1819	SAMUEL	BLACK	s./ SAMUEL & HANNAH	Labourer
31	OCT	1819	THOS	LUN	s./ JOSEPH & MARY	Labourer
09	MAY	1820	JOHN BROWN	MILES	s./ HENRY & MARY	Farmer
25	JUN	1820	JOSEPH	KING	-/ WILLIAM & ANN	Wool-comber
17	SEP	1820	CHARLOTT	BRANSON	d./ WM & SARAH	Carpenter
29	OCT	1820	THOS	FARMER	-/ WM & FRANCIS	F.W.K.
29	OCT	1820	JOHN	DEXTER	base born -/ CATHARINE of Belton	Spinster
11	FEB	1821	GEORGE	KING	s./ THOS & MARY	Laborer
11	FEB	1821	ELIZATH	KING	d./ JOHN & MARY	Laborer
11	FEB	1821	WIL	KING	s./ WM & SARAH	Laborer
20	MAY	1821	EMMA	MALTAS	d./ THOS & SARAH	Inkeeper
20	MAY	1821	JANE	MALTAS	d./ THOS & SARAH	Inkeeper
10	AUG	1821	GEORGE BRANSON	UNDERWOOD	base born -/ MARY	Spinster
16	SEP	1821	CATHARINE	WARD	-/ BENJAMIN & CATHARINE	Farmer
14	OCT	1821	THOMAS	GILBERT	-/ THOMAS & MARTHA	Hosier
12	MAY	1822	THOS	KING	s./ JOHN & MARY	Laborer
06	JUN	1822	MARY	MILES	d./ HENRY & MARY	Farmer
28	JUL	1822	ROSANNAH	KING	d./ WM & SARAH	Laborer
19	JAN	1823	SARAH	FARMER	d./ WM & FRANCES	F.W.K.
02	MAR	1823	SARAH	KING	d./ THOS & MARY	Laborer
27	APR	1823	JAMES	MATCHETT	s./ WILLIAM & ELIZABETH	Laborer
27	APR	1823	SAMUEL	MATCHETT	s./ WILLIAM & ELIZABETH	Laborer
27	APR	1823	WILLIAM	MATCHETT	s./ WILLIAM & ELIZABETH	Laborer
21	SEP	1823	SARAH	HURST	d./ WILLIAM & MARY	Laborer

[1] 'Bap 21 Feb 1815', possibly refers to the date that ELIZABETH, the mother, was baptised.

25	DEC	1823	JOHN WILLIAM	BRANSON	s./ WILLIAM & SARAH	Wheelwright
25	DEC	1823	MARY ANN	BRANSON	d./ WILLIAM & SARAH	Wheelwright
20	JUN	1824	SOPHIA MARY	BRANSON	d./ JOSIAH & CASSANDRA	Carrier
22	JUN	1824	SAMUEL	DERBY	s./ WILLIAM & ANN	Clark
07	NOV	1824	JONATHAN	KING	s./ WILLIAM & SARAH	Laborer
23	JAN	1825	HANNAH	OSBORN	d./ GEORGE & ELIZABETH	Laborer
23	JAN	1825	ANN	OSBORN	d./ GEORGE & ELIZABETH	Laborer
23	JAN	1825	GEORGE	CLIFF	s./ THOS & MARY	Laborer

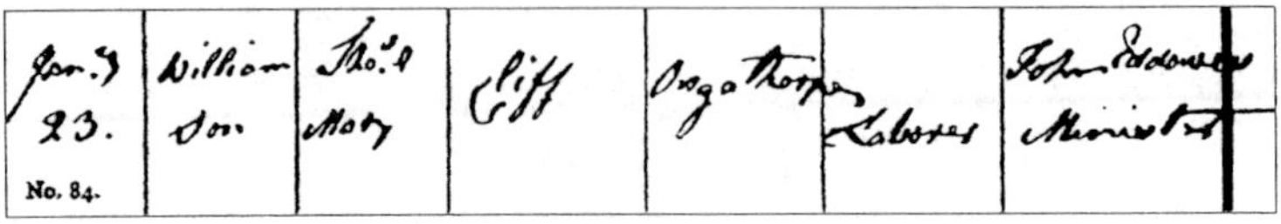
Jan.y 23. No. 84. | William Son | Thos & Mary | Cliff | Osgathorpe | Laborer | Minister

23	JAN	1825	WILLIAM	CLIFF	s./ THOS & MARY	Laborer
23	JAN	1825	SARAH	WALDRAM	d./ JAMES & MARY	Laborer
02	FEB	1825	ELIZABETH	MILES	d./ HENRY & MARY	Farmer
06	FEB	1825	ELIZTH	SHELDON	d./ SAMUEL & MARY	Laborer
19	JUN	1825	FANNY	KING	d./ THOS & MARY	Laborer
12	AUG	1825	CHAROLINE ELIZABETH	KELK	b. 12 Aug 1824 -/ WILLM HYDE & MARY ISABELLA	Farmer
21	AUG	1825	THOS	POXON	s./ SAMUEL & MARTHA	Laborer
21	AUG	1825	JOHN	POXON	s./ SAMUEL & MARTHA	Laborer
21	AUG	1825	SAMUEL	POXON	s./ SAMUEL & MARTHA	Laborer
21	AUG	1825	GEORGE	POXON	s./ SAMUEL & MARTHA	Laborer
28	AUG	1825	FRANCIS	JAMES	s./ FRANCIS & HANNAH	Laborer
04	SEP	1825	ELIZABETH	DAVENPORT	b. 12 Nov 1810 d./ WILLIAM & SARAH	Clark
04	SEP	1825	WILLIAM	DAVENPORT	b. 30 Sep 1812 s./ WILLIAM & SARAH	Clark
04	SEP	1825	ANN	YOUNG	d./ CHRISTOPHER	F.W.K.
18	SEP	1825	SARAH	SMITH	d./ JOHN & ANN	Laborer
16	OCT	1825	MARY	HURST	d./ THOS & HANNAH	Laborer
16	OCT	1825	SARAH	HURST	d./ THOS & HANNAH	Laborer
26	FEB	1826	JANE	FARMER	d./ WILLIAM & FRANCES	Manifactor
09	APR	1826	WILLIAM	MALTAS	s./ THOS & SARAH	Publican
09	APR	1826	SARAH	MALTAS	d./ THOS & SARAH	Publican
15	OCT	1826	DANIEL	KING	s./ WILLIAM & SARAH	Laborer
03	DEC	1826	REBECKAH	WALDRAM	-/ JAMES & REBECKAH	Laborer
04	FEB	1827	CATHERINE	BRANSON	d./ WILLIAM & SARAH	Farmer
21	MAR	1827	JOHN DELAP HASTINGS	KELK	s./ WM HYDE & MARY ISABELLA	Farmer
03	JUL	1827	CAROLINE ELIZABETH	MEAKIN	d./ GEORGE ILLSLEY & MARY CAROLINE CHARLOTTE	Grocer
21	SEP	1827	ANN	WOODCOCK	aged 13 -/ JOSEPH & SARAH	Spinster
12	OCT	1827	FRANCES H.	NEEDHAM base born	-/ SARAH ELIZABETH HASTINGS[1]	Spinster
08	JUN	1828	JOHN	SMITH	s./ WILLIAM & CATHARINE	Spinster[2]

[1] Sex of child not stated: H. most probably = Hastings, the same *middle* name as the mother.

[2] BT & register both gave spinster.

Day	Month	Year	Forename	Surname	Parents	Occupation
21	SEP	1828	MARY ANN	BRADLEY	d./ WILLIAM & SOPHIA	F.W.K.
21	SEP	1828	ELIZABETH	BRADLEY	d./ WILLIAM & SOPHIA	F.W.K.
21	SEP	1828	DINAH	BRADLEY	d./ WILLIAM & SOPHIA	F.W.K.
21	SEP	1828	ANN	BRADLEY	d./ WILLIAM & SOPHIA	F.W.K.
21	SEP	1828	PETER	KING	s./ JOHN & MARY	Labourer
21	SEP	1828	CHARLES	KING	s./ THOMAS & MARY	Labourer
18	JAN	1829	LEVI	BAKER	s./ JOSEPH & ELIZABETH	Labourer
27	APR	1829	MARY	MEAKIN	d./ GEORGE ILESLEY & M.C.C.[1]	Mercer
27	APR	1829	SOPHIA SARAH	MEAKIN	d./ GEORGE ILESLEY & M.C.C.	Mercer
31	MAY	1829	CHARLES	BRANSON	d./ WILLIAM & SARAH	Farmer
26	JUL	1829	ELIZAH	HOULT	d./ GEORGE & REBECKAH	Laborer
09	AUG	1829	BENJAMAN	CLIFF	s./ THOMAS & MARY of Worthington	Laborer
09	AUG	1829	HANNAH	CLIFF	d./ THOMAS & MARY of Worthington	Laborer
09	AUG	1829	RACHEL	WALDRAM	d./ JAMES & SARAH	Laborer
20	SEP	1829	JOSEPH	KING	s./ WILLIAM & SARAH	Laborer
29	NOV	1829	THOMAS BONSER	OSBOURN	s./ GEORGE & ELIZTH	Laborer
29	NOV	1829	DANIEL GEORGE	OSBOURN	s./ GEORGE & ELIZTH	Laborer
26	FEB	1830	THOMAS	WOODCOCK	s./ JOHN & PHEBY of Codner Park, Derbys	Labourer
28	FEB	1830	ALFRED	SMITH	s./ WILLIAM & CATHARINE	Labourer
28	MAR	1830	SARAH ELIZABETH	HAIGHTON	d./ JOHN & SARAH ELIZABETH	Labourer
28	MAR	1830	FERDINANDO HENRY	NEEDHAM	base born s./ ~~JOHN~~ & SARAH ELIZABETH[2]	Spinster
09	MAY	1830	STEPHEN	WOOD	s./ STEPHEN COX & ANN	Joiner
27	FEB	1831	SARAH	KING	d./ SAMUEL & MARY	Stock'g Maker
27	FEB	1831	MARY ANN	BENNIT	d./ JOHN & ANN	Laborer
05	JUN	1831	MARY	BRADLEY	base born d./ SARAH	Spinster
21	AUG	1831	JOSEPH	KING	s./ WILLIAM & SARAH	Labourer
18	SEP	1831	LOUISA	BRANSON	d./ SARAH & WILLIAM	Farmer
18	SEP	1831	SARAH	KING	d./ JOHN & MARY	Labourer
18	SEP	1831	HANNAH	HURST	d./ WILLIAM & MARY of Worthington	Labourer
31	OCT	1831	BENJAMIN	OSBORNE	s./ GEORGE & ELIZABETH	Labourer
13	JAN	1832	GEORGE	YOUNG	natural s./ MARY (P.C.)[3]	Stock'g Maker
05	FEB	1832	WILLIAM	JARVIS	b. 7 Aug 1818 -/ SAMUEL & MARY	Stock'g Maker
05	FEB	1832	CHARLES	JARVIS	b. 4 Sept 1820 -/ SAMUEL & MARY	Stock'g Maker
05	FEB	1832	JOHN	JARVIS	b. 11 Sept 1823 -/ SAMUEL & MARY	Stock'g Maker
05	FEB	1832	CHARLOTTE	JARVIS	b. 8 Nov 1825 -/ SAMUEL & MARY	Stock'g Maker
05	FEB	1832	HANNAH	JARVIS	b. 20 Jun 1828 -/ SAMUEL & MARY	Stock'g Maker
05	FEB	1832	MARY	JARVIS	b. 25 Aug 1831 -/ SAMUEL & MARY	Stock'g Maker
05	FEB	1832	GEORGE	NEWMANS	b. 25 May 1831 -/ EDWARD & RACHAEL	Labourer
15	APR	1832	JOHN	WOOD	-/ STEPHEN COX & ANN	Carpenter
16	MAY	1832	ROBERT	BLACK	-/ SAMUEL & HANNAH	Laborer
03	JUN	1832	ANNE	POXON	-/ SAMUEL & MARTHA	Labourer

1 ILESLEY was father's middle name. M.C.C. was the abbreviation used for Mary Caroline Charlotte.

2 John was crossed out in register; BT only gave s./ SARAH.

3 P.C. probably refers to a private christening.

10	JUN	1832	JOSEPH	STATHAM	s./ WILLIAM & MARY	Labourer
24	JUN	1832	DAVID SEDGWICK	WOODCOCK	s./ JOHN & PHABE of Codner Park in pa. of Selstone, Derbys	Engineer
19	AUG	1832	HANNAH	SMITH	aged 17 d./ THOMAS & ELIZABETH	Labourer
19	AUG	1832	THOMAS	SMITH	aged 11 s./ THOMAS & ELIZABETH	Labourer
19	AUG	1832	WILLIAM	MOORE	aged 17 s./ JOSEPH & MARY	Stock'g Maker
19	AUG	1832	JOSEPH	KING	aged 12 s./ SAMUEL & MARY	Stock'g Maker
18	NOV	1832	ELIZABETH	KING	-/ THOMAS & MARY of Breedon Brand	Labourer
18	NOV	1832	RUTH	WALDRAM	-/ JAMES & SARAH	Labourer
16	DEC	1832	JOHN RICHARD	MATCHETT	-/ WILLIAM & ELIZABETH	Labourer
16	DEC	1832	SARAH CATHARINE	MATCHETT	-/ WILLIAM & ELIZABETH	Labourer
16	DEC	1832	CHARLOTTE	MATCHETT	-/ WILLIAM & ELIZABETH	Labourer
16	DEC	1832	MARIA	MATCHETT	-/ WILLIAM & ELIZABETH	Labourer
26	MAY	1833	FANNY	ROE	-/ EPHRAIM & HANNAH	Labourer
26	MAY	1833	JOSEPH	ROE	-/ EPHRAIM & HANNAH	Labourer
20	JUL	1833	JOSIAH	PERRY	-/ GEORGE & MARY (P.)	Hawker
20	NOV	1833	WILLIAM	BENNETT	-/ JOHN & ANNE (P.R.)	Labourer
12	JAN	1834	WILLIAM	DARBY	-/ JOHN & SARAH	Labourer
19	JAN	1834	JANE	BRADLEY	-/ WILLIAM & SOPHIA	F.W.K.
19	JAN	1834	WILLIAM	BRADLEY	-/ WILLIAM & SOPHIA	F.W.K.
02	FEB	1834	MARY	QUENBY	-/ BENJAMIN JOHN & ANN (P.R.)	F.W.K.
09	FEB	1834	BESSY	KING	-/ WILLIAM & SARAH of Breedon Brand	Labourer
18	FEB	1834	THOMAS	MALTAS	-/ THOMAS & SARAH (P.)	Victualler
18	FEB	1834	JOSEPH	MALTAS	-/ THOMAS & SARAH (P.)	Victualler
23	FEB	1834	WILLIAM	NEWMANS	-/ EDWARD & RACHAEL	Labourer
09	MAR	1834	ELIZABETH	QUENBY	-/ BENJAMIN JOHN & ANN	F.W.K.
30	MAR	1834	THOMAS	HURST	base born. -/ MARY	Servant
30	MAR	1834	GEORGE	BIRD	-/ THOMAS & MARY	Labourer
13	APR	1834	WILLIAM	HURST	-/ WILLIAM & MARY of Breedon Brand	Labourer
20	APR	1834	SARAH	ASHER	-/ JOHN & MARY	Cordwainer
25	APR	1834	JANE ELIZABETH CHRISTIAN	BRANSON	-/ WILLIAM & SARAH	Farmer
06	MAY	1834	MARY	ROE	-/ JAMES & SARAH	Labourer
03	JUN	1834	MARY	WOODCOCK	-/ JOHN & PHABE of Codner Parks in pa. Selstone, Derbys	Engineer
12	JUN	1834	JOSEPH	ALLT	natural s./ FRANCES	Servant
04	JUL	1834	GEORGE	STATHAM	-/ WILLIAM & MARY	Labourer
03	AUG	1834	SOPHIA	YOUNG	-/ CHRISTOPHER & SARAH	F.W.K.
03	AUG	1834	MARIA	YOUNG	-/ CHRISTOPHER & SARAH	F.W.K.
10	AUG	1834	CHARLOTTE	MORE	aged 13 -/ JOSEPH & MARY	F.W.K.
10	AUG	1834	LEAH	MORE	aged 9 -/ JOSEPH & MARY	F.W.K.
10	AUG	1834	ELIZABETH	ALLT	aged 13 -/ SAMUEL & MARY	Labourer
10	AUG	1834	EMMA	ALLT	aged 5 -/ SAMUEL junr & MARY	Labourer
12	AUG	1834	BRIDGET	HADDON	-/ FRANCIS & SARAH	F.W.K.
08	OCT	1834	HANNAH	PICKARD	-/ THOMAS & CHARLOTTE	Bookkeeper at the Whitwick Colliery
01	FEB	1835	WILLIAM	WOOD	-/ STEPHEN COX & ANNE	Carpenter

11	MAR	1835	ROBERT	IRONMONGER	-/ THOMAS & HANNAH	Wheelwright
05	APR	1835	JOSEPH	MATCHETT	-/ WILLIAM & ELIZABETH	Potter
22	JUN	1835	JOSIAH	BRANSON	-/ WILLIAM & SARAH	Farmer
26	JUL	1835	ROSAN	WALDROM	-/ JAMES & SARAH	Labourer
20	SEP	1835	JOHN	DARBY	-/ JOHN & SARAH	Parish Clerk
27	SEP	1835	ELIZABETH	POXON	-/ SAMUEL & MARTHA	Labourer
27	DEC	1835	ELIZABETH	SIDDONS	-/ JOSEPH & ANN	Labourer
17	JAN	1836	JOHN	STATHAN	-/ WILLIAM & MARY	Labourer

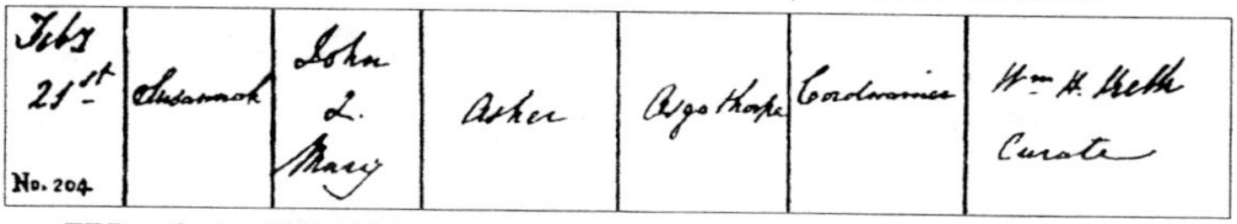

21	FEB	1836	SUSANNAH	ASHER	-/ JOHN & MARY	Cordwainer
28	FEB	1836	ELIZABETH	ROE	-/ JAMES & SARAH	Labourer
27	MAY	1836	SAMUEL	BENNETT	-/ JOHN & ANNE	Labourer
01	AUG	1836	SUSANNAH	MOSELEY	-/ ELIZABETH	Servant
14	AUG	1836	MARY	ROE	-/ EPHRAIM & HANNAH	Labourer
10	SEP	1836	MARIA	JOHNSON	-/ THOMAS & ESTHER	Butcher
11	SEP	1836	WILLIAM	YOUNG	-/ MARY	Spinster
06	NOV	1836	JAMES	WEBSTER	-/ SAMUEL & ELIZA	Labourer
06	NOV	1836	ELIZABETH	WEBSTER	-/ SAMUEL & ELIZA	Labourer
06	NOV	1836	HANNAH	WEBSTER	-/ SAMUEL & ELIZA	Labourer
15	JAN	1837	JAMES	BRADLEY	aged 2 -/ JAMES & SUSANNAH	Publican
15	JAN	1837	WILLIAM	BRADLEY	-/ JAMES & SUSANNAH	Publican
05[1]	FEB	1837	WILLIAM ROBERT	KING	-/ WILLIAM & SARAH of Breedon Brand	Labourer
14	FEB	1837	SARAH	GILBERT	-/ THOMAS & HARRIET (P.)	Shoe Maker
19	MAR	1837	WILLIAM	YOUNG	-/ CHRISTOPHER & SARAH	F.W.K.
28	MAY	1837	BETSY	FLETCHER	-/ JOHN & JULIA	Labourer
09	JUN	1837	GEORGE	MATCHETT	-/ WILLIAM & ELIZABETH	Potter
09	JUN	1837	MARY	MATCHETT	-/ SAMUEL & ELIZABETH	Labourer
09	JUN	1837	HENRY	MATCHETT	-/ SAMUEL & ELIZABETH	Labourer
30	JUN	1837	MARY	JOHNSON	aged 19 -/ THOMAS & ESTHER	Butcher
30	JUN	1837	MARTHA	JOHNSON	aged 17 -/ THOMAS & ESTHER	Butcher
30	JUN	1837	HANNAH	JOHNSON	aged 15 -/ THOMAS & ESTHER	Butcher
30	JUN	1837	ELIZABETH	JOHNSON	aged 13 -/ THOMAS & ESTHER	Butcher
30	JUN	1837	CATHERINE	JOHNSON	aged 11 -/ THOMAS & ESTHER	Butcher
30	JUN	1837	THOMAS	JOHNSON	aged 7 -/ THOMAS & ESTHER	Butcher
30	JUN	1837	JAMES	NEEDHAM	aged 2½ -/ FRANCIS & MARY	Parish Clerk
02	JUL	1837	GEORGE	BLACK	-/ SAMUEL & HANNAH	Carpenter
02	JUL	1837	CATHARINE	BLACK	-/ SAMUEL & HANNAH	Carpenter
02	JUL	1837	JOSEPH	BLACK	-/ SAMUEL & HANNAH	Carpenter
07	JUL	1837	SARAH ANNE	MILES	-/ WILLIAM & HANNAH	Farmer

[1] Appears to be 15 in register; however, entry was smudged and is certainly 5. See actual register not microfiche.

11 AUG 1837 CHARLES HALLAM -/ THOMAS & HANNAH F.W.K.
17 SEP 1837 SAMUEL BRANSON -/ WILLIAM & SARAH Farmer
17 SEP 1837 JANE KING -/ EDWARD & MARY Labourer
22 OCT 1837 SARAH IRONMONGER -/ THOMAS CLIVE & HANNAH Carpenter
07 DEC 1837 EDWARD PERRY -/ MATILDA (P.) Lace Runner
16 FEB 1838 CHARLOTTE LUCY KATHARINE KELK
-/ WILLIAM HASTINGS & LUCY HENRIETTA (P.) Rector
04 MAR 1838 THOMAS JARVIS -/ SAMUEL & MARY (P.) F.W.K.

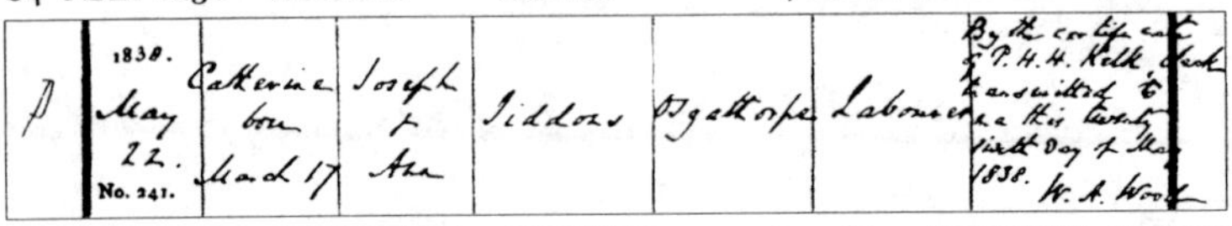
P 1838. May 22. No. 241. | Catherine born March 17 | Joseph & Ann | Siddons | Osgathorpe | Labourer | By the certificate of W. H. H. Kelk Clerk transmitted to me this twenty sixth Day of May 1838. W. A. Wood

22 MAY 1838 CATHERINE SIDDONS b. 17 Mar -/ JOSEPH & ANN (P.) Labourer
27 MAY 1838 SAMUEL SKERMER ASHER b. 26 May -/ JOHN & MARY Inn Keeper
08 JUN 1838 WILLIAM BRADLEY b. 4 Jun -/ WILLIAM & MARY (P.) Shoemaker
24 JUN 1838 GEORGE HASTINGS NEEDHAM b. 30 May -/ FRANCIS & MARY Parish Clerk
02 SEP 1838 MARTHA ROE -/ JAMES & SARAH Labourer
02 SEP 1838 REUEL WALDROM -/ JAMES & SARAH Labourer
16 SEP 1838 ANNE REBECCA MOSELEY -/ JOSEPH & MARY Farmer
11 NOV 1838 HENRY MILES -/ WILLIAM & HANNAH Farmer
16 DEC 1838 JAMES WOOD -/ STEPHEN COX & ANNE Carpenter
23 DEC 1838 CHARLOTTE WEBSTER -/ SAMUEL & ELIZA Coal Miner
11 MAR 1839 WILLIAM HENRY HASTINGS KELK
-/ WILLIAM HASTINGS & LUCY HENRIETTA (P.) Clerk
05 MAY 1839 JOSEPH THOMAS DARBY -/ JOHN & SARAH Labourer
12 MAY 1839 EMMA KING -/ EDWARD & MARY Labourer
05 JUN 1839 MARY CLARKE -/ JAMES & ELIZABETH (P.) Farmer
12 AUG 1839 WILLIAM STEVENSON -/ GEORGE & SARAH Labourer
25 AUG 1839 WILLIAM PERRY -/ MATILDA Lace Runner
22 SEP 1839 HEZEKIAH BAKER -/ ELIZABETH F.W.K.
25 DEC 1839 JOSEPH BENNET -/ JOHN & ANN Labourer
02 FEB 1840 THOMAS BRADLEY -/ JAMES & SUSANNA Farmer
02 FEB 1840 LUCY OLIVER -/ HANNAH Spinster
16 FEB 1840 ANNE WOOD -/ STEPHEN COX & ANNE Parish Clerk
03 MAY 1840 GEORGE ROE -/ JAMES & SARAH Labourer
03 MAY 1840 ADAH SMITH WALDROM -/ ANNE Spinster
28 JUN 1840 JOHN ASHER -/ JOHN & MARY Publican
09 SEP 1840 ELIZABETH SIDDONS -/ JOSEPH & ANN Labourer
20 NOV 1840 AUGUSTUS HASTINGS KELK -/ WILLIAM HYDE & MARY ISABELLA Gentleman
29 NOV 1840 WILLIAM HENRY MOSELEY -/ JOSEPH & MARY Farmer
02 MAY 1841 RICHARD WALDROM -/ JAMES & SARAH Labourer
09 MAY 1841 JOHN DARBY -/ JOHN & SARAH Labourer
30 MAY 1841 MATTHEW WHITE -/ MATTHEW & ELIZABETH Labourer
30 MAY 1841 JOSEPH THOMAS KING -/ EDWARD & MARY Labourer
26 JUL 1841 JOHN YOUNG -/ CHRISTOPHER & SARAH F.W.K.

26	JUL	1841	THOMAS	YOUNG	-/ CHRISTOPHER & SARAH	F.W.K.
30	JUL	1841	SARAH	CLARKE	aged 6 -/ JAMES & ELIZABETH	Farmer
30	JUL	1841	HANNAH	CLARKE	aged 3 -/ JAMES & ELIZABETH	Farmer
30	JUL	1841	ANN	CLARKE	-/ JAMES & ELIZABETH	Farmer
11	AUG	1841	PRISCILLA	WEBSTER	-/ SAMUEL & ELIZA	Coal Carrier
03	OCT	1841	WILLIAM	SMITH	-/ TOBIAS & MARY	Labourer
30	DEC	1841	WILLIAM	WOOD	-/ STEPHEN COX & ANNE	Parish Clerk
20	MAR	1842	ELIZABETH HANDFORD	STEVENSON	-/ GEORGE & SARAH	Labourer
29	JUN	1842	WILLIAM	CLARKE	-/ JAMES & ELIZABETH	Farmer
16	JUL	1842	MARY ANN	KING	-/ WILLIAM & MATILDA	Labourer
05	AUG	1842	ELIZA	ASHER	-/ JOHN & MARY	Publican
21	AUG	1842	ALICE HALLAM	BRADLEY	ELIZABETH 'NB. Methodist'[1]	F.W.K.
21	AUG	1842	SAMUEL GILBERT	WALDROM	ELIZABETH 'NB. Methodist'	Lace Runner
30	AUG	1842	SARAH	HALL	-/ JOHN & MARY	F.W.K.
27	NOV	1842	SAMUEL	ROE	-/ JAMES & SARAH	Labourer
27	NOV	1842	GEORGE	OSBORNE	-/ JOHN & ELIZABETH	Labourer
10	FEB	1843	THOMAS	BENNETT	-/ JOHN & ANN	Labourer
16	MAR	1843	THOMAS	WHEATLEY now BAGGERLEY	-/ JANE of Osga' late of Diseworth	-[2]
29	MAY	1843	MARY JANE	MILES	about 2 yrs old -/ WILLIAM & HANNAH	Farmer
29	MAY	1843	HANNAH	MILES	-/ WILLIAM & HANNAH	Farmer
04	JUN	1843	JAMES WARRIS	GREEN	-/ JOHN & SARAH	Bricklayer
16	JUL	1843	THOMAS	KING	-/ EDWARD & MARY	Labourer
14	AUG	1843	WILLIAM	KING	-/ WILLIAM & MATILDA	Labourer
20	AUG	1843	JOHN	SIDDONS	-/ JOSEPH & ANN	Labourer
02	NOV	1843	ELIZA	ROE	-/ SARAH ANN 'Baptist'[3]	Servant
17	DEC	1843	MARY ANN	PERRY	-/ GEORGE & CATHERINE	Miner
25	FEB	1844	HANNAH	HALL	-/ JOHN & MARY	F.W.K.
06	MAR	1844	EMMA	WOOD	-/ STEPHEN COX & ANNE	Parish Clerk
07	APR	1844	KIDGER	DARBY	s./ JOHN & SARAH	Labourer
07	APR	1844	SARAH	BLACK junr	-/ SAMUEL & CATHERINE	Carpenter
11	MAY	1844	MARY	CLARKE	-/ JAMES & SARAH	Farmer
11	MAY	1844	ELIZA	CLARKE	-/ JAMES & SARAH	Farmer
28	JUL	1844	SARAH ANN	BLACK	-/ GEORGE & ELIZABETH	Laborer
13	OCT	1844	HANNAH	WHITE	-/ MATHEW & ELIZABETH	Labourer
13	OCT	1844	WILLIAM	ASHER	-/ JOHN & MARY	Publican
24	NOV	1844	MARY	BURTON	-/ JOSEPH & CHARLOTTE	Labourer
24	NOV	1844	MAHALA	PEMBERTON	-/ ESAU & DINAH	Coal Miner
12	JAN	1845	GEORGIENA	KING	-/ JOSEPH & ELIZABETH	Labourer
04	MAY	1845	RACHEL	WALDROM	-/ JAMES & SARAH	Labourer
22	JUN	1845	GEORGE	MOORE	-/ JOSEPH & HANNAH	F.W.K.
15	SEP	1845	MARTHA	MORGAN	-/ BENJ & CHARLOTTE	Potter
12	OCT	1845	JOSEPH GEORGE	GREEN	-/ JOHN & SARAH	Carrier

[1] Revd T.N. Bland, rector of Osgathorpe, performed this & the following baptism.
[2] BT & register both gave spinster, which was crossed out.
[3] Revd T.N. Bland, rector of Osgathorpe, performed this baptism.

12	OCT	1845	JOSEPH	ROE	-/ JAMES & SARAH	Labourer
24	DEC	1845	SARAH	KING	-/ EDWARD & MARY	Labourer
10	JAN	1846	SUSANNAH	PERRY	-/ GEORGE & CATHARINE	Miner
04	MAR	1846	WILLIAM	SIDDONS	-/ JOSEPH & ANN	Labourer
22	APR	1846	JEMIMA	BENNETT	-/ CHARLES & ELIZABETH BERRIDGE	Farmer
25	SEP	1846	CAROLINE	CLARKE	-/ JAMES & SARAH	Farmer
25	OCT	1846	JOHN	ASHER	-/ JOHN & MARY	Publican
22	NOV	1846	EMMA	BLACK	-/ GEORGE & ELIZABETH	Labourer
28	FEB	1847	GEORGE	KING	-/ JOSEPH & ELIZABETH	Labourer
28	FEB	1847	JAMES	ROE	-/ WILLIAM & ANN	Labourer
01	JUN	1847	ELIZA	DARBY	-/ JOHN & SARAH	Labourer
04	JUN	1847	GEORGE DAWKINS	WALE b.18 Oct 1822	-/ THOMAS WARD & ELIZABETH	Farmer
23	AUG	1847	SARAH	HALL	-/ JOHN & MARY of Belton	Labourer
19	SEP	1847	JOHN WILLIAM	KING	-/ THOMAS & ELIZABETH	Labourer
07	DEC	1847	MARTHA	MORGAN	-/ BENJ & CHARLOTTE	Potter
01	JAN	1848	THOMAS	DARBY	-/ SAMUEL & ELIZABETH	Labourer
14	MAR	1848	MATILDA REBECCA	WALE aged 13	-/ THOMAS WARD & ELIZABETH	Farmer
02	APR	1848	SARAH ANN	GREEN	-/ JOHN & SARAH	Carrier
30	JUL	1848	JANE	HALLAM	-/ THOS & ELIZTH	F.W.K.
22	SEP	1848	HENRY	ROE	-/ JAMES & SARAH	Labourer
15	OCT	1848	WILLIAM	ROE	-/ JAMES & SARAH	Labourer
10	DEC	1848	ELIZA	KING	-/ THOMAS & ELIZABETH	Labourer
17	DEC	1848	MARY ANN	KENDRICK	-/ THOS & SARAH	Labourer
31	DEC	1848	SARAH ANN	GILBERT	-/ WILLIAM & JANE	Blacksmith
25	FEB	1849	JOSEPH	POPE	-/ HANNAH 'Methodist'[1]	Servant
22	JUL	1849	WILLIAM	KING	-/ JOSEPH & ELIZABETH	Labourer
03	AUG	1849	JAMES	CLARKE	-/ JAMES & SARAH	Farmer
12	AUG	1849	SARAH ANN	BENNETT	-/ JOHN & ANN	Labourer
02	DEC	1849	ELIZA	KING	-/ EDWARD & MARY	Labourer
27	FEB	1850	ELIZABETH	JEFFCOAT	-/ THOMAS & ELIZABETH	Labourer
13	MAR	1850	SARAH ELIZA	WALE an adult	-/ THOMAS WARD & ELIZABETH	Farmer
12	MAY	1850	EMMA	GREEN	-/ JOHN & SARAH	Carrier
21	JUL	1850	SARAH ANN	KING	-/ THOMAS & ELIZABETH	Carrier
22	SEP	1850	JAMES	GILBERT	-/ WILLIAM & JANE	Blacksmith
22	DEC	1850	WILLIAM	DARBY	-/ SAMUEL & ELIZABETH	Labourer
05	JAN	1851	EMMA	KENDRICK	-/ THOMAS & SARAH	Labourer
23	JAN	1851	THOMAS	SHARPE	-/ JAMES & MARY	Labourer
26	JAN	1851	RUTH	HALLAM	-/ THOMAS & ELIZTH	F.W.K.
16	MAR	1851	CHARLES	ROE	-/ JAMES & SARAH	Labourer
16	MAR	1851	HANNAH	SIDDONS	-/ JOSEPH & ANN	Labourer
19	OCT	1851	WILLIAM	MILLWOOD	-/ JAMES & CHARLOTTE	Labourer
19	OCT	1851	HARRIET	MORGAN	-/ BENJAMIN & CHARLOTTE	Potter
25	OCT	1851	SUSANNAH	PERRY	-/ CAROLINE ?spinster	Lace Runner
26	OCT	1851	MARY	MOSELEY	-/ JOSEPH & MARY	Farmer

[1] Revd T.N. Bland, rector of Osgathorpe, performed this baptism.

09 NOV 1851 JAMES ASHER -/ JOHN & MARY Publican
09 NOV 1851 TOM COOPER ASHER -/ JOHN & MARY Publican
07 JAN 1852 JOHN WILLIAM CLARKE -/ JAMES & SARAH (P.B.) Farmer
25 JAN 1852 JOSEPH KING -/ JOSEPH & ELIZABETH Labourer
11 APR 1852 MARY ANN DARBY -/ SAMUEL & ELIZABETH Labourer
02 MAR[1] 1852 THOMAS GADSBY -/ WILLIAM & ANN (P.B.) Labourer
04 JUL 1852 WILLIAM KING -/ EDWARD & MARY Labourer
19 SEP 1852 ALICE BRADLEY b. 22 Dec 1842 [parents see below]

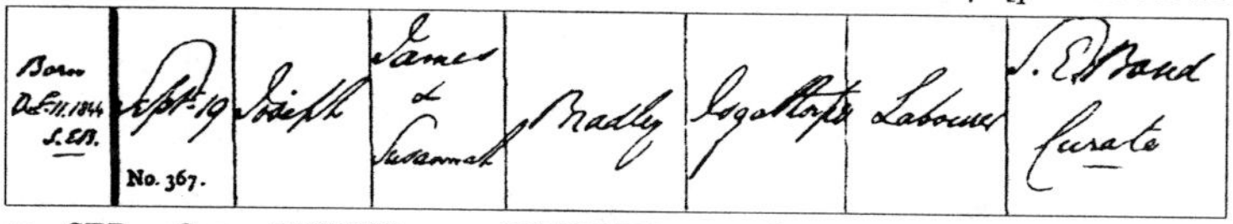
Born Dec 11. 1844 S.E.B. | Sept 19 No. 367. | Joseph | James & Susannah | Bradly | [illegible] | Labourer | S. E. Band Curate

19 SEP 1852 JOSEPH BRADLEY b. 11 Dec 1844 "
19 SEP 1852 FREDERICK BRADLEY b. 23 Dec 1847 "
19 SEP 1852 ISRAEL BRADLEY b. 15 Nov 1849 "
19 SEP 1852 SUSANNAH BRADLEY -, -/ JAMES & SUSANNAH Labourer
30 JAN 1853 MARY KING -/ THOMAS & ELIZABETH Carrier
20 FEB 1853 MATILDA PERRY -/ FREDERIC & HANNAH Coal Miner
04 APR 1853 CLARA BURTON -/ JOSEPH & CHARLOTTE Coal Miner
08 MAY 1853 MARY JANE GILBERT -/ WILLIAM & JANE Blacksmith
29 MAY 1853 JOSEPH MOSELEY -/ JOSEPH & MARY Farmer
26 JUN 1853 JANE ASHER -/ JOHN & MARY Publican
10 AUG 1853 JOHN GREEN s./ ELIZABETH Servant
21 AUG 1853 JOHN KENDRICK s./ THOMAS & SARAH Labourer
05 JAN 1854 JOHN CLIFFORD HAYWOOD s./ SAMUEL & ELIZABETH Miner
26 FEB 1854 SARAH ANN BRADLEY -/ JAMES & HANNAH Farmer
08 OCT 1854 CHARLES SMITH -/ JOHN & CAROLINE F.W.K.
02 NOV 1854 HANNAH MEE -/ WILLIAM & MARTHA Wheelwright
11 NOV 1854 SAMUEL JEFFCOAT -/ THOMAS & ELIZABETH Labourer
12 NOV 1854 ANNIE MARY MATCHETT -/ LOUISA Servant
13 NOV 1854 SARAH ANN YOUNG -/ MARIA Seamstress
29 NOV 1854 HANNAH MILLWOOD -/ JAMES & CHARLOTTE Labourer
03 JAN 1855 SAMUEL DARBY -/ GEORGE & ANN Labourer
15 APR 1855 THOMAS KING -/ THOMAS & ELIZABETH Carrier
15 JUL 1855 THOMAS SMITH -/ WILLIAM & HANNAH Miner
18 AUG 1855 MARY ANN HORROBIN -/ JOHN & HANNAH Labourer
09 SEP 1855 GEORGE DARBY -/ SAMUEL & ELIZABETH Labourer
16 SEP 1855 CHARLES JARVIS -/ SAMUEL & MARY ANN Labourer
30 SEP 1855 CLARA PERRY d./ JOSIAH & ANN Miner
30 SEP 1855 WILLIAM PERRY s./ JOSIAH & ANN Miner
26 DEC 1855 JOHN WALDROM s./ SOPHIA Seamstress
13 JAN 1856 SARAH ANN COWLEY -/ JOHN & ELIZA Labourer
13 JAN 1856 ARTHUR HURST -/ GEORGE & SARAH Miner

[1] Out of chronological order in both register & BT.

28 MAR 1856 ALFRED WOODWARD LEES -/ JOHN & SUSAN ANNE Master Miner
13 APR 1856 MARY JANE SMITH -/ JOHN & CAROLINE F.W.K.
19 APR 1856 GEORGE WRIGHT s./ THOMAS & SARAH Labourer
01 JUN 1856 EMILY DARBY -/ WILLIAM & ELIZA Labourer
27 JUL 1856 DANIEL ELIJAH WOLSEY -/ WILLIAM & MARY Labourer
31 AUG 1856 JOHN ALFRED COGGAN -/ GEORGE BARTLETT & HARRIET JANE of Rapps near Ashill, Somerset Gentleman
21 SEP 1856 PETER KING -/ THOMAS & ELIZABETH Carrier

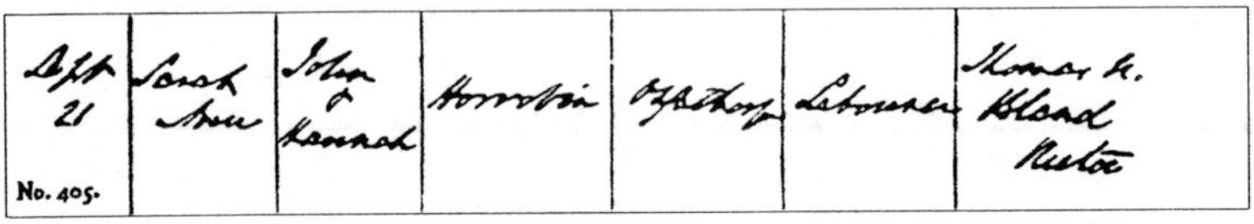

Sept 21 No. 405.	Sarah Ann	John & Hannah	Horrobin	Osgathorpe	Labourer	Thomas K. Bland Rector

21 SEP 1856 SARAH ANN HORROBIN -/ JOHN & HANNAH Labourer
21 SEP 1856 JOSEPH DARBY -/ GEORGE & ANN Labourer
25 DEC 1856 HANNAH ELIZA GREEN now HAYWOOD -/ ELIZABETH Seamstress
25 DEC 1856 JANE HANNAH BRIGGS -/ JOHN & MARY ANN of Barton in the Wolds Labourer
24 JAN 1857 SAMUEL JEFFCOAT -/ THOMAS & ELIZABETH Labourer
15 MAR 1857 JOSEPH THOMAS DARBY -/ WILLIAM & ELIZA Labourer
20 SEP 1857 FREDERICK PERRY -/ JOSIAH & ANN Miner
20 SEP 1857 MARY ANN HALLAM -/ THOMAS & ELIZABETH F.W.K.
19 DEC 1857 ANN ELIZABETH GILBERT -/ WILLIAM & JANE Blacksmith
25 DEC 1857 WILLIAM GADSBY b. 28 Nov 1849 -/ WILLIAM & ANN Miner
24 JAN 1858 ADELINE SMITH -/ JOHN & CAROLINE F.W.K.
24 JAN 1858 ELIAS DARBY -/ GEORGE & ANN Labourer
04 APR 1858 EMMA ROE -/ JAMES & SARAH Labourer
04 APR 1858 ELIZABETH MANN -/ JAMES & JANE Blacksmith
04 APR 1858 JOHN MANN -/ JAMES & JANE Blacksmith
20 JUN 1858 ELIZABETH MILLWOOD -/ WILLIAM & SARAH Miner
20 JUN 1858 CHARLES SIDDONS -/ JOSEPH & ANN Labourer
15 JUL 1858 JOHN WRIGHT -/ THOMAS & SARAH Labourer
19 SEP 1858 GEORGE JOHNSON CLARKE b. 24 Dec 1851 -/ SARAH [Blank]
19 SEP 1858 BENJAMIN CLARKE b. 9 Nov 1854 -/ SARAH [Blank]
19 SEP 1858 THOMAS JOHNSON -/ THOMAS & SARAH Farmer
03 OCT 1858 ISAAC WOLSEY -/ WILLIAM & MARY Labourer
20 FEB 1859 BENJAMIN MORGAN -/ GILES & SARAH Miner
27 MAR 1859 WALTER PERRY -/ JOSIAH & ANN Miner
27 MAR 1859 ELIZABETH KING -/ THOMAS & ELIZABETH Carrier
08 APR 1859 WILLIAM JEFFCOAT -/ THOMAS & ELIZABETH Labourer
08 APR 1859 THOMAS JEFFCOAT age 7 -/ THOMAS & ELIZABETH Labourer
08 APR 1859 PRISCILLA YOUNG age 13 -/ CHRISTOPHER & SARAH F.W.K.
08 APR 1859 HANNAH YOUNG age 7 -/ SARAH Seamstress
08 APR 1859 SAMUEL YOUNG age 5 -/ SARAH Seamstress
08 APR 1859 EDWARD YOUNG age 3 -/ SARAH Seamstress
09 JUL 1859 HARRIET HURST -/ GEORGE & SARAH Miner
13 NOV 1859 SELINA MILLWOOD -/ JAMES & CHARLOTTE Labourer

25	DEC	1859	JOHN LAWRENCE RENNOCKS		-/ WILLIAM & ELIZABETH	Shoe Maker
06	APR	1860	ELIZA	BURTON	b. Dec 1850 [parents see below]	
06	APR	1860	THOMAS CLIFFORD BURTON		b. Mar 1854 "	
06	APR	1860	JAMES	BURTON	b. Feb 1859 -/ JOSEPH & CHARLOTTE	Miner
06	APR	1860	ALLEN	TAYLOR	-/ WILLIAM & ELIZA	Miner
29	APR	1860	GEORGE THOMAS SMITH		-/ JOHN & CAROLINE	F.W.K.
12	MAY	1860	THERESA	WOLSEY	-/ WILLIAM & MARY	Labourer
13	JUL	1860	CHARLES	WRIGHT	-/ THOMAS & SARAH	Labourer
30	SEP	1860	PHEBE	DARBY	-/ GEROGE & ANN	Labourer
30	SEP	1860	JANE ELIZABETH HARTSHORNE		-/ JOHN & JANE	Labourer
30	SEP	1860	HANNAH	KING	-/ THOMAS & ELIZABETH	Labourer
30	SEP	1860	JOSEPH	BAKER	-/ LEVI & SARAH	Labourer
30	SEP	1860	CATHARINE	HEYWOOD	-/ DAVID & ELIZABETH	Miner
30	SEP	1860	SARAH ANN EMMA HEYWOOD		-/ DAVID & ELIZABETH	Miner
24	FEB	1861	THOMAS JAMES JOHNSON		-/ THOMAS & SARAH	Farmer
07	APR	1861	WILLIAM ARTHUR BROOKS		-/ FANNY[1]	Servant
28	APR	1861	AMELIA	MORGAN	-/ GILES & SARAH	Miner
04	JUN	1861	ADA	BURTON	-/ JOSEPH & CHARLOTTE	Miner
16	FEB	1862	GEORGE	TAYLOR	-/ WILLIAM & ELIZA	Miner
08	JUN	1862	ANNIE	RENNOCKS	-/ WILLIAM & ELIZABETH	Shoemaker
15	JUN	1862	ANN	DARBY	-/ WILLIAM & ELIZA	Labourer
15	JUN	1862	SARAH	DARBY	-/ WILLIAM & ELIZA	Labourer
15	JUN	1862	WILLIAM	HORROBIN	-/ JOHN & HANNAH	Labourer
03	AUG	1862	HENRY	BAKER	-/ LEVI & SARAH	Labourer
03	AUG	1862	ELIZA ANN	BRADLEY	about 3 yrs -/ JAMES & ANN first wife	Labourer
09	NOV	1862	JOSIAH	PERRY	-/ JOSIAH & ANN	Miner
30	NOV	1862	SELINA	KING	-/ THOMAS & ELIZABETH	Carrier
30	NOV	1862	JOSEPH	BURTON	-/ JOSEPH & CHARLOTTE	Miner
08	FEB	1863	CHARLES	SHAW	-/ JACOB & HANNAH	Miner
22	FEB	1863	JAMES	WRIGHT	-/ THOMAS & SARAH	Labourer
05	APR	1863	ADA	WALKER	-/ GEORGE & SOPHIA	Labourer
24	APR	1863	ELIZABETH	GILBERT	b. 16 May 1860 -/ WILLIAM & JANE	Blacksmith
29	SEP	1863	JOSEPH HENRY FREEMAN		-/ HENRY & MARY ANN	Farmer
18	OCT	1863	WILLIAM ALFRED GILBERT		-/ WILLIAM & JANE	Blacksmith
28	FEB	1864	JOSEPH	BRADLEY	-/ JAMES & ANN	Labourer
28	FEB	1864	ELIZABETH	MILLWOOD	-/ JAMES & CHARLOTTE	Labourer
17	APR	1864	GEORGE	BAKER	-/ LEVI & SARAH	Labourer
17	APR	1864	FEDERICK JAMES BAKER		-/ HEZEKIAH & EMMA	Labourer
29	MAY	1864	GEORGE	BRADLEY	-/ THOMAS & ANN	Labourer
19	JUL	1864	GEORGE	FIELD	-/ GEORGE & MARY ANN	Labourer
27	NOV	1864	ANN	SHAW	-/ JACOB & HANNAH	Miner
25	DEC	1864	HERBERT	WALKER	-/ GEORGE & SOPHIA	Labourer
12	MAR	1865	LUCY ANN	JARVIS	-/ JOSEPH & HANNAH	Labourer
09	APR	1865	HENRY TAYLOR BURBIDGE		-/ HENRY & JANE of Breedon	Game Keeper

[1] Register also gave 'came into this parish to be confined does not belong to this parish'.

30	APR	1865	MARY ANNIE	FREEMAN	-/ HENRY & MARY ANN	Farmer
14	MAY	1865	MARK	BRADLEY	-/ JAMES & ANN	Labourer
27	AUG	1865	FANNY	WARNER	-/ CHARLES EDWIN & ANN	Master of the Grammar School
31	DEC	1865	CHARLES HENRY	BROOKS	-/ JOSEPH & MARTHA	Labourer
31	DEC	1865	EDITH ANN	PERRY	-/ JOSIAH & ANN	Labourer
31	DEC	1865	WILLIAM	HARTSHORNE	-/ JOHN & JANE	Labourer
31	DEC	1865	ANNIE	HARTSHORNE	-/ JOHN & JANE	Labourer
25	FEB	1866	JOHN THOMAS	HOROBIN	-/ JOHN & HANNAH	Collier
04	MAR	1866	WILLIAM	DAVILL	-/ STEPHEN & MARY	Blacksmith
15	APR	1866	SARAH ANN	BAKER	-/ LEVI & SARAH	Engine Tenter
06	MAY	1866	JOSIAH	GILBERT	-/ WILLIAM & JANE	Farmer
20	MAY	1866	SEPTIMUS JOSEPH	JERVIS	-/ JOSEPH & HANNAH	Collier
01	JUL	1866	ELJAH	HORROBIN	-/ ELIZA MARY	Servant
12	AUG	1866	CHARLES	HENSON	-/ WILLIAM THOMAS & HARRIET	F.W.K.
21	OCT	1866	ELIZABETH	SHAW	-/ JACOB & HANNAH	Miner
21	OCT	1866	ELIZABETH ANN	DARBY	-/ GEORGE & ANN	Labourer
11	NOV	1866	AMOS	WALKER	-/ GEORGE & SOPHIA	Labourer
25	DEC	1866	MINNIE	BRADLEY	-/ JAMES & ANN	Miner
24	MAR	1867	SARAH EDITH	FIELD	-/ GEORGE & MARY ANN	Farmer
21	APR	1867	ABNER SAM	JARVIS	-/ JOSEPH & HANNAH	Miner
01	JUN	1867	SAMUEL HENRY	WEBSTER	-/ HENRY & SARAH of Breedon	Labourer
14	JUL	1867	FRANK REGINALD	WALKER	s./ THOMAS & FANNY	Farmer
25	AUG	1867	HANNAH MATILDA	BAKER	-/ HEZEKIAH & EMMA of Thringstone	Labourer
25	AUG	1867	EDITH REBECCA	BILLING	-/ WILLIAM & CHARLOTTE	Miner
25	AUG	1867	JOHN	RICHARDS	-/ SAMUEL & ALICE	Miner
22	SEP	1867	MARY ELIZABETH	WALL	-/ JOHN & MARY ANNIE [see below]	
22	SEP	1867	LUCY HANNAH	WALL	-/ JOHN & MARY ANNIE "	
					of Sutton in Ashfield, near Mansfield	Baker
19	JAN	1868	MARY ELIZABETH	DEAVILLE	-/ STEPHEN & MARY	Blacksmith
15	MAR	1868	MARY ANN	WALKER	-/ GEORGE & SOPHIA	Miner
22	MAR	1868	RUTH	HARTSHORNE	-/ JOHN & JANE	Labourer
22	MAR	1868	WILLIAM ARTHUR	SIDDONS	-/ JOHN & MARY ANN	Miner
17	MAY	1868	FLORENCE	HOLLINGSHEAD	d./ HERBERT & ELIZABETH SARAH	Farmer
23	AUG	1868	SARAH ANN	BRADLEY	d./ JAMES & ANN	Miner
23	AUG	1868	ELIZA ELEANOR	DARBY	d./ GEORGE & ANN	Miner
23	AUG	1868	HANNAH LAVINA	HORROBIN	d./ JOHN & HANNAH	Labourer
30	AUG	1868	HARRIET ELIZA	HENSON	d./ WILLIAM THOMAS & HARRIET	Clerk in Colliery
06	SEP	1868	ELIZA JANET ALEXANDA	WILLIAM[S]	d./ WALTER AUGUSTUS & JANET	Rector
20	SEP	1868	HARRIETT	BAKER	d./ LEVI & SARAH	Engine Tenter
20	SEP	1868	JAMES	LEESON	s./ JAMES ORTON & CATHARINE	Miner
20	SEP	1868	JULIA	PERRY	d./ JOSIAH & ANN	Miner
22	NOV	1868	THOMAS	GILBERT	s./ WILLIAM & ELIZABETH	Farmer
24	JAN	1869	EMMA	RICHARDS	d./ SAMUEL & ALICE	Miner
17	MAR	1869	WILLIAM	BAKER	s./ ELIZABETH	Servant
24	MAR	1869	ADA	BURTON	d./ WILLIAM & HARRIETT	Miner
18	APR	1869	THOMAS	SIDDONS	s./ WILLIAM & LOUISA	Miner

18	APR	1869	ELEANOR MARY HINDS		d./ GEORGE & ELIZA of Thringstone	Labourer
20	JUN	1869	ALFRED	BRADLEY	s./ JOSEPH & FRANCES	Miner
20	JUN	1869	JARVIS	MILLWOOD	s./ JAMES & CHARLOTTE	Labourer
20	JUN	1869	CONSTANCE GRACE JERVIS		d./ JOSEPH & HANNAH	Miner
11	JUL	1869	ELLEN	WALKER	d./ GEORGE & SOPHIA	Miner
16	JAN	1870	WALTER DAVID WILLIAMS		d./ WALTER AUGUSTUS & JANET	Rector
14	FEB	1870	THOMAS WILLIAM BARNES		s./ ENOCH & SARAH ANN	Miner
03	MAR	1870	JOSEPH	DARBY	s./ WILLIAM & ELIZA	Miner

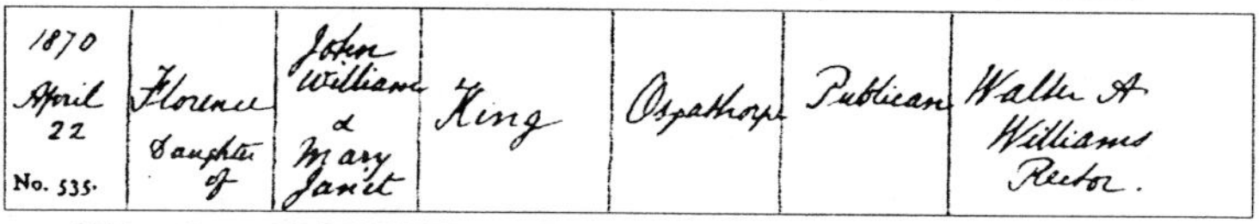
1870 April 22 No. 535. | Florence daughter of | John William & Mary Janet | King | Osgathorpe | Publican | Walter A Williams Rector.

22	APR	1870	FLORENCE	KING	d./ JOHN WILLIAM & MARY JANET	Publican
24	APR	1870	OLIVER	BRADLEY	s./ JAMES & ANN of St George's, Thringstone	Publican
24	APR	1870	CATHARINE	LEESON	d./ JAMES ORTON & CATHARINE	Miner
15	APR	1870	EMILY	SMITH	d./ JOHN & MARY	Labourer
14	AUG	1870	LUCY	GILBERT	d./ WILLIAM & ELIZABETH	Farmer
14	AUG	1870	GEORGE	GADSBY	s./ b. 1864 WILLIAM & MARY	Miner
14	AUG	1870	WILLIAM	GADSBY	s./ b. 1866 WILLIAM & MARY	Miner
14	AUG	1870	ROBERT	GADSBY	s./ WILLIAM & MARY	Miner
14	AUG	1870	FRANCES SARAH DARBY		d./ GEORGE & ANN	Miner
14	AUG	1870	ELIZABETH ANN BAKER		d./ HEZEKIAH & EMMA of Thringstone	Labourer
11	SEP	1870	ANNIE DRUSILLA DEAVILLE		d./ STEPHEN & MARY	Blacksmith
18	SEP	1870	ALBERT ARTHUR PERRY		s./ JOSIAH & ANN	Miner
18	SEP	1870	HARRIETT	WALKER	d./ GEORGE & SOPHIA	Miner
18	SEP	1870	ANNIE STATHAM WALL		d./ JOHN & MARY ANNIE of Sutton in Ashfield, near Mansfield	Baker
01	JAN	1871	WALTER ISRAIL BRADLEY		s./ JOSEPH & FRANCES	Miner
01	JAN	1871	MARY ANN	BURTON	d./ WILLIAM & HARRIETT	Miner
10	APR	1871	WILLIAM MORRIS WILLIAMS		s./ WALTER AUGUSTUS & JANET	Rector
14	MAY	1871	MARY ANNE	BILLINGS	d./ JOSEPH & RUTH	Blacksmith
21	MAY	1871	LOUISA	DARBY	d./ SAMUEL & ELIZA	Labourer
21	MAY	1871	GEORGE THOMAS BENNETT		s./ SARAH ANNE	Servant
21	MAY	1871	JOSEPH	BENNETT	s./ SARAH ANNE	Servant
21	MAY	1871	AGNES ELIZABETH SIDDENS		d./ JOHN & MARY ANNE	Labourer
21	MAY	1871	MARY ANNE	BRADLEY	d./ SUSANNAH of Thringstone	Servant
21	MAY	1871	CHARLES ELIJAH BILLINGS		s./ WILLIAM & CHARLOTTE	Labourer
21	MAY	1871	ALBERT	HOROBIN	s./ ELIZA	Servant
21	MAY	1871	ALICE	RICHARDS	d./ SAMUEL & ALICE	Collier
04	JUN	1871	LAURA	HOLLINGSHEAD	d./ HERBERT & ELIZABETH SARAH	Farmer
04	JUN	1871	ERNEST	HOLLINGSHEAD	s./ HERBERT & ELIZABETH SARAH	Farmer
04	JUN	1871	IDA	UPTON	d./ RANDAL JOSEPH & SARAH ANNE	Farmer
17	SEP	1871	WALTER	SIDDONS	s./ WILLIAM & LOUISA	Miner
17	SEP	1871	BERTHA	BURTON	d./ WILLIAM & HARRIETT	Miner
08	OCT	1871	EMILY	GADSBY	d./ WILLIAM & ELIZA	Blacksmith

15	OCT	1871	WILLIAM	DARBY	s./ WILLIAM & ELIZA	Miner & Labourer
15	OCT	1871	JOHN	DARBY	s./ WILLIAM & ELIZA	Miner & Labourer
15	OCT	1871	JOSEPH	DARBY	s./ WILLIAM & ELIZA	Miner & Labourer
31	DEC	1871	GEORGE	BILLING	s./ JOSEPH & RUTH	Blacksmith
28	JAN	1872	HERBERT	DARBY	s./ WILLIAM & MARY ANN	Miner
28	JAN	1872	ANNIE	BAXTER	d./ FREDERICK & ELIZA	Wagoner
28	JAN	1872	THOMAS	LEESON	s./ JAMES ORTON & CATHARINE	Miner
28	JAN	1872	CLARA	BRADLEY	d./ JAMES & ANN	Miner

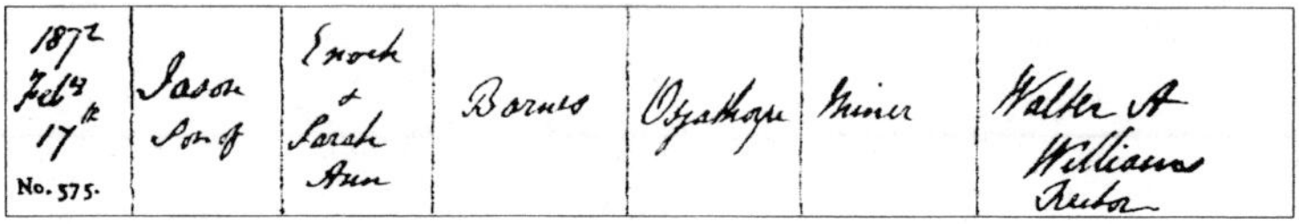
1872 Feb 17th No. 575. | Jason Son of | Enoch & Sarah Ann | Barnes | Osgathorpe | Miner | Walter A Williams Rector

17	FEB	1872	JASON	BARNES	s./ ENOCH & SARAH ANN	Miner
18	FEB	1872	MARGARET	KING	d./ MARY	Servant
25	FEB	1872	HANNAH	WALKER	d./ GEORGE & SOPHIA	Miner
28	APR	1872	SARAH AGNES	BAKER	d./ HEZEKIAH & EMMA of Thringstone	Labourer
28	APR	1872	AGNES KATE	PERRY	d./ JOSIAH & ANN	Miner
12	MAY	1872	RUTH	RICHARDS	d./ SAMUEL & ALICE	Miner
18	AUG	1872	ROSETTA ELIZABETH	BILLINGS	d./ WILLIAM & CHARLOTTE	Labourer
08	DEC	1872	HARRIETT ELIZA	BURTON	d./ WILLIAM & HARRIETT	Miner
08	DEC	1872	THOMAS	GADSBY	s./ WILLIAM & ELIZA	Blacksmith
12	JAN	1873	MARY BERTHA	WILLIAMS	d./ WALTER AUGUSTUS & JANET of Osgathorpe Rectory	Clerk in Holy Orders
12	JAN	1873	SARAH REBECCA	DEAVILLE	d./ STEPHEN & MARY	Blacksmith & Farmer
12	JAN	1873	SARAH ANN	BRADLEY	d./ JOSEPH & FRANCES	Miner
12	JAN	1873	WILLIAM	BAXTER	s./ FREDERICK & ELIZA	Miner
04	MAY	1873	EMILY	KING	d./ WILLIAM & MARY	Miner
11	MAY	1873	GEORGE EDWARD	CHAPLIN	aged 3 s./ SAMUEL & FANNY	Miner
11	MAY	1873	JOHN THOMAS	CHAPLIN	aged 1yr 8mths s./ SAMUEL & FANNY	Miner
22	JUN	1873	BERNARD	HOLLINGSHEAD	s./ HERBERT & ELIZABETH SARAH	Farmer
06	JUL	1873	LUCY ANNIE MARIA	HORROBIN	d./ JOHN & HANNAH of Belton	Labourer
16	JUL	1873	ALBERT	HINDS	b.17 Jul 1870 s./ [parents see below]	
16	JUL	1873	VIOLET ANN	HINDS	b.Apr 1873 d./ GEORGE & ELIZA (P.B.)	Labourer
26	JUL	1873	SOPHIA	RICHARDS	d./ SAMUEL & ALICE	Miner
24	AUG	1873	ELIZABETH	BILLING	d./ JOSEPH & RUTH	Blacksmith
24	AUG	1873	THOMAS HENRY	LEESON	s./ JAMES ORTON & CATHARINE of Worthington	Miner
24	AUG	1873	THOMAS	BRADLEY	s./ JAMES & ANN of St George's, Thringstone	Miner
21	SEP	1873	GEORGE WILLIAM	BAKER	s./ HEZEKIAH & EMMA of Thringstone	Labourer
23	NOV	1873	ISAAC	GADSBY	s./ WILLIAM & MARY of Hucknall Torkard, Notts	Miner
07	DEC	1873	AGNES	KING	d./ GEORGE & SARAH	Shoe Maker
13	DEC	1873	WILLIAM	UPTON	s./ RANDAL JOSEPH & SARAH ANNE (P.B.)	Farmer
19	APR	1874	GEORGE	HORROBIN	s./ GEORGE & EMILY	Labourer
30	APR	1874	JOHN WILLIAM	KING	aged 3 s./ JOHN WILLIAM & MARY JANET	Miner
24	MAY	1874	PERCIVAL AUSTIN	HINES	s./ GEORGE & ELIZA	Labourer
28	JUN	1874	JOHN ELISHA	BILLING	s./ WILLIAM & CHARLOTTE	Labourer

28	JUN	1874	FRANCES AMY SIDDONS		d./ JOHN & MARY ANN	Labourer
16	AUG	1874	HERBERT	SIDDONS	s./ WILLIAM & LOUISA	Miner
16	AUG	1874	GEORGE	KING	s./ WILLIAM & MARY	Miner
05	SEP	1874	WILLIAM WILSON STATHAM		s./ WILLIAM WILSON & ANN	Labourer
18	OCT	1874	EDMUND	BAKER	s./ ELIZABETH (P.)	[Blank]
19	OCT	1874	JANE ELIZABETH HALLAM		d./ MARY ANN (P.)	Servant
25	OCT	1874	JAMES ERNEST HARRIS WILLIAMS		s./ WALTER AUGUSTUS & JANET of Osgathorpe Rectory	Clerk in Holy Orders
25	OCT	1874	SAMUEL	RICHARDS	s./ SAMUEL & ALICE	Miner
25	OCT	1874	FANNY	BILLING	d./ JOSEPH & RUTH	Blacksmith
25	OCT	1874	LAURA LYDIA	BRADLEY	d./ JOSEPH & FRANCES	Miner
25	OCT	1874	JOHN THOMAS BAXTER		s./ FREDERICK & ELIZA	Miner
25	OCT	1874	HENRY	BURTON	s./ WILLIAM & HARRIETT	Miner
25	OCT	1874	ELIZABETH ANNIE WEBSTER		aged 3 d./ HENRY & SARAH	Labourer
22	DEC	1874	HANNAH	DARBY	d./ SAMUEL & [Blank]	Labourer
03	JAN	1875	WALTER	BARNES	s./ ENOCH & SARAH ANN	Labourer
14	MAR	1875	JAMES	ROWE	s./ JAMES & LOIS	Labourer
02	MAY	1875	ERNEST EDWARD DARBY		s./ THOMAS & ELLEN	Pit Labourer
20	JUN	1875	IDA	HOLLINGSHEAD	d./ ROBERT & ELIZABETH SARAH	Farmer
19	SEP	1875	ARTHUR HENRY BAKER		s./ HEZEKIAH & EMMA of Thringstone	Labourer
19	SEP	1875	MARY CATHARINE WEBSTER		d./ HENRY & SARAH	Labourer
19	SEP	1875	MARY FREDERICA PEMBERTON		d./ AARON & ANNIE of Whitwick	Miner
14	NOV	1875	FRANCIS JOSEPH GEORGE MATCHETT		s./ EDWARD & GEORGINA	Miner
14	NOV	1875	JOSEPH	KING	s./ GEORGE & SARAH	Shoe Maker
14	NOV	1875	CHARLES SMITH SLEATH		s./ WILLIAM & PRISCILLA of Whitwick	Miner
02	JAN	1876	SARAH EMILY JOHNSON		d./ GEORGE & MARY	Farmer
02	JAN	1876	ISAAC	BAKER	s./ LEVI & PHOEBE	Engine Tentee [Tenter]
20	FEB	1876	GEORGE HALLAM RICHARDS		s./ SAMUEL & ALICE	Miner
07	MAY	1876	ANN	GOLDSTRAW	d./ PHOEBE	[Blank]
07	MAY	1876	AMY ELIZABETH KING		d./ WILLIAM & MARY	Miner
11	JUN	1876	JOHN THOMAS BURTON		s./ GEORGE & SARAH	Miner
13	JUN	1876	THOMAS	UPTON	s./ RANDAL JOSEPH & SARAH ANNE	Farmer
25	JUN	1876	ARTHUR	BILLING	s./ JOSEPH & RUTH	Blacksmith
25	JUN	1876	LAURA	BENNETT	d./ JOHN & ELIZA	Labourer
25	JUN	1876	EMILIA	HINDS	d./ GEORGE & ELIZA	Labourer
02	JUL	1876	JAMES	ROE	s./ EMMA	Servant
02	JUL	1876	MARGARET LOUISA KING		d./ JOHN WILLIAM & MARY JANET	Miner
06	AUG	1876	MARY HANNAH STATHAM		d./ WILLIAM WILSON & ANN	Labourer
03	SEP	1876	SAMUEL	JARVIS	s./ CHARLES & MARY ANN	Collier
05	NOV	1876	HANNAH	BRADLEY	d./ JOSEPH & FRANCES	Miner
05	NOV	1876	JOSEPH	BURTON	s./ WILLIAM & HARRIETT	Miner
15	JAN	1877	AMELIA	KING	d./ JOHN WILLIAM & MARY JANET	Miner
04	FEB	1877	LAURA GRACE SIDDONS		d./ JOHN & MARY ANN	Miner
04	FEB	1877	FREDERICK JAMES BILLING		s./ WILLIAM & CHARLOTTE	Labourer
25	FEB	1877	FANNY MARIA	COLEMAN	aged 28 wife of JOHN CUFFLINS d./ JOSEPH & SABINA	[Blank]

25	MAR	1877	JOSEPH	HARTSHORNE	s./ JOHN & MARY JANE	Miner
15	APR	1877	GEORGE	WEBSTER	s./ HENRY & SARAH	Labourer
15	APR	1877	ERNEST	SIDDONS	s./ WILLIAM & LOUISA	Miner
10	JUN	1877	LUCY	LEESON	d./↓	
10	JUN	1877	HENRY	LEESON	s./ JAMES ORTON & CATHARINE of Worthington	Miner
17	JUN	1877	JAMES FREDERICK	RICHARDS	s./ SAMUEL & ALICE	Miner
17	JUN	1877	HENRY ALBERT	MOSELEY	s./ WILLIAM HENRY & SARAH ANN	Farmer
17	JUN	1877	HENRY MORRISON	WILLIAMS	s./ WALTER AUGUSTUS & JANET of Osgathorpe Rectory	Clerk in Holy Orders
14	OCT	1877	ISABEL	DARBY	d./ THOMAS & HANNAH ELIZABETH	Labourer
14	OCT	1877	NELLY GRACE	WRIGHT	d./ JOSEPH & SELINA	F.W.K.
02	DEC	1877	GEORGE HARRY	BARNES	s./ ENOCH & SARAH ANN	Labourer
02	DEC	1877	GEORGE	KING	s./ THOMAS & MARY ANN	Labourer
17	FEB	1878	MARY	FLAMSON	aged 24 yrs wife of JOSEPH DARBY d./ GEORGE & FANNY of Thringstone	Labourer
24	FEB	1878	FREDERICK	BAKER	s./ JOSEPH & ANN	Labourer
24	FEB	1878	DORA	JARVIS	d./ CHARLES & MARY ANN	Miner
10	MAR	1878	CATHARINE	ROE	d./ JAMES & LOIS	Labourer
10	MAR	1878	WILSON	KING	s./ WILLIAM & MARY	Miner
12	MAY	1878	ALBERT	BILLING	s./ JOSEPH & RUTH	Blacksmith
12	MAY	1878	FREDERICK	BURTON	s./ WILLIAM & HARRIETT	Miner
02	JUN	1878	ARTHUR HERBERT	BAKER	s./ HEREKIAH & EMMA of Thringstone	Labourer
09	JUN	1878	KELLY	BRADLEY	d./ JOSEPH & FRANCES	Miner
03	JUL	1878	SARAH ANN	THOMPSON	d./ HENRY & MARY of Kings Newton, Melbourne	Labourer
22	SEP	1878	AGNES	HARTSHORNE	d./ JOHN & MARY JANE	Miner
22	SEP	1878	REGINALD JAMES	HAYWOOD	s./ JOHN & HANNAH	Miner
22	SEP	1878	KATE	RICHARDS	d./ SAMUEL & ALICE	Miner
22	SEP	1878	THOMAS	TIVEY	s./ JOHN & FANNY	Farmer & Publican
22	SEP	1878	JOSEPH	BIRD	s./ JOHN & ELIZABETH of Worthington	Labourer
01	DEC	1878	ELLEN ELIZA	DARBY	d./ WILLIAM & ELIZA	Labourer
01	DEC	1878	SARAH ANN	STATHAM	d./ WILLIAM WILSON & ANN	Labourer
01	DEC	1878	JOSEPH WILSON	STATHAM	s./ WILLIAM WILSON & ANN	Labourer
16	MAR	1879	ELLEN	BILLING	d./ JOSEPH & RUTH	Blacksmith
16	MAR	1879	LOUISA HARRIETTE	WILLIAMS	d./ WALTER AUGUSTUS & JANET of Osgathorpe Rectory	Clerk in Holy Orders
11	MAY	1879	GEORGE HENRY	HINES	s./ GEORGE & ELIZA	Labourer
11	MAY	1879	JOSEPH HENRY	ROE	s./ JAMES & LOIS	Labourer
19	OCT	1879	MARGARET ANN	BILLING	d./ WILLIAM & CHARLOTTE	Labourer
19	OCT	1879	ERNEST	KING	s./ THOMAS & MARY ANN	Labourer
04	JAN	1880	LYDIA	BENNETT	d./ JOHN & ELIZA	Labourer
04	JAN	1880	JOSEPH	JARVIS	s./ CHARLES & MARY ANN	Miner
04	JAN	1880	JAMES WILLIAM	BAKER	s./ JOSEPH & ANN	Labourer
22	FEB	1880	AMELIA	HARTSHORNE	d./ JOHN & MARY JANE	Miner

Date	Forename(s)	Surname	Parents	Occupation
21 MAR 1880	ERNEST JOSEPH	HAYWOOD	s./ JOHN & HANNAH	Miner
28 MAR 1880	EDWARD HUGH	BRADLEY	s./ JOSEPH & FRANCES	Miner
29 MAR 1880	SARAH CATHARINE	RICHARDS	d./ SAMUEL & ALICE	Miner
31 MAR 1880	CLARA	WALKER	d./ GEORGE & SOPHIA	Miner
31 MAR 1880	FRANCES ELLEN	WALKER	d./ GEORGE & SOPHIA	Miner
31 MAR 1880	GEORGE	WALKER	s./ GEORGE & SOPHIA	Miner
18 JUL 1880	JOHN HENRY	SIDDONS	s./ JOHN & MARY ANN	Miner
25 JUL 1880	PRISCILLA MATCHETT	CAWRAH	d./ SARAH ANN	[Blank]

1880 July 25 No. 699.	Sarah daughter of	Edward & Sarah Ann	Matchett Young	Osgathorpe	Miner	Walter A. Williams Rector

Date	Forename(s)	Surname	Parents	Occupation
25 JUL 1880	SARAH	MATCHETT/YOUNG	d./ EDWARD MATCHETT & SARAH ANN YOUNG	Miner
25 JUL 1880	ALBERT	BURTON	s./ WILLIAM & HARRIETT	Miner
04 SEP 1880	WILLIAM HENRY	STEVENSON	s./ WILLIAM & HANNAH of Hall Farm	Farmer
07 NOV 1880	ELIZA	BLACKWELL	aged 10. d./ [parents see below]	
07 NOV 1880	REBECCA ELIZABETH	BLACKWELL	aged 9. d./ "	
07 NOV 1880	TOM ALLEN	BLACKWELL	aged 7. s./ "	
07 NOV 1880	ISAAC ERNEST	BLACKWELL	aged 5. s./ "	
07 NOV 1880	SARAH ANN	BLACKWELL	aged 3. d./ CHARLES & ELIZA	Publican
28 NOV 1880	ALBERT ERNEST	SMITH	s./ CHARLES & MARTHA	F.W.K.
28 NOV 1880	LAURA	KING	d./ WILLIAM & MARY	Miner
16 JAN 1881	ELIZABETH ELLEN	KING	d./ PETER & ELIZA	Miner
16 JAN 1881	JOHN JOSEPH	BURTON	s./ JOHN GEORGE & EMMA MARIA	Publican & Joiner
16 JAN 1881	AMOS	BILLING	s./ JOSEPH & RUTH	Blacksmith
17 APR 1881	MILLICENT	KING	d./ THOMAS & MARY ANN	Labourer
05 JUN 1881	HENRY GARNER	KING	s./ JOHN WILLIAM & MARY JANET	Miner
05 JUN 1881	MARY	BROOKS	d./ JAMES & MARY ANN	Farmer
29 JUN 1881	WILLIAM	STATHAM	s./ WILLIAM WILSON & ANN	Labourer
25 SEP 1881	FAITH	RICHARDS	d./ SAMUEL & ALICE	Miner
16 OCT 1881	MARY JANE	HARTSHORNE	d./ JOHN & MARY JANE of Griffy Dam Worthington	Miner
05 FEB 1882	HENRY KIDGER	DARBY	s./ WILLIAM & ELIZA	Labourer
05 FEB 1882	SARAH ANN	BAKER	d./ JOSEPH & ANN	Labourer
05 FEB 1882	JOHN	MATCHETT/YOUNG	s./ EDWARD MATCHETT & SARAH ANN YOUNG	Miner
14 APR 1882	FREDERICK	BRYERS	s./ GEORGE & ELIZABETH of Lewknor, Oxfordshire	Coachman
07 MAY 1882	MARY ELIZABETH	SIDDONS	d./ WILLIAM & LOUISA	Farmer
07 MAY 1882	EDITH MAUD	WILLIAMS	d./ WALTER AUGUSTUS & JANET of Osgathorpe Rectory	Clerk in Holy Orders
08 MAY 1882	FANNY	GRIMLEY	d./ ELIZABETH of Sheepshed	Employed in factory
28 MAY 1882	JAMES	BROOKS	s./ JAMES & MARY ANN	Farmer
23 JUL 1882	CLARA	JARVIS	d./ CHARLES & MARY ANN	Miner

03 SEP 1882 AMY BRADLEY d./ JOSEPH & FRANCES Miner
01 OCT 1882 MINNIE BILLING d./ JOSEPH & RUTH Blacksmith
01 OCT 1882 DAVID STATHAM s./ WILLIAM WILSON & ANN Labourer
01 OCT 1882 EDITH KING d./ PETER & ELIZA Miner
23 FEB 1883 ALFRED JOHN WILLIAMS s./ WALTER AUGUSTUS & JANET
of Osgathorpe Rectory Clerk in Holy Orders
25 MAR 1883 MINNIE KATE SIDDONS d./ JOHN & MARY ANN Miner
22 APR 1883 ELLEN ANDERSON PURDY d./ THOMAS & REBECCA of Ibstock Miner

1883 April 22 No. 734.	Charles William Son of	Samuel & Alice	Richards	Osgathorpe	Miner	Walter A. Williams Rector.

22 APR 1883 CHARLES WILLIAM RICHARDS s./ SAMUEL & ALICE Miner
08 JUL 1883 THOMAS EDWYN KNIGHT s./ FREDERICK & HARRIET
of Stordon Grange, Thringstone Farmer
29 JUL 1883 ADA ELIZABETH KING d./ THOMAS & MARY ANN Labourer
18 NOV 1883 ALBERT HEDLEY LAKIN s./ JAMES & HANNAH Cordwainer & Farmer
18 NOV 1883 FRANCES GERTRUDE LAKIN d./ JAMES & HANNAH Cordwainer & Farmer
18 NOV 1883 MARY ANN DARBY d./ ELIAS & ELLEN Labourer
18 NOV 1883 ALBERT KING s./ WILLIAM & MARY Miner
08 DEC 1883 EDWARD MATCHETT/YOUNG s./ EDWARD MATCHETT &
SARAH ANN YOUNG Miner
27 JAN 1884 ALBERT JARVIS s./ CHARLES & MARY ANN Miner
09 MAR 1884 FLORIE CLARK DEAN d./ ABRAHAM BROOKS & ELIZABETH Farmer
09 MAR 1884 WILLIAM SIDDONS s./ WILLIAM & LOUISA Farmer
09 MAR 1884 LOUISA HARRIETT BAKER d./ JOSEPH & ANN Labourer
13 APR 1884 WINIFRED ELIZABETH HARTSHORNE d./ JOHN & MARY JANE
of Gelsmoor, Worthington Miner
12 JUN 1884 LOUISA RICHARDS d./ SAMUEL & ALICE Miner
17 AUG 1884 ELYAH DARBY s./ ELIAS & ELLEN Labourer
24 AUG 1884 MARGARET FRANCES BRADLEY d./ JOSEPH & FRANCES Miner
24 AUG 1884 JOHN TWIGG s./ [parents see below]
24 AUG 1884 JAMES TWIGG s./ "
24 AUG 1884 HERBERT HENRY TWIGG s./ THOMAS & SUSANNAH
of St George's, Swannington Miner
25 SEP 1884 JOHN HENRY BRYERS s./ GEORGE & ELIZABETH Coachman
18 JAN 1885 ANNIE BILLING d./ JOSEPH & RUTH Blacksmith
21 MAY 1885 GEORGE HENRY LEVI BAKER s./ JOSEPH & ANN Labourer
24 MAY 1885 JOHN HENRY PERRY s./ EDITH ANN Servant
31 MAY 1885 EDITH VERA SERRES d./ JOHN JAMES & EDITH BRUMMELL Surgeon
19 JUL 1885 CLARA BURTON d./ THOMAS & ANNIE Miner
19 JUL 1885 GERTRUDE MAUD SIDDONS d./ JOHN & MARY ANN Farmer
19 JUL 1885 MATILDA MAUD CLARKE d./ GEORGE & MAUD MARY Farmer
19 JUL 1885 CATHARINE DARBY d./ ELIAS & ELLEN Labourer
22 NOV 1885 IDA BEATRICE LAKIN d./ JAMES & HANNAH Cordwainer & Farmer

22	NOV	1885	BERTHA	KING	d./ WILLIAM & MARY	Miner
06	DEC	1885	MARY	GIDLOW	d./ WILLIAM & CATHARINE of Breedon Brand	Gamekeeper
06	DEC	1885	LYDIA	PEPPER	d./ WILLIAM & EMMA	Inn Keeper
06	DEC	1885	SARAH	PEPPER	d./ WILLIAM & EMMA	Inn Keeper
02	MAY	1886	JOSEPH DAVIS	ALLARD	s./ EDWIN & MARY ANN	Clerk to Aspalte Co.
30	MAY	1886	BERTHA MAY	SERRES	d./ EDWARD EDMUND & BERTHA	Master of the Grammar School
15	AUG	1886	LILY	BENNETT	d./ JOHN & ELIZA	Labourer
31	OCT	1886	LILIAN	EDWARDS	d./ HARRIET	[Blank]
21	NOV	1886	EVA DENT	MILLWOOD	d./ ELIZABETH	[Blank]
21	NOV	1886	LUCY ANN	RICHARDS	d./ SAMUEL & ALICE	Miner
12	DEC	1886	ERNEST DOMINIC	SERRES	s./ JOHN JAMES & EDITH BRUMMELL	Surgeon
20	FEB	1887	HERBERT	KING	s./ THOMAS & MARY ANN	Labourer
20	FEB	1887	FLORENCE	HICKLIN	d./ GEORGE & EMMA	Labourer
20	FEB	1887	ERNEST	JARVIS	s./ CHARLES JANE	Miner
20	FEB	1887	ADALINE MATILDA	KING	d./ JOSEPH & MARY JANE	Farmer
27	MAR	1887	RAYMOND	BRYERS	s./ GEORGE & ELIZABETH	Servant
10	APR	1887	JOHN THOMAS CLIFFORD	BURTON	s./ THOMAS & ANN	Miner
10	APR	1887	EDWARD	PARKER	s./ AMOS FRANCIS & ANN	Publican
15	MAY	1887	ALFRED ERNEST	KNIGHT	s./ [parents see below]	
15	MAY	1887	FLORENCE ELIZA	KNIGHT	d./ "	
15	MAY	1887	HARRY PRICE	KNIGHT	s./ JOHN WILLIAM & SARAH HANNAH of Stordon Grange, Thringstone	Farmer
15	MAY	1887	EDITH HANNAH	LAKIN	d./ JAMES & HANNAH	Cordwainer & Farmer
15	MAY	1887	ORIEL	SIDDONS	s./ WILLIAM & LOUISA of Holywell, Ashby de la Zouch	Farmer
15	MAY	1887	ALFRED	BILLING	s./ JOSEPH & RUTH	Blacksmith
03	JUL	1887	FREDERICK WILLIAM	SERRES	s./ EDWARD EDMUND & BERTHA	Master of the Grammar School
18	SEP	1887	ARTHUR JOSEPH	BAKER	s./ JOSEPH & ANN	Labourer
02	OCT	1887	ANN	LEECH	d./ AMY of Griffy Dam, Worthington	Char Woman
02	OCT	1887	HANNAH	ROWELL	d./ CHARLES & ANN of Griffy Dam Breedon on the Hill	Brickmaker
02	OCT	1887	ALICE	MARSHALL	d./ EDWARD & HARRIET	Farmer
13	OCT	1887	GEORGE	DARBY	s./ ELIAS & ELLEN	Labourer
03	JUN	1888	FREDERICK WILLIAM	RICHARDS	s./ THOMAS & HARRIET	Miner
06	JUL	1888	JOHN THOMAS	BAKER	s./ GEORGE & SARAH	Labourer
05	AUG	1888	GEORGE	KING	s./ JOSEPH & MARY JANE	Farmer
02	SEP	1888	ELIZABETH	STATHAM	d./ WILLIAM WILSON & ANN	Labourer
02	SEP	1888	ANNIE	STATHAM	d./ WILLIAM WILSON & ANN	Labourer
07	NOV	1888	ELIZABETH	DARBY	d./ LOUISA	Labourer
02	DEC	1888	JOHN HENRY	HICKLIN	s./ GEORGE & EMMA	Labourer
02	DEC	1888	JOHN ARTHUR	JARVIS	s./ CHARLES & JANE	Miner

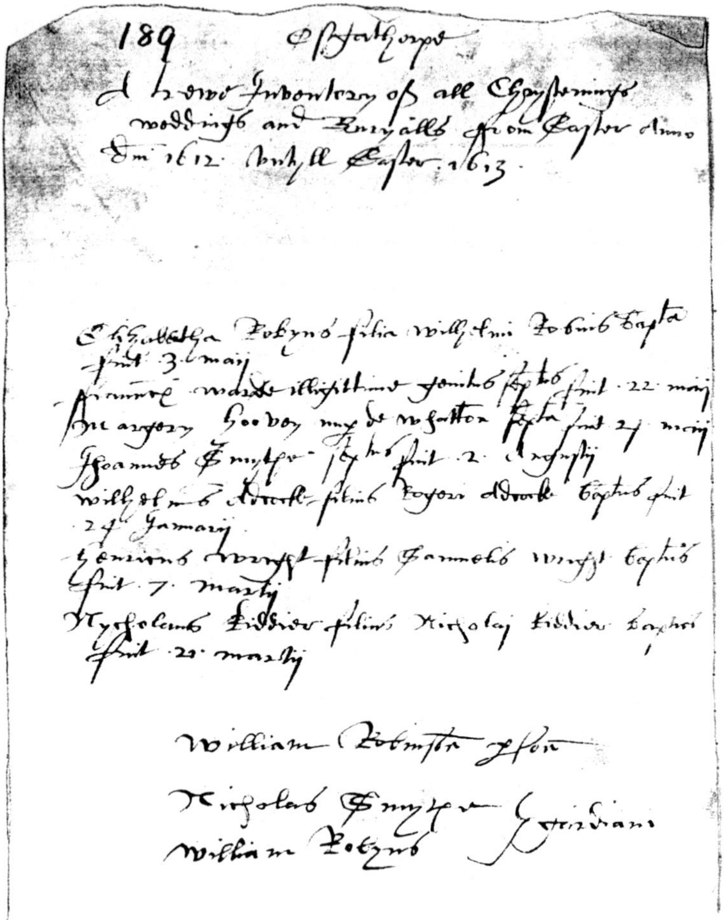

The 1612 Bishop's Transcript

Recording the burials of FFrannce Ward, Margery Harvey
& Jhoannes Smythe [John Smith]
John's entry was written in Latin and reads
'Jhoannes Smythe Sep[ul]tus fuit 2 Augustis' = John Smith buried he 2 August

6. BURIALS 1583 – 1891

An asterisk* after a surname indicates, that the person being buried is known to have left a Will or Letters of Administration. However, this will *not* include those who, for whatever reason, did not state Osgathorpe as their abode. An [MI] denotes that a Monumental Inscription was erected. The reader should note that some entries were written in Latin (See Latin names & words) and that before 1752 the year began on Lady Day, 25 March. (See introduction: Dates)

Date	Forename	Surname	Notes
[1583–1679]	[This period has been transcribed from the surviving bishop's transcripts]		
1583	No Burials		
17 APR 1584	WILLM	HOYOSON	-
08 JUL 1584	THOMAS	JONSON	-
1585–1603	[No BTs]		
27 SEP 1604	*?duo filie*	ADCOCK	d./ *HENRIRI et sepult eadem ?postemodo*[1]
1605	[No BT]		
1606	No Burials		
22 APR 1607	ISABELL	BARTON	w./ RYCHARD
13 JUL 1607	ALES	NORTH	widdow
19 MAR 1608	ROBERTE	COTTON	servannte of WILLIAM ROBINSON
02 JAN 1609	*EDWARDUS*	HYLL	-
1610–1611	[No BTs]		
22 MAY 1612	*FFRANNCE*	WARDE	*illigittme genitis*[2]
24 MAY 1612	*MARGERY*	HARVEY	?mrs. of Whatton
02 AUG 1612	*JIIOANNES*	SMYTHE*	-
1613	[No BT]		
21 JUL 1614	WILLIAM	TOPP	-
24 SEP 1614	ANN	NORTHE	d./ JULIAN[3]
04 OCT 1614	JOAN	COOPER	-
1615–1616	[No BTs]		
04 OCT 1617	ISABELL	KIDDIAR	w./ NICOLAS
1618–1620	[No BTs]		
28 JUN 1621	JANE	ROBERTS	w./ WILLIAM
01 FEB 1621	ELIZABETH	KIDDIER	-
1622–1624	[No BTs]		

---

[1] *?duo filie* = ?two daughters: *et sepult eadem ?postemodo* = and buried the same afterwards [were baptised & buried the same day].

[2] *illigittme genitis* = illegitimate begotten.

[3] BT gave 'baptized the 16 September & buried 24'.

14	DEC	1625	HAMLETT	MASON alias BALIE*	-
10	APR	1626	NICHOLAS	HALL	*predictus sepuliebatur*[1] [s./ *ZACHARIE*]
11	MAY	1627	ELIZABETH	FFRANNCIS	w./ JOHN
07	AUG	1628	THOMAS	DAWSON	*pedict Sepultus erat*[2] [s./ *THOME*]
01	MAY	1629	*JOHANNES*	MASON*	-
23	JUN	1629	HENRY	BROWETT	-
11	DEC	1630	NICHOLAS	SMITH	-
		1631	[No BT]		

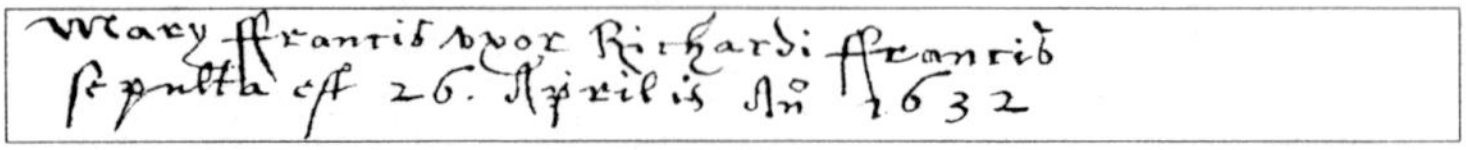
Mary ffrancis uxor Richardi ffrancis sepulta est 26. Aprilis Ano 1632

26	APR	1632	MARY	FFRANCIS	w./ *RICHARDI*
25	MAY	1632	MARGARET	ROBINS	d./ *GULIELMS*
19	SEP	1633	CATHARINE	BROWET	w./ *HENRIEI*
13	JAN	1634	ELIZABETH	ONESBY	w./ *RICHARDI*
		1635	[No BT]		
14	MAY	1636	THOMAS	RAGGS*	Labourer
05	DEC	1636	JOANE	MARSHALL	w./ JAMES a Yeoman
		1637–1638	No Burials		
09	JUN	1639	*SARA*	DAWSON	w./ EDWARD a Tanner
26	SEP	1639	WILLIAM	FFAIRFIELD*	Collier
30	SEP	1639	MARY	FFAIRFIELD*	widdow
04	DEC	1639	ANNE	PARSONS	d./ THOMAS & MARGARIE
14	DEC	1639	NICHAUS	PARSONS	s./ THOMAS *pedict*[3] [MARGARIE]
17	JAN	1639	ROBERT	WOOTTON	s./ THOMAS & ANNE
22	FEB	1639	JOHN	COLTON	s./ GEORGE & ELIZ. a Yeoman[4]
		[1640–1668]	[No BTs for the Civil War & Commonwealth period]		
03	SEP	1669	ANNE	JERUAS alias KIDDIER	w./ GEORGE
10	OCT	1669	MARY	PARSO[N]S	d./ THOMAS & KATHERINE
11	OCT	1669	ELIZABETH	BAYLY	w./ JOHN
19	OCT	1669	JANE	BROWET alias ADCOCKE	w./ THOMAS
[5]		1670	[THOMAS]	[HARLEY][MI]	-
04	OCT	1671	THOMAS	LOATON	-
08	JAN	1671	ELIZABETH	BAYLEY	-
19	MAY	1672	WILL	SHAW	-
27	MAY	1672	MARGERY	HALL	-
04	JUN	1672	MARY	BAYLEY	-
24	JUN	1672	ELIZABETH	BROWITT	-
08	APR	1673	JANE	ROBINS	widdow

[1] *predictus sepuliebatur* = above-mentioned was buried. BT recorded his baptism above this.

[2] *p[r]edict[us] Sepultus erat* = above-mentioned he was buried. BT recorded his baptism above this.

[3] *p[r]edict[us]* = above-mentioned [i.e. Thomas & Margarie].

[4] BT gave 'baptized Feb 9 and buried Febr 22'.

[5] BT did not record any burials for 1670, however a monumental inscription in the church gave 'Near to this place lies the body of Thomas Harley, of Osgathorpe... died 17 January 1670'.

22	APR	1673	THOMAS	PARSONS	senior
22	AUG	1673	RUTH	SMITH	-
19	SEP	1673	JOHN	ERRINGTON	-
23	NOV	1673	ELEANOR	GREENE	-
04	DEC	1673	WILLIAM	SHAW	-
11	JAN[1]	1674	THOMAS	WOOD	-
06	MAY	1674	JOHN	MARSHALL	-
26	AUG	1674	ELIZABETH	ROBINS	w./ WILLIAM senior
16	JUN	1675	JANE	WHITE	-
11	AUG	1675	WILLIAM	HATHAWAY	-
03[2]	MAR	+1676	ELIZABETH	GILBERT	d./ SAMUEL & ELIZ
13	MAR	+1676	MARY	WRIGHT	widdow
03	APR	1676	ANNE	WOOTTON	w./ THOMAS
19	APR	1676	ANNE	RIDYARD alias JARUAS	w./ GEORGE
13	AUG	1676	HENRY	FULGIUM	s./ CHARLES & ELIZABETH
16	SEP	1676	SARAH	HALL	d./ GEORGE & SUSANNA
16	JUN[3]	1676	MARGARET	BAILY alias MASON	w./ JOHN
07	DEC	1676	RUTH	SHAW	w./ JOHN
16	JAN	+1677	MARY	WHITE	d./ HENRY & JANE
19	FEB	+1677	HAMLET	LITHERLAND	s./ HUMFREY & ANNE
11	MAR	+1677	JOHN	SHERWIN	Traveller
28	MAY	1677	EDWARD	BELTON	s./ EDWARD & ANN
01	SEP	1677	JOHN	BOYER	Traveller
21	JUN	1678	KATHARINE	GREENE	-
24	JUN	1678	MARY	PARSONS	-
12	JAN	1678	THOMAS	BROWET	-
11	APR	1679	MARGERY	PARSONS	widdow
22	JUN	1679	JOHN	ROSSE	Rector of Osgathorpe
24	AUG	1679	MARGARET	HOLLAND	widow of Mr HOLLAND a Minister
30	AUG	1679	MARY	PARSONS	d./ JAMES & MARY
			[The oldest surviving register starts in 1680]		
07	MAY	1680	WILLIAM	BROWET	-
06	JUN	1680	MARY	BELTON	-
10	JUN	1680	ANE	BELTON	infant
07	JUL	1680	RUTH	FOLIAMBE	infant
02	AUG	1680	THOMAS	GREEN	infant
09	AUG	1680	FRANCIS	HARLEY[MI]	infant
04	NOV	1680	ANE	FOLIAMBE	infant
27	JAN	1680	ANE	RAGG	-

[1] The following 6 entries marked with a plus sign+, appear to be dated using 1 January as the beginning of the year and not Lady Day (25 March). This undoubtedly persisted from the Commonwealth period, when 1 January was the official start of the year.

[2] Another BT, confusingly gave '*Baptised 4* March 1676'. This however, appears to be an error in both event & date, as Elizabeth had been baptised on the 20 April 1675.

[3] Out of chronological order on the BT.

24	APR	1681	EDWARD	HATHAWAY*	Clerke
28	JUL	1681	WILLIAM	WICKES	-
01	AUG	1681	MILLICENT	FOLIAMBE	-
24	OCT	1681	JAMES	PARSONS*	-
24	NOV	1681	SARAH	BOUND	-
04	FEB	1681	JOHN	HALL	-
08	MAR	1681	EDWARD	BELTON	-
18	MAY	1682	DOROTHY	SHEFFIELD	-
02	JAN	1682	EDWARD	PALMER*	Attarney
26	JAN	1682	GEORGE	HALL	-
22	FEB	1682	DOROTHY	BROWET	-
18	MAR	1682	THOMAS	HARLEY[MI]	infant
30	MAR	1683	ALICE	WHITE	wid
12	APR	1683	GEORGE	BROWET	-
17	JUL	1683	THOMAS	MOORE	-
03	AUG	1683	MILLICENT	FOULIAMB	-
28	DEC	1683	MARY	CLARK	-
31	DEC	1683	ANA	VAUGHAN	-
24	JAN	1683	RACHEL	BELTON	twins
24	JAN	1683	LEAH	BELTON	twins
16	FEB	1683	ISABEL	MORRICE	ministers wid
07	MAY	1684	EDWARD	FOLIAMB	-
20	JUN	1684	JOHN	NORTH	-
16	SEP	1684	JOHN	BAYLY*	-
31	MAR	1685	MARY	BELTON	d./ EDWARD & ANE
20	APR	1685	-	WHITE	still borne male child of HEN & JANE
30	JUN	1685	ALICE	BELTON	wid
04	JUL	1685	JUDITH	SCAMPTON	-
07	JUL	1685	THOMAS	BAILY*	-
30	SEP	1685	FRANCIS	HARLEY[MI]	infant
08	OCT	1685	JOHN	WILLOWES	infant
12	MAR	1685	WILLM	BELTON	infant
22	MAR	1685	MARY	SMEDLEY	w./ CORNELIUS. Schoolmaster
27	MAY	1686	JOHN	ROBINS	infant
10	JUN	1686	JANE	RAGG	-
26	JUL	1686	SUSANA	HALL	infant
07	OCT	1686	ELIZABETH	PORT	w. [widow]
29	NOV	1686	SARAH	HARLEY	wid
25	JAN	1686	ANE	SMITH	w./ JOHN
24	JAN[1]	1686	-	BELTON	still born child of WM & MARY
10	JUN	1687	JAMES	RAGG	-
31	JUL	1687	FRANCES	NEEDHAM	-
24	MAR	1687	ANE	GREEN	-
11	JAN	1688	SARAH	WIGHTMAN	wid

[1] Out of chronological order in register.

08	FEB	1688	ABIGAIL	FOE	ministers wid
08	MAR	1688	ROBERT	NORTH	-
13	MAY	1689	CATHERINE	ORTON	-
07	MAR	1689	EDWARD	HALL	infant
15	MAR	1689	WILLIAM	CARRINGTON	-
16	MAR	1689	WILLIAM	ROBINS	junior
27	SEP	1690	THOMAS	NORTH	-
28	MAY	1691	GEORGE	KIDGER	-

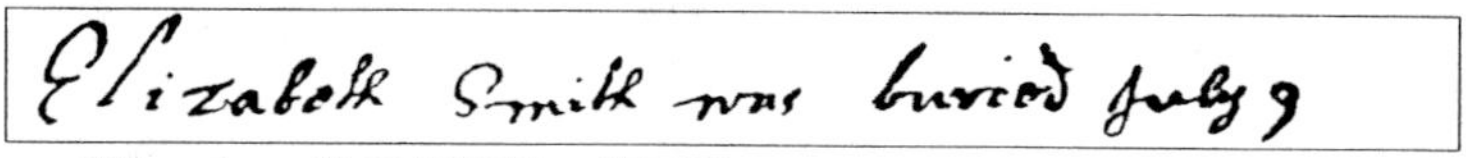
Elizabeth Smith was buried July 9

09	JUL	1691	ELIZABETH	SMITH	-
31	JUL	1691	JOHN	GREEN	-
23	AUG	1691	JOANE	WHATTON	-
10	NOV	1691	GEORGE	RIGARD	-
30	DEC	1691	JOHN	ABEL	-
26	DEC	1691	ANE	GREEN	-
04	MAY	1692	THOMAS	WOOTTON	-
01[1]	JAN	1692	HANAH	NORTH	-
04	JUL	1693	THOMAS	BOUND	-
08	AUG	1693	SUSANA	MASON alias BAILY	-
06	FEB	1693	ELIZABETH	KIDDIER	-
16	FEB	1694	JOHN	SHAW	junior
12	MAR	1694	ALICE	KIDDIER	-
08	SEP	1695	CATHERINE	BELTON	-
04	MAR	1695	JOHN	SHAW*	-
17	JUL	1696	MARY	SYMKIN	infant[2]
01	OCT	1696	ELIZABETH	COULTON[MI]	-
09	FEB	1696	MARGERY	WILLOWS	-
18	APR	1697	NICHOLAS	KIDDIER	-
30	APR	1697	ANN	SHILTON	-
11	DEC	1698	-	LEATHERLAND	man child of WM & ELIZABETH[3]
18	APR	1699	JOHN	DOEWELL	-
06	AUG	1699	JANE	BROWN	-
30	SEP	1699	JOHN	BROWN	-
30	SEP	1699	MARY	BROWN	-
29	OCT	1699	WILLIAM	SHAW	-
29	OCT	1699	ANE	SUMERFIELD	M.W. [ministers widow]
14	NOV	1699	ELIZABETH	BROWN	-
09	DEC	1699	ELIZABETH	BELTON	-

---

1 BT gave 18 January.

2 Infant was crossed out in the register, but not on the BT.

3 Entry recorded on a separate page of the register, immediately prior to the start of the Marriages; 'A man child of WM LEATHERLAND & ELIZABETH his wife borne December 5. The same child departed this life December ii [11]'.

12	JAN	1699	CADWALLADER	VAUGHAN[MI]	jun
30	MAY	1700	JANE	WOOTTON	-
18	JUL	1700	MICHAEL	FRITH	-
28	JUL	1700	NICHOLAS	KIDDIER	-
16	FEB	1700	JAMES	DOEWELL	-
20	SEP	1701	ABIA	HATHAWAY	-
31	OCT	1701	MARY	GILBERT	-
12	APR	1702	THOMAS	FARMER	-

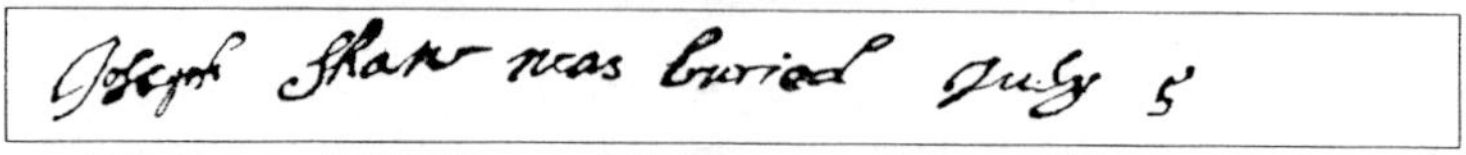

05	JUL	1702	JOSEPH	SHAW	-
03	DEC	1702	EDWARD	BELTON	-
05	JAN	1702	ANNE Mrs	HAZARD	wid
22	JAN	1702	ANN	BOULTBY	infant
10	MAR	1702	SUSANNAH	SLEITH	-
27	APR	1703	SUSANNA	TOOLY	-
29	MAY	1703	MARY	JOYNES	-
07	JUN	1703	DOROTHY	STINSON	-
14	SEP	1703	FRANCIS	MORLEY	infant
03	MAR	1703	ELIZABETH	GODDARD	-
21	MAR	1703	JOSEPH	SHAW	s./ THOS & ELLEN
13	JUN	1704	MARGARET	NORTH	-
08	NOV	1704	THOMAS	GREEN*	-
14	DEC	1704	THOMAS	NORTH	senior
13	FEB	1704	JOHN	HALL	-
05	MAR	1704	JOHN	BROWN	s./ H. [HENRY] & ANE[1]
		1705	No Burials		
27	APR	1706	WINIFFRID	VAUGHAN	-
12	DEC	1706	MARY	JEPHCOAT	-
25	DEC	1706	ANE	HEATHERLY	-
27	JUN	1707	MARGARET	MEAD[MI]*	-
25	NOV	1707	MARY	HUSKINSON	junr
02	DEC	1707	MARY	HUSKINSON	senr
03	OCT	1708	HENRY	WHITE*	-
14	MAY	1709	ELIZABETH	RIDYARD	-
27	JUN	1709	ROBERT	BLUNT	-
19	AUG	1709	JOSEPH	SHAW	infant
21	JAN	1709	ELIZABETH	HUSKINSON	senr
01	MAR	1709	GEORGE	COULTON[MI]	senior
03	APR	1710	ELIZABETH	COULTON[MI]	-
21	MAY	1710	SARAH	WILLOWS	-
31	OCT	1710	ELIZABETH	HUSKINSON	junr
17	DEC	1710	DOROTHY	KIDDIER	-

[1] Fathers name from son John's baptism in 1703.

30	JAN	1710	THOMAS	GODDARD	-
10	FEB	1710	THOMAS	PARSONS	-
14	FEB	1710	ELIZABETH	HALL	-
18	MAY	1711	ANE	NORTH	-
28	OCT	1711	WILLIAM	SWAINE	infant
11	NOV	1711	ANNA	SWAINE	infant
16	NOV	1711	BRIDGET	SWAINE	ye mother
18	NOV	1711	ANN	BELTON	widdow
19	FEB	1711	ANE	WOOTON	-
03	DEC	1712	JOHN	STINSON	infant
29	JAN	1712	RICHARD	RAGG	-
15	FEB	1712	JOSEPH	TOMLINSON	-
01	OCT	1712	DOROTHY	SPENCE	-[1]
27	MAR	1713	THOMAS	MORLEY	infant
08	APR	1713	MARY	ORTON	-
09	OCT	1713	JOHN	NORTH*	-
12	MAR	1713	DAVID	VAUGHAN[MI]	-
20	MAR	1713	MARY	BRADLEY	-
24	MAR	1713	CORNELIUS	SMEDLEY[MI]*	Schoolmaster
30	AUG	1714	ELIZABETH	GILBERT	-
13	OCT	1714	THOMAS	ORTON	-
11	JAN	1714	ROBERT	CHURCHILL	infant
15	MAR	1714	MARY Mrs	ROUSE	widdow
11	MAY	1715	SUSANAH	HALL	wid
28	MAY	1715	ELIZABETH	HEMSLEY	-
23	OCT	1715	FRANCIS Mr	HARLEY[MI]*	-
28	OCT	1715	JOHN	HALL	-
24	FEB	1715	JONE	RICHARDSON	-
21	APR	1716	JANE	QUINBURROW	wid
28	DEC	1717	SAMUEL	GILBERT	-
17	SEP	1718	DORCAS	HARLEY[MI]	wid
21	OCT	1718	SARAH	JOYNES	infant
21	MAY	1719	THOMAS	BUSH	-
03	JUN	1719	ELIZ	WILLIAMSON	infant
18	JUL	1719	GRACE	MOSELY	min'trs widow
17	NOV	1719	MARY	GILLET	sen
03	FEB	1719	MARY	GILLET	junr
23	MAY	1720	HANNAH	WOOTTON	-
21	JUN	1720	JOHN	BRADLEY*	-
20	JUL	1720	NATHANIEL	JOYNES	infant
20	DEC	1720	MARY	STINSON	infant
30	JAN	1720	WILLIAM	PEAT	infant
19	APR	1721	MARY	PIERCESON	-[2]

[1] Out of chronological order in register and entry does not appear on two BTs for 1712.
[2] BT gave SARAH for MARY.

24	APR	1721	MARY	BELTON	-
11	SEP	1721	THOMAS	STINSON*	-
24	SEP	1721	JANE	WHITE	-
22	FEB	1721	SUSANNAH	TWINBURY	-
07	MAY	1722	JAMES	TATENAL	infant
01	SEP	1722	ELIZABETH	BROWN	infant
19	DEC	1722	CATHARINE	CHURCHMAN	min'trs widow
10	DEC	1723	SARAH	WILLIAMSON	-
24	JAN	1723	RICHARD	WRIGHT	infant
28	JAN	1723	JOHN	SMITH*	-
26	MAR	1724	JOSHUA	SENYOR	infant
09	JUN	1724	MARY Mrs	BAINBRIGGE[MI]	widow of JOHN late of Lockinton Esq[1]
02	NOV	1724	ANNE	BELTON	infant
13	JAN	1724	ANNE	ASHBURY	-
22	SEP	1725	WILLIAM	ALLEN*	sen
21	MAR	1725	WILLIAM Mr	HARLEY	-
22	MAR	1725	THOMAS	CLARK[MI]	sen
12	MAY	1726	ANNE	TOMLINSON	infant
08	SEP	1726	THOMAS	TATENAL[MI]	infant
21	NOV	1726	MARY	SIMPSON	infant
10	MAR	1726	ANNA	VAUGHAN	infant
16	APR	1727	SARAH	CLARK[MI]	widow
18	APR	1727	THOMAS	NORTH	-
03	NOV	1727	GEORGE	JOYNES	-
13	NOV	1727	JOHN	BROWN	-
24	DEC	1727	WILLIAM	KIDDIER	-
31	JUL	1728	WILLIAM	SIMPSON	-
07	AUG	1728	GEORGE	HALL	-
04	SEP	1728	WILLIAM	ALLEN*	-
01	JAN	1728	CADWALLADER	VAUGHAN[MI]*	Rector of this parish
10	FEB	1728	ABRAHAM	DAKIN	-
19	MAR	1728	JANE	GADSBY	-
05	APR	1729	DORCAS	VAUGHAN	infant
18	JUN	1729	RICHARD	WRIGHT	-
29	JUN	1729	THOMAS	BROWN	-
17	SEP	1729	ELIZ	WRIGHT	d./ widow WRIGHT
04	NOV	1729	wid	SMITH	-
02	DEC	1729	JAMES	HALL	-
31	MAR	1730	Mrs	LITTIL	clergymans wid
12	MAY	1730	WILL	SHAW	*juvenis*[2]
15	OCT	1730	wid [MARY]	ALLEN*	senr[3]

[1] Register also gave 'only daughter of Thomas Harley citizen of London ye sole founder of ye free school & hospital house here was buried'.

[2] *Juvenis* = young man.

[3] MARY from her Will.

03	NOV	1730	JOHN	GODDERD*	-
03	JAN	1730	- [ANN]	TOMLINSON	w./ GEORGE[1]
10	JAN	1730	- [ELLEN]	SHAW	w./ THO[2]
14	MAR	1730	JOHN	JOYNES	-
16	JUN	1731	JOHN	JOYNES	bastard of MARY
09	JUL	1731	JOHN	STANSON	-
23	AUG	1731	Mrs	TWINBURY	clergymans wid
31	OCT	1731	SARAH	WILLIAMSON	infant

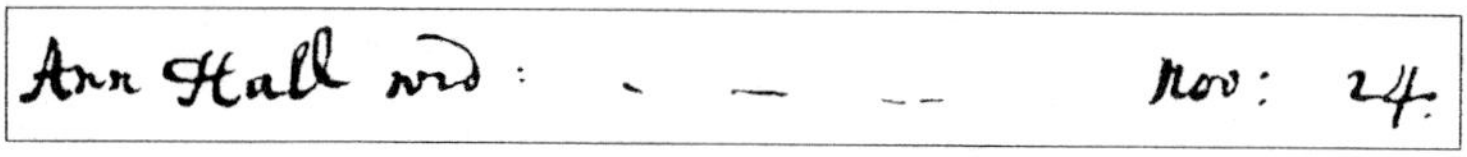
Ann Hall wid : - — -- Nov: 24.

24	NOV	1731	ANN	HALL	wid
05	MAR	1731	wid	FALLOWS	-
08	APR	1732	SUSANNA	TATENAL	w./ JOHN
10	APR	1732	-	BELTON	child of THO
15	APR	1732	JOHN	PARSONS	s./ THO
08	FEB	1732	- [ELIZABETH]	PEACH[MI]	d./ Mr PEACH of Derby[3]
18	APR	1733	HANNAH Mrs	HOYLAND	clergymans wid
06	OCT	1733	Mrs [MARY]	GILBERT	clergymans wid[4]
01	MAR	1733	ELIZ	SLEATH	d./ THO
01	JUN	1734	GEORGE	TOMLINSON	-
02	FEB	1734	Mrs [ELIZABETH]	SMEDLEY[MI]	clergymans widow[5]
18	SEP	1735	Revrd Mr [CHARLES]	CLARKE[MI]*	Schoolmaster & Vic[a]r of Whitick[6]
23	DEC	1736	BARBARA	HALL	wid
20	FEB	1736	Mrs	SHERWIN	clergymans wid
12	APR	1737	SARAH Mrs	PEACH[MI]	w./ HENRY of Darby
17	APR	1737	THOMAS	CLERK*	-
15	JUN	1737	Mrs [ELIZABETH]	HOLBROOKE[MI]	-[7]
23	NOV	1737	THO	PARSONS	senr
09	JUN	1738	SARAH	PEACH[MI]	d./ Mr PEACH of Derby
12	AUG	1738	RUTH	BOULTBEE[MI]	w./ Mr WILL
17	DEC	1738	TIMOTHY	CHURCHILL[MI]*	-
07	JAN	1738	WILL	RICHARDS	s./ SIMON
10	MAR	1738	ELIZ	BELTON	d./ THO
13	APR	1739	HANNAH	BELTON	d./ THO
13	APR	1739	SARAH	BELTON	d./ THO
26	APR	1739	EDW	HALL	s./ EDW
20	JUN	1739	THO	SHAW	-

---

1 ANN from her children's baptisms.
2 ELLEN from her children's baptisms.
3 ELIZABETH from monumental inscription.
4 MARY from her being witness to numerous marriage bonds 1723–28.
5 ELIZABETH from monumental inscription & 1687 marriage licence, at Newbold Verdon.
6 CHARLES from monumental inscription.
7 ELIZABETH from monumental inscription.

22	AUG	1739	JOHN	SMITH	s./ JOHN
27	DEC	1739	JAMES	GILLET*	-
02	JUN	1740	WILL	MATCHET	infant
07	JAN	1740	ROBERT	MORLY*	-
05	APR	1741	DOROTHY	HILL	clergymans wid
13	JUN	1741	widow	HEMSLY	-
21	JUL	1741	-	BRADLY	d./JOHN
23	DEC	1741	Mrs	TURNER	clergymans wid

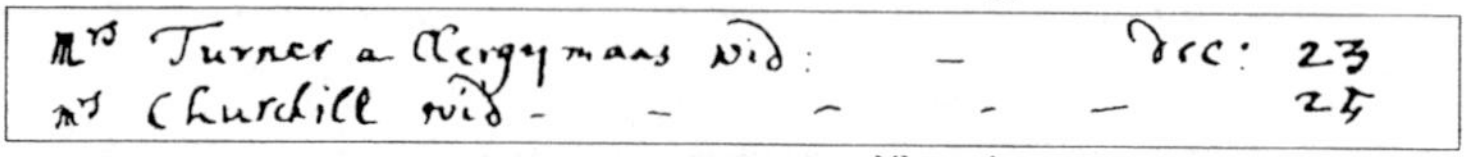
Mrs Turner a Clergymans wid: — Dec: 23
Mrs Churchill wid - - - - - 25

25	DEC	1741	Mrs [ELIZABETH]	CHURCHILL[MI]	wid[1]
28	DEC	1741	Mrs	MORLY	wid
03	JAN	1741	MARY	TATENAL	d./ J. [JOHN][2]
13	AUG	1742	SAM	TATENAL	s./ JOHN
24	MAR	1742	- [ABIA]	HEMMESLY	w./ JOHN[3]
31	MAR	1742	RACHEL	SHAW	-
17	MAY	1743	JOHN	TATENAL*	the younger
24	DEC	1743	JOHN	BADHAM	a Blind Fidler
06	JAN	1744	DANIEL	HEMSLY	-
07	JAN	1745	-	BRADLY	child of JOHN
09	JAN	1745	MARY	BAILY	pauper
08	MAY	1746	WILLIAM	SKENSON[MI]	-
28	FEB	1746	MARY	ASHUR[MI]	w./ SAM
07	MAY	1747	ELIZABETH	PEGG	w./ JOS
25	JUL	1747	MARY	TATENAL	d./ ROBERT
14	SEP	1747	HANNAH	SKENSON	child of HANNAH
12	JAN	1747	ROBERT	BRADFORD	the younger
17	JAN	1747	ROBERT	BRADFORD	the elder
25	FEB	1747	ELIZ	HODGKINSON	pauper / a poor woman
11	APR	1748	ELIZTH	CLERK*	widow
05	JUL	1748	Mrs [MARY]	ROBINSON[MI]	clergymans widw[4]
14	NOV	1748	SAML Revd Mr	HOLBROOKE[MI]	Rector of this parish buried at Osgathorpe
28	DEC	1748	JAMES	HALL*	the elder
12	FEB	1748	RICHARD	DANE	s./ RICHD & JANE
17	SEP	1749	MARTHA	JOYNES	d./ TIMOTHY & ELIZABETH
11	DEC	1749	MARY	YOUNGE	d./ MOSES & SARAH
03[5]	DEC	1749	THOMAS	PLANT	s./ ROBT & SARAH
27	APR	1750	THOMAS	WARD	s./ THOMAS & JANE

---

1 ELIZABETH from monumental inscription.

2 Fathers name from daughter Mary's baptism in 1729.

3 ABIA from her children's baptisms.

4 MARY from monumental inscription.

5 Appears to be 13 in register, but 1 is probably a later accidental ink mark on the parchment. Possibly done when the BT was written. (See actual register not microfiche). BT gave 3 December.

20	MAY	1750	JOSEPH	WARD	s./ THOMAS & JANE
02	JUN	1750	MARTHA	BROWNE	d./ SAMUEL & ELIZABETH
09	JUN	1750	CHRISTIANA	ALLEN	widow
15	SEP	1750	ALICE	HALL[MI]	w./ EDWARD
01	APR	1751	SAMUEL	BROWNE	s./ SAMUEL & ELIZATH
01	MAY	1751	JOHN	MATCHET	-
28	MAY	1751	ELIZABETH	SIMPSON	-
19	SEP	1751	MARY	BELTON	-
06	OCT	1751	JOHN	ASTBURY	-
12	NOV	1751	ABIGAIL	GLOVER	-
17	NOV	1751	MARY	TABERNOR*	of Worthington
14	FEB	1752	ROBERT	TATNELL	s./ ROBT & SARAH
19	FEB	1752	HENRY Mr	PEACH[MI]	of Derby
19	APR	1752	ELIZABETH	ROW	d./ WILL & ANN
04	JUL	1752	JOSEPH	BRADLEY	s./ JNO & TRYPHENA of Grace Dieu
15	AUG	1752	SARAH	SMITH	w./ JOHN
22	APR	1753	SAMUEL	GILBERT	-
10	JUN	1753	JOHN	HEMSLEY*	-
18	OCT	1753	ELIZABETH	PARSONS	w./ THOMAS
16	NOV	1753	ANN	SHAW	w./ THOMAS
06	MAY	1754	MARY	GODDARD	widow
17	MAY	1754	EDWARD	HALL[MI]*	-
24	OCT	1754	JOHN	CLARKE*	-
19	NOV	1754	MARY	PLANT	d./ ROBT & SARAH
25	NOV	1754	SARAH	PLANT	w./ ROBERT
05	FEB	1755	GILBERT	ILLSLEY	-
18	FEB	1755	HANNAH	KENDRICK	w./ RICHARD
24	MAR	1755	SARAH	BENNET	d./ JOHN & SARAH
23	JUL	1755	MARY	BRADFORD	widow
25	SEP	1755	ANNE Mrs	BOULTBEE[MI]	d./ WILLIAM
13	NOV	1755	ELIZABETH	JOYNES	widow
19	NOV	1755	ELIZABETH	BROWNE	d./ SAMUEL & ELIZABETH
11	JAN	1756	THOMAS	PARSONS	
06	FEB	1756	SAMUEL	BROWNE	s./ JOHN
15	JUL	1756	ROBERT	CORBET	s./ ROBERT
13	APR	1757	ELIZABETH	JOYNES	w./ TIMOTHY
18	JUN	1757	NICHOLAS	KIDDIAR*	-
06	OCT	1757	WILLIAM Mr	BOULTBEE[MI]*	-
20	NOV	1757	MARY	ASTBURY	-
07	DEC	1757	MARY	BROWNE	d./ JOHN
13	JAN	1758	TRYPHENA	BRADLEY	w./ JNO of Grace Dieu
04	FEB	1758	ANN	ORTON	-
10	MAR	1758	ANN	BOWLEY	d./ THOMAS
24	MAR	1758	SARAH Mrs	VILLIERS[MI]	-
24	APR	1758	MARY	STEVENSON	widow
02	OCT	1758	WILLIAM	ROPER	s./ RICHD & JANE

18	OCT	1758	HENRY	DANIELS	-
16	JAN	1759	JOHN	BROWN*	-
19	JUN	1759	JANE	NEWBALD	d./ THOMAS & ANNE
06	JUL	1759	MARY	BARRET	d./ RICHARD & SARAH
19	SEP	1759	JOSEPH	UNDERWOOD	s./ JOSEPH & ELIZABETH of Dyseworth
28	FEB	1760	ELIZABETH	GLOVER	d./ WILLIAM & SARAH
26	APR	1760	FRANCIS	DALBY*	-
27	APR	1760	MARY	MATCHET	widow
01	FEB	1761	WILLIAM	GLOVER	s./ WILLIAM & SARAH
08	FEB	1761	RICHARD	KENDRICK	-
[Blank]		1761	JOHN	PLATT	s./ HUGH Mr & CATHARINE[1]
19	MAY	1761	RUTH Mrs	BOULTBEE[MI]	-
28	JUL	1761	JANE	GODDARD	w./ THOS
07	SEP	1761	JANE	ILLSLEY	widow
26	NOV	1761	ELIZABETH Mrs	COOPER	clergymans widow
29	NOV	1761	JAMES	CHAPLIN	s./ JAMES & ELIZABETH
05	FEB	1762	THOMAS	BELTON	-
18	FEB	1762	ELIZABETH	ALT	-
07	APR	1762	SAMUEL	BROWN	s./ SAMUEL & ELIZABETH
09	MAY	1762	SAMUEL	ASHER*	of the pa. of Breedon
16	JUN	1762	JANE Mrs	BAGE	of Stordon Grange
26	JUN	1762	Mrs	WESTMORELAND	clergymans widow
02	AUG	1762	JOHN	BRADLEY	s./ JOHN of Grace Dieu
20	AUG	1762	JAMES	LAKINS	s./ THOMAS & SARAH
21	APR	1763	THOMAS	NEWBALD	s./ THOMAS & ANN
05	JUN	1763	JOHN	NORTH	of the village of Thringstone
15	JUL	1763	MARY	WALKER	-
23	AUG	1763	MARY	ELLIS*	-
24	AUG	1764	CATHARINE	BAILEY*	widow of Thringstone
23	MAR	1765	MARY Mrs	HARDY*	widow
13	MAY	1765	THOMAS	BAILEY	-
15	MAY	1765	WILLIAM Mr	BOULTBEE*	-
27	MAY	1765	HENRY	FORD	s./ JAMES & JANE
02	JUL	1765	Mrs	SPARKS	widow
06	AUG	1765	JANE	ROPER	w./ RICHD
31	OCT	1765	SAMUEL	MATCHET	-
02	NOV	1765	HANNAH	BROWN	d./ SAML & ELIZ
15	DEC	1765	JARVIS	LACEY	-
21	DEC	1765	JAMES	DANIEL	s./ HENY & JANE
11	JAN	1766	ELIZ	SWAN	d./ THOS & ANN
08	APR	1766	JAMES	CHAPLIN	s./ JAMES
28	APR	1766	WILLIAM	ROSE	s./ JOHN
17	JUN	1766	JOSEPH	PEGG	-
19	SEP	1766	SARAH	ROSE	d./ ROBT & ANN

[1] This entry was crossed out in the register and did not appear on the BT.

10	DEC	1766	ELIZ	TIVY	w./ EDWD
18	MAY	1767	WILLIAM	ASHER*	-
31	JUL	1767	THOS	TIVY	s./ EDWD & ELIZ
30	AUG	1767	THOS	ASHER	s./ THOS & MARY
21	JAN	1768	JOHN	MANSFIELD	s./ RICHD & BARBARA
11	MAR	1768	ELIZ	FORD	w./ HENRY
22	APR	1768	ELIZ	MUGLESTON	widow
08	MAY	1768	THOS	CLARK[MI]	s./ JOHN & DOROTHY

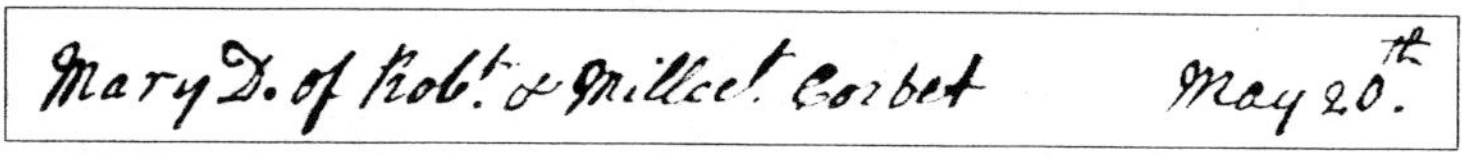
Mary D. of Robt. & Millcet Corbet May 20th.

20	MAY	1768	MARY	CORBET	d./ ROBT & MILLCET
28	JUN	1768	WILLIAM	LACEY	-
19	JUL	1768	MARY	ROSE	d./ JOHN & ELIZ
16	SEP	1768	THOS	WARD	-
14	MAR	1769	ANN Mrs	FLOYER	widow
03	AUG	1769	MARY	BROWN	widow
07	AUG	1769	HANNAH	ASHER	widow
15	AUG	1769	WILLIAM	HARRIS	-
25	OCT	1769	MARY	HARRIS	d./ WM & MARY
25	OCT	1769	HELEN	HARRIS	d./ WM & MARY
11	NOV	1769	THOS	WOODWARD	s./ THOS & SARAH
28	DEC	1769	SARAH	DEXTER	d./ GEORGE & ELIZ
27	JAN	1770	ANN	HALL	widow
02	FEB	1770	JOHN	DARBY*	-
04	FEB	1770	ANN	ROE	w./ WILLIAM
19	MAR	1770	SARAH	BAILEY	w./ EDWD
03	APR	1770	WILLIAM	MATCHET	natural s./ SARAH
09	SEP	1770	JAMES	CHURCHILL[MI]*	-
18	SEP	1770	JOSHUA	BAILEY	-
07	DEC	1770	JANE	CHAPLIN	d./ JAMES & ELIZ
17	FEB	1771	JOSEPH	MATCHET	-
09	APR	1771	RICHARD	MUGISSON	-
26	JUL	1771	THOMAS	GODDARD	-
28	JUL	1771	DOROTHY	SWAN	d./ THOS & ANN
04	DEC	1771	SARAH	JOHNSON[MI]*	widow
23	MAY	1772	EDWARD	BAILEY	s./ EDWD
01	JUN	1772	JOSEPH	MORLEY	-
04	JUL	1772	WILLIAM	GIBSON	s./ WM & SUSANNA
16	JUL	1772	JAMES	ASHER*	-
29	AUG	1772	Mrs	BARNARD	widow
20	SEP	1772	SUSANNA	GIBSON	-
13	OCT	1772	JOSEPH	DARBY	s./ WM & ELIZ
04	FEB	1773	SARAH	LAKIN	d./ THOS & SARAH
12	FEB	1773	SARAH	HUSKISSON	w./ THOS
04	MAR	1773	HANNAH	HARRIS	widow

14	MAY	1773	THEOPHILA	DALBY	widow
11	JUN	1773	ROBERT	CORBET	-
20	JUN	1773	THOMAS	BRADLEY	s./ WILLIAM & DEBORAH
27	JUL	1773	ELIZABETH	DEXTER	w./ GEORGE
29	SEP	1773	EDWARD	HALL	-
05	DEC	1773	JOHN	CORBET	-
23	AUG	1774	MARY	ASHER	w./ THOS
25	NOV	1774	WILLIAM	GIBSON	-

> Judith D. of Robt. & Judith Mountney buried 22d. Jany. 1775.

22	JAN	1775	JUDITH	MOUNTNEY	d./ ROBT & JUDITH
02	JUN	1775	HELEN[1]	GILBERT	widow
14	JUL	1775	THOMAS	SHAW	-
02	AUG	1775	ELIZABETH Mrs	BRALESFORD[MI]	widow
06	JAN	1776	JOSEPH	KELLEY	natural s./ SARAH
23	JAN	1776	ELIZABETH Mrs	WEBSTER	widow
26	JAN	1776	ANN	WILLIERS*	widow
30	SEP	1776	WILLIAM	WILSON*	of the pa. of Worthington
12	OCT	1776	ANN Mrs	DOWNS	widow
01	FEB	1777	MATTHEW	WHITINGHAM	-
21	FEB	1777	DOROTHY	CLARK[MI]	-
25	APR	1777	JOHN	ROSE*	-
08	MAY	1777	ROBERT	TATNEL[MI]*	-
10	AUG	1777	THOMAS	HUSKISSON*	-
07	SEP	1777	JANE	YOUNG	-
18	DEC	1777	MARY	MOUNTNEY	w./ ROBERT
03	JAN	1778	MARY	KEMPSON	d./ WILLIAM & ELIZ
21	APR	1778	ELIZABETH	CHAPLIN	w./ JAMES
10	OCT	1778	ROWLSON	BEER[MI]	s./ THOMAS & SARAH
15	OCT	1778	SARAH	BEER[MI]*	w./ THOMAS
05	NOV	1778	ELIZABETH	GILBERT	w./ SAMUEL
07	NOV	1778	MARY	WHITINGHAM	-
11	NOV	1778	JANE	WARD	-
14	JAN	1779	THOMAS	WHITINGHAM	-
24	JAN	1779	MARY	KIDDIER	-
09	MAR	1779	SARAH	LAKIN	d./ THOS & SARAH
20	APR	1779	SARAH	LAKIN	w./ THOS
31	MAY	1779	CHARLES	MATCHET	s./ ANN widow[2]
03	JUN	1779	ELI	MARLER	s./ STARKEY & MARY
08	JUN	1779	ELIZABETH	PARSONS	w./ THOS
18	JUN	1779	BENJAMIN	JOHNSON[MI]*	-
19	NOV	1779	MARY	BRADLEY	w./ JOHN

---

[1] BT gave ELLEN.

[2] BT gave s./ JOSEPH & ANN.

03	DEC	1779	SUSANNA Mrs	RAINSFORD[MI]	widow
05	FEB	1780	SARAH	ROE	d./ WILLM & MARY
23	OCT	1780	TIMOTHY	JOYNES	widower
23	APR	1781	CATHERINE Mrs	BARSBY	widow
29	OCT	1781	THOMAS	SWANN	-
11	MAR	1782	ANN	HALL	widow of Worthington
22	JUL	1782	JOSEPH WOOLLEY	DARBY	natural s./ JOHN[1]
19	JAN	1783	MARY	GLOVER	d./ WILLIAM & SARAH
16	FEB	1783	DIANAH	BAGNAL	d./ SAMUEL & ANN
07	MAR	1783	EDWARD	BAILEY	widower
10	JUL	1783	BARBARA	ROSE	widow of the late JOHN ROSE
13	AUG	1783	DEBORAH	BRADLEY	w./ WILLIAM
07	OCT	1783	HENRY	FORD	widower
01	NOV	1783	WILLIAM	ROE	widower
28	MAR	1784	MARY	CHARLESWORTH	d./ STEPHEN & SARAH
09	APR	1784	THOMAS	BOWLEY	-
14	MAY	1784	SARAH	NORTH	widow of Thringston
25	MAY	1784	RICHARD	HUMBER	s./ JOHN & KATHERIN
09	JUL	1784	RICHARD	ROPER	widower
31	OCT	1784	RACHEL	BERRISFORD	w./ CHARLES
03	NOV	1784	JOHN	MATCHETT	s./ JOHN & ELIZABETH
17	DEC	1784	WILLIAM	SWANN	s./ THOMAS & ANN
29	JAN	1785	MARY	YONGE	d./ ROBERT & SARAH
02	MAR	1785	MILICENT	CORBETT	d./ ROBERT & MILICENT poor
05	MAR	1785	JAMES	GIBSON	s./ WILLIAM & SUSANNAH poor
27	APR	1785	SARAH	GLOVER	w./ WILLIAM poor
13	JUL	1785	THOMAS Gent	BOULTBEE[MI]	of Stordon Grange
19	AUG	1785	SAMUEL	BAGNALL	s./ SAMUEL & ANN poor
21	AUG	1785	JOHN	CORBETT	s./ MILICENT poor
21[2]	AUG	1785	THOMAS	WOODCOCK	s./ DANIEL & MARTHA
21	AUG	1785	SARAH	WOODCOCK	d./ DANIEL & MARTHA
15	MAR	1786	MARGARET	JOHNSON[MI]*	widow of BEN[JAM]IN deceased
25	MAY	1786	JOHN	MATCHETT	s./ JOHN & ELIZABETH poor
17	SEP	1786	THOMAS	BOULTBEE	s./ JOSEPH & SARAH
13	OCT	1786	REBECCAH	MATCHETT	widow poor
01	FEB	1787	MARY	ASHER	w./ WILLIAM
11	FEB	1787	ANN	HUSKINSON	d./ THOMAS & SARAH
16	FEB	1787	CHARLES	BERRISFORD	widower
25	FEB	1787	WILLIAM	ASHER	s./ WILLIAM & MARY
06	MAR	1787	THOMAS	BRADLEY	s./ JOHN & TRYPHENA
16	MAR	1787	SARAH	CHARLESWORTH	w./ STEPHEN
19	MAR	1787	JOHN	HALL	s./ JAMES & ANN
19	MAY	1787	WILLIAM	BRADLEY	s./ WILLIAM & SARAH

[1] Register & BT both gave JOHN as the only parent.

[2] BT gave this entry & the next as 28 August.

26	JUN	1787	JAMES	GILBERT	-
03	MAR	1788	THOMAS	YOUNG	s./ JAMES & ANN poor
03	MAY	1788	HANNAH	GIBSON	d./ JOHN & HANNAH
16	JUN	1788	JOSEPH	BARRATT	s./ RICHARD & SARAH
17	SEP	1788	ELIZABETH	SHAW	widow poor
28	SEP	1788	HANNAH	FISHER	d./ JOSEPH & TAMER[1]
30	NOV	1788	JOHN	SIDDON	poor
23	DEC	1788	SARAH	BOULTBEE	d./ THOS & JANE
06	APR	1789	JANE	BOULTBEE[MI]	widow of THOMAS of Stordon Grange
18	JUN	1789	WILLIAM	MOSELEY	-
08	OCT	1789	ANN	BAGGALEY	w./ SAMUEL poor
28	OCT	1789	ANN	BAGGALEY	d./ SAMUEL & ANN poor
07	JAN	1790	RACHEL	BRAILSFORD[MI]	d./ the Revd JOHN
14	FEB	1790	SARAH	WOODCOCK	d./ DANIEL & MARTHA
06	APR	1790	ELIZABETH	BOWLEY	widow poor
07	APR	1790	THOMAS	HEAP	poor
13	APR[2]	1790	THOMAS	ASHER	widower of Barleston
21	APR	1790	SARAH	TATENALL[MI*]	widow of ROBT
14	MAY	1790	WILLIAM	MATCHETT	poor
18	JUL	1790	ELIZABETH	BRADLEY	w./ THOMAS
04	AUG	1790	SAMUEL	BROWN	parish clerk 34 years. poor
08	APR	1791	ELIZABETH	DARBY	w./ JOHN
02	JUL	1791	HANNAH	ILLSLEY	w./ GEORGE
23	SEP	1791	MARY	MATCHETT	widow poor
20	JUN	1792	JOHN	EARPE[MI]	-
29	JUN	1792	WILLIAM	ASHER	widower
06	MAR	1793	ALICE	NADIN*	w./ THOMAS
03	MAY	1793	THOMAS	PARSONS	widower
19	JUN	1793	MARY	PEAT	w./ GEORGE
04	OCT	1793	ELIZABETH	NEWBOLD	widow p.[Poor]
12	NOV	1793	JOSEPH	WOODCOCK	s./ JOSEPH & SARAH
28	NOV	1793	JANE	CROWSON	w./ JOSEPH
14	DEC	1793	HANNAH	EVERARD[MI]	w./ FRANCIS
12	JAN	1794	SARAH	YOUNG	w./ MOSES p.[Poor]
13	FEB	1794	JAMES	GODDARD	s./ THOMAS & ELIZABETH p.[Poor]
27	APR	1794	FRANCIS	HARVEY	s./ FRANCIS & CATHARINE
08	JUN	1794	THOMAS	BARRAT	s./ RICHARD & SARAH
22	NOV	1794	FRANCIS	EVERARD[MI]	widower
05	JAN	1795	MARY	JOHNSON	d./ JACOB & MARY
14	JAN	1795	SAMUEL	BROWN	s./ WILLIAM & URSULA
09	FEB	1795	ELIZABETH	ROSE	w./ JOHN
12	MAR	1795	WILLIAM	HOUTON	-
12	MAR	1795	JOHN	DEXTER	s./ STEPHEN & LETITIA

---

[1] BT gave TAMAR for TAMER.

[2] Register gave 13 MAY and was out of chronological order: BT gave 13 APRIL and was in order.

23	MAR	1795	JOSEPH	YOUNG	s./ ROBERT & SARAH
06	MAY	1795	WILLIAM	BROWN	s./ WILLIAM & URSULA
10	MAY	1795	RICHARD	BARRAT	-
01	JUN	1795	MARY	DEXTER	d./ STEPHEN & LATITIA
09	SEP	1795	MARY	BRAUNSON	w./ JOHN
21	SEP	1795	STEPHEN	BEALEY	s./ WILLIAM & ANN
04	OCT	1795	ANN	EDWARDS	d./ RICHARD & ROSE
02	NOV	1795	JOHN	WHITE	s./ MATTHEW & HANNAH

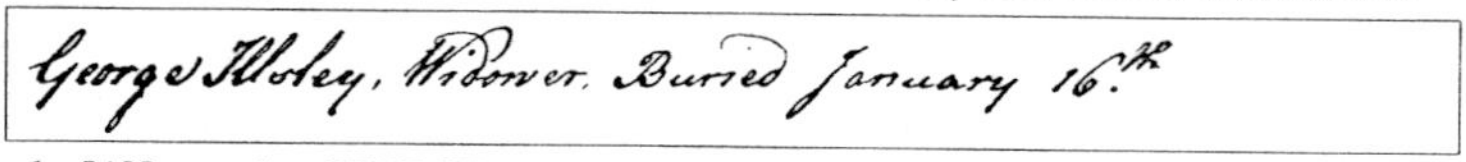
George Illsley, Widower. Buried January 16th

16	JAN	1796	GEORGE	ILLSLEY	widower
06	MAY	1796	WILLIAM	GLOVER	widower
22	MAY	1796	ANN	FARMER	w./ FRANCIS
23	JUL	1796	ANN	FARMER	d./ FRANCIS
11	OCT	1796	ELIZABETH	FARMER	w./ JOHN
01	NOV	1796	REBECCA	MATCHET	d./ JOHN & ELIZABETH
19	NOV	1796	ANN	HALL	w./ JAMES of Liberty of Worthington
19	MAR	1797	JANE	HUSKINS	widow
26	APR	1797	JAMES	FORD*	-
12	NOV	1797	ROBERT	WILLOWS	-
28	DEC	1797	ELIZABETH	GOODARD	w./ T. [THOMAS][1]
10	JAN	1798	THOMAS	HALL	s./ JAS & ANN
13	MAR	1798	CATHERINE	MATCHIT	widdow
04	APR	1798	ELIZABETH	MITCHIL	-
04	JUN	1798	CHARLES	HARRIS	-
12	AUG	1798	MARY	DARBY	widow
09	SEP	1798	HANNAH	ASHER	-
17	OCT	1798	JOHN	MASON	-
05	NOV	1798	ELIZABETH	KING	-
14	APR	1799	JOHN	WOODCOCK	of Witwick
17	APR	1799	MARY	CROSON	-
10	JUN	1799	RACHAEL	FARMER	w./ FRANCIS
21	JUL	1799	MARY	ORCHARD	d./ WILLM & FRANCES
18	AUG	1799	THOMAS	STINSON	-
08	NOV	1799	CATHERINE	SWAN	d./ THOMAS & CATHERINE
20	JAN	1800	MARY	FARMER	d./ FRANCIS & ANN
06	MAY	1800	ELENOR	HARRIS	d./ JAMES & MARY
17	AUG	1800	MARY	HARRIS	d./ JAMES & MARY
30[2]	AUG	1800	THOMAS	BRADLEY	-
15	NOV	1800	ANN	GODDARD	d./ MARY STINSON[3]

[1] THOMAS from his marriage at Osgathorpe in 1764.

[2] BT gave 31 August.

[3] ANN GODDARD was baptised, 28 July 1786, the illegitimate daughter of MARY GODDARD. After which Mary married Thomas Stinson, 7 March 1791.

28	NOV	1800	ALICE	MEAKIN	w./ WM
30	NOV	1800	P. Miss	RUSSEL	-
15[1]	MAR	1801	JOHN	KING	s./ THOMAS & SARAH
01	APR	1801	JAMES	TETLEY	s./ ANN
24	MAY	1801	CATHERINE	CORBET	d./ ROBERT & MILLICENT
19	JUN	1801	HANNAH	NICHOLLS	w./ JOHN
06	JUL	1801	CHARLES	FARMER	s./ FRANCIS & RACHAL
16	AUG	1801	ELIZABETH	DARINGTON	d./ WILLIAM & ELIZABETH
17	SEP	1801	WILLIAM	DARINGTON	s./ WILLIAM & ELIZABETH
12	OCT	1801	ELIZABETH	DAVENPORT	d./ WILLIAM & FRANCES
22	DEC	1801	SARAH	BARFOOT	widow
29	JAN	1802	JAMES	DARINGTON	s./ WILLIAM & ELIZABETH
01	APR	1802	Mrs	BOWLEY	widow
08	APR	1802	JOSEPH	WOODCOCK	s./ JOSEPH & SARAH
13	JUN	1802	ANN	SMITH	d./ DANIEL & ELIZABETH
30	OCT	1802	JOHN	GIBSON	-
28	NOV	1802	THOMAS	EARP[MI]*	-
06	JAN	1803	WILLIAM	FARMER	-
03	FEB	1803	MARY	DARBY	d./ JOHN & ELIZABETH
06	FEB	1803	THOMAS	GODDARD	-
06	FEB	1803	ELIZABETH	BROWN	-
23	FEB	1803	ALICE	HARRIS	d./ JAMES & MARY
31	MAY	1803	WILLIAM	MOORE	-
24	JUN	1803	DANIEL	WOODCOCK	s./ DANIEL & MARTHA
25	SEP	1803	ANN	DARBY	d./ MARY
16	NOV	1803	RACHEL	YOUNG	d./ JAMES & ANN
27	NOV	1803	WILLIAM	STINSON	-
06	DEC	1803	ANN	MOORE	-
01	APR	1804	JOHN	DARBY	s./ WILLIAM & ELIZABETH
23	MAY	1804	MOSES	YOUNG	-
23	JUL	1804	THOMAS	NORMAN	-
03	SEP	1804	MARY	WORTHINGTON	-
27	SEP	1804	WILLIAM WILSON	WOODCOCK	s./ JOSEPH & SARAH
28	FEB	1805	MARY	WOODCOCK	d./ DANIEL & MARTHA
28	FEB	1805	CHARLES	HARRIS	s./ CHARLES & ANN
16	APR	1805	LEONARD	DEXTER	s./ STEPHEN & LETITIA
28	JUN	1805	MARY	HUTCHINSON	w./ WILLIAM
11	AUG	1805	FANNY	GLOVER	w./ WILLIAM
15	OCT	1805	JOSEPH	HARRIS	s./ JAMES & MARY
27	AUG	1806	MICHAEL	HARDY	s./ WILLIAM & SARAH
24	OCT	1806	NICHOLAS KIDGER	DARBY	s./ JOHN
28	OCT	1806	SAMUEL	GILBERT*	-
02	NOV	1806	HANNAH	HICKLIN	w./ WILLIAM
09	NOV	1806	ANN	PICKARD	w./ WILLIAM

[1] BT gave 5 March.

27	NOV	1806	THOMAS	KENDRICK	-
01	DEC	1806	THOMAS	PICKARD	s./ WILLIAM
20	JAN	1807	JOHN	ASHER	-
06	MAR	1807	JAMES	YOUNG	-
07	APR	1807	MARY	MATCHET	of the pa. of Thringstone
19	APR	1807	ANN	FARMER	d./ FRANCIS & MARY
05[1]	JUN	1807	MARTHA	WOODCOCK	w./ DANIEL of Whitwick
23	OCT	1807	GEORGE	ILLSLEY[MI]*	-
19	FEB	1808	BENJAMIN	STINSON	s./ WM & MILICENT
10	APR	1808	ELIZABETH	DARBY	w./ WM
13	APR	1808	SARAH	HARRIS	w./ THOS MATON
18	APR	1808	SAMUEL	HARRIS	s./ JAMES & MARY
18	MAY	1808	WILLIAM	GLOVER	-
04	JAN	1809	JAMES	MITCHEL	-
01	MAR	1809	ANN	MOORE	d./ JOSEPH
05	MAR	1809	SARAH	MOORE	w./ JOSEPH
13	JUL	1809	MARY	DEXTER	d./ STEPHEN & LITISHER
15	DEC	1809	SARAH	BOWLEY*	-
16	FEB	1810	HANNAH	MEAKIN	d./ JOHN & SARAH
02	MAR	1810	WILLIAM	HARRIS	s./ JAMES & MARY
03	APR	1810	MARY	NORMAN	-
06	APR	1810	WILLIAM	BRADLEY*	-
16	APR	1810	HANNAH	BROWN	d./ WILLIAM & URSULA
29	APR	1810	WILLIAM	HARRIS	-
31	MAY	1810	SARAH	RICHARDS	w./ JOHN
24	JUN	1810	JOHN	GODDARD	-
07	OCT	1810	JOSEPH	VICKARS	-
17	JAN	1811	MARY	BRADLEY	d./ SARAH
15	MAR	1811	MARY	EVERAD	-
18	MAR	1811	CATHARINE ELIZABETH	FOWLER	d./ RICHARD & MARY
30	APR	1811	JAMES	HALL*	-
19	MAY	1811	THOS	HARDY	s./ WILLIAM & SARAH
22	MAY	1811	SAML	HARDY	s./ WILLIAM & SARAH
24	MAY	1811	DANIEL	HARDY	s./ WILLIAM & SARAH
09	JUN	1811	THOMAS	SWAN	s./ THOMAS & CATHARINE
19	JUN	1811	JOHN	SWAN	s./ THOS & CATHARINE
18	JUL	1811	JAMES	HARRIS	-
24	JUL	1811	JAMES	HEAP	s./ HUMPHREY & FRANCES
01[2]	AUG	1811	ANN	STINSON	d./ WILLIAM & MILLICENT
11	AUG	1811	MARY	NEWBOUND	-
15	AUG	1811	MARY	DEXTER	d./ STEPHEN & LATITIA[3]
27	AUG	1811	FRANCES	HARVEY	-

---

[1] BT gave 6 June.

[2] BT gave 7 August.

[3] BT gave ELIZ instead of LATITIA.

20	SEP	1811	WILLM	SLEATH	-
21	SEP	1811	WILLM	WOODCOCK	s./ JOSEPH & SARAH[1]
02	OCT	1811	SARAH	BOULTBY	w./ ROBERT
20	NOV	1811	ELIANOR	VICKERS	-
16[2]	DEC	1811	ANN	DEVENPORT	-
13	APR	1812	PATIENCE	COOPER	-
05	MAY	1812	HANNAH	WILLOWS	-
29	MAY	1812	ANN	TWO [TOW]	d./ WM & SARAH
26	DEC	1812	DOROTHY	KELK	-

From 1813, all the burial entries included the deceased's age and place of abode. However, due to the limitations of space & for clarity, Osgathorpe has been omitted. All other places of abode have been included.

19	FEB	1813	MARY	BRANSON	-	50
21	MAR	1813	DANIEL	WOODCOCK	of Whitwick	81
13	APR	1813	MARY	ILLSLEY[MI]*	-	73
14	APR	1813	DAWSON	YOUNG	-	32
04[3]	SEP	1813	SARAH	ROE	-	5
07	DEC	1813	ELIZATH	MASON	-	69
13	JAN	1814	JAMES	BRADLEY*	-	37
21	FEB	1814	ANN	YOUNG	-	62
28	FEB	1814	MARY	HARRIS	-	80
27	MAR	1814	ELIZTH	MOOR	-	60
15	APR	1814	ANN	SWAN	-	78
22	APR	1814	MARY	MITCHELL	-	48
24	APR	1814	SARAH	PICKARD	-	63
27	APR	1814	SAMUEL	WOODCOCK	-	infant
29	APR	1814	WILLIAM	HARVY	-	22
19	SEP	1814	HARAN	SMITH	-	3
02	OCT	1814	ANN	SWAN	-	infant
27	NOV	1814	ANN	STINSON	-	80
22	JAN	1815	THOS	SLINGSBY	baseborn s./ SARAH	infant
01	JUL	1815	MARY	FARMER	w./ FRANCIS	32[4]
12	AUG	1815	MARY ROMSLEY	MEAKIN	d./ SARAH	27[5]
27	SEP	1815	DANIEL	SMITH	-	66
27	SEP	1815	JANE	ROSE[MI]*	-	66
18	OCT	1815	HANNAH	GIBSON	-	76
15	NOV	1815	SARAH	WALDROM	-	infant

---

[1] This entry was crossed out in the register, but not on the BT.

[2] BT gave 20 December.

[3] BT gave 5 September.

[4] BT gave 27 yrs, which appears to have been transposed with the next entry.

[5] BT gave 32 yrs, which appears to have been transposed with the previous entry.

21	JAN	1816	JAMES	ASHER*	-	34
22	JAN	1816	MARY	JOHNSON	of Thringstone	49
28	JAN	1816	WILLIAM	SMITH	-	79
21	FEB	1816	ELIZTH	BOULTBY	of Staudons	18
28	FEB	1816	JACOB	JOHNSON*	of Thringstone	54
08	MAY	1816	JOHN	FARMER*	-	89
04	JUN	1816	ANN	HARVEY	-	34
18	JUL	1816	CATHARINE	SWAN	d./ THOS & CATHARINE	infant

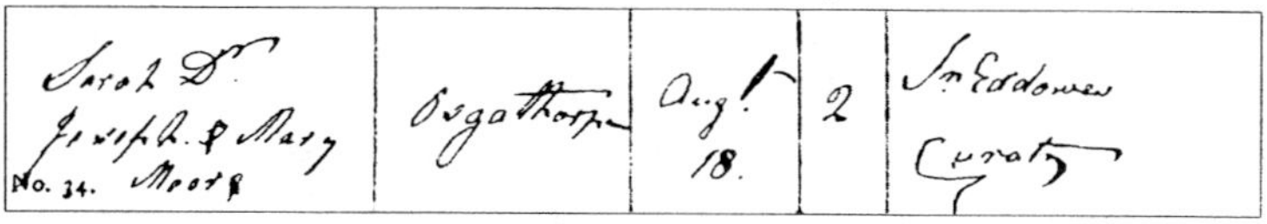
Sarah Dr. Joseph & Mary Moore No. 34. | Osgathorpe | Aug. 18. | 2 | Jn Eddowes Curate

18	AUG	1816	SARAH	MOORE	d./ JOSEPH & MARY	2
26	SEP	1816	BENJAMIN	JOHNSON*	-	60
13	FEB	1817	WILLIAM	WILLIAMSON	baseborn	infant
19	JUN	1817	JAMES	MACKIE[MI]*	-	75
28	SEP	1817	THOS	BOULTBEE*	of Staudens	28
07	DEC	1817	ELIZTH	SMITH	-	70
31	DEC	1817	ANN	BAGGERLEY	w./ SAMUEL	73
04	JAN	1818	FRANCES	DARBY	w./ JOHN	23
20	FEB	1818	JOHN	DARBY*	-	83
24	FEB	1818	MARY	DARBY	d./ WILLIAM	11
12	APR	1818	SAMUEL	BAGGERLEY	-	80
11	MAY	1818	ANN	WOODWARD	w./ WM	75
24	JUN	1818	ABRAHAM	ENSOR	-	56
19	NOV	1818	JOSEPH	ASHER	of Coleorton	84
19	NOV	1818	WILLIAM	MILES	-	62
30	NOV	1818	SARAH	BUCKLEY	w./ THOS	50
18[1]	JAN	1819	THOMAS	ORSBORN	s./ GEORGE & ELIZABETH	1
21	FEB	1819	WILLIAM	OSBORN	s./ SARAH	16
04	MAR	1819	ELIZTH	MORE	d./ JOSEPH & MARY	1
09	MAY	1819	FRANCES	BRADLEY	d./ WM & SOPHIA	2
05	JUN	1819	ANN	WILLIAMSON	baseborn d./ ELZTH	infant
24	JUN	1819	MARTHA	ENSOR	-	55
02	OCT	1819	CATHERINE	WARD	d./ BENJ & CATH	infant
13	MAR	1820	ELZTH	SIDDONS	d./ CATHARINE HARVEY	35
07	MAY	1820	WILLIAM	BLADDON	-	74
21	MAY	1820	WM	HOW	s./ JOHN & MARY	11
24	MAY	1820	SARAH	YOUNG	w./ ROBERT of Coleorton	71
23	JUN	1820	FRANCES	JONES	-	74
13	AUG	1820	WM	ROE*	of Worthington	79
01	SEP	1820	MATTHEW	WHITE	-	55
31	DEC	1820	ANN	BLADON*	-	75

[1] BT gave 10 January.

26	JAN	1821	MARY	ROE*	-	75
08	APR	1821	HANNAH	ROADLEY	-	35
09	AUG	1821	REBEKAH	BAILEY	d./ WM & ANN	25
27	AUG	1821	SUSANNAH	ROBERTS	of Whitwick	46
16	JAN	1822	THOS	KING	-	73
01	FEB	1822	MARY	GILBERT	d./ THOS & ANN	infant
26	MAY	1822	FRANCES	WALDROM	baseborn d./ MARY	2
02	JUN	1822	CHARLES	KELK	s./ ELIZTH CATHARINE	26

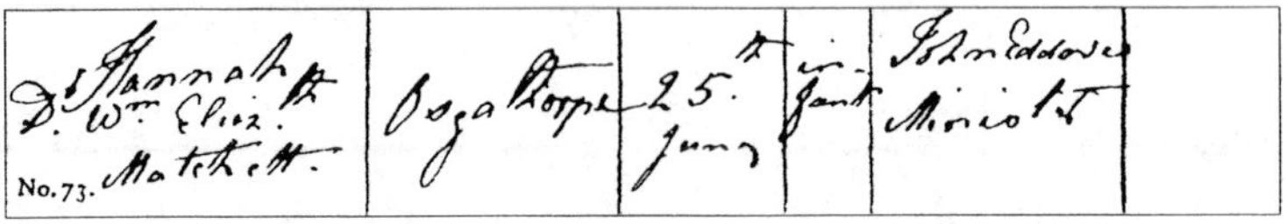

Hannah D. Wm. Eliz. Matchett No. 73.	Osgathorpe	25th June	infant	John Eddowes Minister	

25	JUN	1822	HANNAH	MATCHETT	d./ WM & ELIZTH	infant
25	AUG	1822	THOS	WILLIAMSON	-	53
20	OCT	1822	ANN	TOTLEY	w./ GEORGE of Worthington	61
09	NOV	1822	THOS	STINSON	-	22
13	NOV	1822	MARTHA	BAILEY	d./ WM & ANN	15
25	MAR	1823	MARY	WILLIAMSON	baseborn d./ ELIZABETH	infant
21	APR	1823	JANE CHARLOTTE	SHARRAR	-	62
26	MAY	1823	SARAH	MACKEY	-	73
25	JUN	1823	WILLIAM	ORCHARD	-	73
11	DEC	1823	JOHN	ROSE*	-	91
29	DEC	1823	MARY ANN	FELL	-	38
10	MAR	1824	BENJAMIN	LUNN	-	infant
25	MAY	1824	HANNAH	YONG	d./ CHRISTOPHER	30
24	JUN	1824	WILLIAM	DARBY	-	49
15	AUG	1824	JOHN	BRADLEY*	of Belton	17
01	SEP	1824	MATILDA	SIMPSON	d./ HANNAH	22
08	SEP	1824	GEORGE	WEBSTER	s./ SAMUEL	infant
05	NOV	1824	THOS	BLACK	s./ SAMUEL & HANNAH	infant
01	FEB	1825	JOHN	BRADLEY[MI]	s./ ALSE [ALICE] of Belton	56
09	FEB	1825	THOMAS	SIDDONS	-	8
22	MAR	1825	JOHN	MATCHET	-	74
16	AUG	1825	GERTRUDE	FELL	-	75
05	NOV	1825	SARAH	MEEKIN	-	50
15	DEC	1825	SARAH	WOODCOCK	-	53
25	DEC	1825	HANNAH	BRADLEY	-	2
05	JAN	1826	SAMUEL	BROWN	-	18
01	FEB	1826	JOHN	WALDROM	-	30
21	FEB	1826	THOS	POXON	s./ SAMUEL & MARTHA	9
19	MAY	1826	JOHN	ANDREWS	s./ ISACK & LEAH	infant
17	JUN	1826	SARAH	TABBARER	w./ ALEXANDER	35
09	AUG	1826	ELIZABETH	MATCHET	-	76
11	AUG	1826	THOS	BRADLEY	s./ WILLIAM & SOPHIA	infant
09	OCT	1826	JANE	WRAGG[MI]	-	82

29	OCT	1826	JANE	FORD	-	81
24	NOV	1826	THOS	JOHNSON[MI]*	-	62
21	MAR	1827	EMMA	HOLLADY	-	82
26	JUN	1827	MARY	ALT	-	52
02	DEC	1827	THOS	SMITH	-	37
09	DEC	1827	JOHN	HARRISON*	-	77
28	DEC	1827	HURSULLA	BROWN	w./ WILLIAM	59
04	MAR	1828	MARY	MOORE	-	36
16	MAR	1828	CATHARINE	SIMPSON	-	24
24	MAR	1828	HANNAH	BRANSON	d./ WILIAM & SARAH	infant
15	APR	1828	WILLIAM	WOODCOCK	-	65
21[1]	MAY	1828	JOHN	STINSON	baseborn s./ MARY	infant
08	JUL	1828	MARY	HARRIS	-	79
08	JUL	1828	CAROLINE ELIZABETH MEAKIN		d./ GEORGE ILLSLEY & MARY CAROLINE CHARLOTTE MEAKIN	infant[2]
11	NOV	1828	JOSEPH	YOUNG	s./ CHRISTOPHER & SARAH	infant
03	FEB	1829	JOSEPH	ALLIN	Stocking maker	33
12	FEB	1829	LYDIA	BROWN	-	23
15	FEB	1829	JOSEPH	SALKELD*	-	52
13	JUN	1829	HANNAH	ROE	-	55
14	JUN	1829	WILLIAM	MEAKIN	-	73
30	JUL	1829	MARY	LUNN	of Belton	31
22	NOV	1829	MARIAH	YOUNG	-	infant
01	DEC	1829	MARY CAROLINE CHARLOTTE MEAKIN		-	21
03	APR	1830	HANNAH	MOOR	d./ JOSEPH & MARY	infant
25	APR	1830	MARY	HOTON	-	77
29	APR	1830	JOSEPH	KING	s./ WM & SARAH	infant
21	MAY	1830	HANNAH	SIMPSON	-	66
26	MAY	1830	GEORGE	BRADLEY	s./ WM & SOPHIA	infant
09	JUN	1830	ELIYAH	MORLEY	s./ WM & ELIZ	2
23	JUN	1830	SARAH	HADDON	w./ FRANCIS	19
11	NOV	1830	WILLIAM	BRADLEY	-	35
22	FEB	1831	ELIZABETH	JOHNSON[MI]	-	54
03	APR	1831	JOSEPH	FARMER	-	70
09	AUG	1831	FRANCIS	SWAN	-	52
10	AUG	1831	WILLIAM	DAVENPORT	-	84
21	AUG	1831	HENRY	HOLLIDAY	-	86
20	SEP	1831	HANNAH	MEAKIN	-	[Blank]
15	NOV	1831	ROBERT	YOUNG	of Coleorton	76
09	FEB	1832	SARAH	BARRATT	-	93
15	APR	1832	GEORGE	NEWMANS	-	10 months
19	APR	1832	GEORGE	PEAT*	-	92
09	MAY	1832	JOHN	ROE	-	7 months

---

1 BT gave 27 May.

2 BT gave age at burial as 1. ILLSLEY was her father's middle name.

18	MAY	1832	JAMES	ROE	-	5
07	APR	1833	GEORGE	TETLEY	-	67
04	OCT	1833	ANNE	MILES	widow of WILLIAM Mr of Birds Hill, Appleby	67
14	JAN	1834	JOHN KNIGHT	GILBERT	-	3
19	FEB	1834	WILLIAM	BRADLEY	-	7 months
09	MAR	1834	FRANCIS	FARMER*	killed by wagon on the rail road	65
11	MAY	1834	SARAH	DEXTER	-	61
31	MAY	1834	JOHN	BRANSON	Master of the free School	70
18	JUN	1834	JOSEPH	ALLT	-	infant
07	JUL	1834	GEORGE	STATHAM	-	infant
15	SEP	1834	BRIDGET	HADDON	-	infant
18	NOV	1834	ROBERT	IRONMONGER	-	3
18	DEC	1834	ELIZABETH CATHARINE	KELK	-	67
25	JAN	1835	ANNE	KING	-	75
27	FEB	1835	ALICE	BRADLEY*	of Belton Low Woods	96
31	MAR	1835	ANNE	GILBERT	-	48
12	APR	1835	THOMAS	HURST	-	87
05	SEP	1835	JANE	WEBSTER	-	36
03	OCT	1835	LEAH	MORE	-	11
20	MAR	1836	WILLIAM	ROE	-	65
27	APR	1836	JAMES	WALDROM	Shardlow House of Industry	17
19	JUN	1836	FRANCES	DEVONPORT	-	88
15	AUG	1836	SOPHIA	BRADLEY	-	43
16	AUG	1836	SUSANNAH	MOSELEY	-	10 months
12	SEP	1836	WILLIAM	YOUNG	-	3 weeks[1]
10	JAN	1837	JOHN	WOOD	Burned to death	4
02	FEB	1837	SARAH	BRADLEY	-	79
19	FEB	1837	SARAH	GILBERT	-	infant
05	MAR	1837	RACHEL	NEWMAN	-	31
12	MAR	1837	WILLIAM ROBERT	KING	of Breedon Brand	infant
19	MAR	1837	JOSEPH	BROWN	Shardlow House of Industry	[Blank]
20	MAR	1837	ANNE	QUENBY	-	33
28	APR	1837	MARY	YOUNGHUSBAND[MI]	-	74
11	JUN	1837	MILICENT	STINSON	-	70
18	JUN	1837	ROSANNA	WALDROM	-	1
11	AUG	1837	WILLIAM	BROWN	-	70
03	OCT	1837	WILLIAM	BAILEY*	-	70
09	JAN	1838	EDWARD	PERRY	-	infant
14	JAN	1838	MARY	JOHNSON*	-	86
25	MAR	1838	MARY	MOSELEY	-	83
27	APR	1838	FRANCIS	FARMER	-	27
13	MAY	1838	JANE	KING	-	7 months
04	SEP	1838	JAMES	ROE	-	27
28	SEP	1838	JOHN	HAYWOOD	-	41

[1] BT gave age at burial as 3 months.

07 NOV 1838 JOSEPH WOODCOCK - 68
06 DEC 1838 MARY ELLIS d./ Rev J. ELLIS vicar of Llanbadric, Anglesea.[1] Osgathorpe Residence 15
18 DEC 1838 JAMES WOOD - infant
20 FEB 1839 WILLIAM JOHNSON of Tringstone 30
11 MAR 1839 CHARLOTTE LUCY KATHARINE KELK - 13 months
19 MAR 1839 HANNAH WHITE - 70
14 APR 1839 MARTHA ROE - 10 months

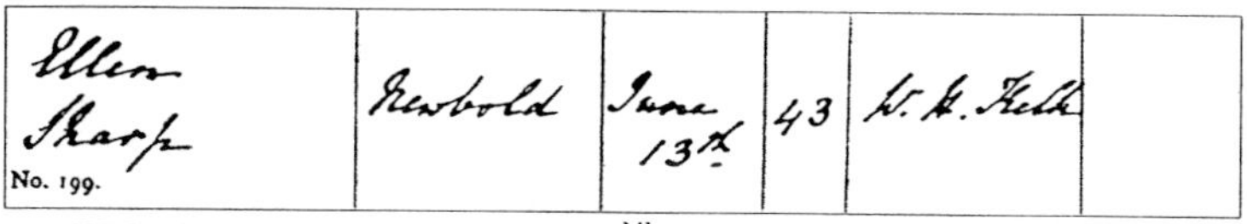
Ellen Sharp No. 199.	Newbold	June 13th	43	W. K. Kelk	

13 JUN 1839 ELLEN SHARP[MI] of Newbold 43
05 SEP 1839 WILLIAM MACKIE of Fritchley in pa. of Crich, Derbys 34
05 OCT 1839 WILLIAM PERRY - infant
09 JAN 1840 SARAH BROWN of Belton Low Woods 59
24 JAN 1840 WILLIAM WOOD - 5
23 FEB 1840 RACHEL WALDROM - 10
02 MAR 1840 MARY CLARKE - 9 months
05 MAR 1840 CATHARINE ANNE JOHNSON[MI] of Spring Vale near Stoke 30
19 APR 1840 ANN HALLAM - 10
27 APR 1840 ELIZABETH HALLAM - 12
27 APR 1840 THOMAS HALLAM - 5
30 APR 1840 JOHN DARBY - 4
01 MAY 1840 EMMA KING - 1
08 MAY 1840 WILLIAM WOODWARD - 79
22 JUN 1840 ELIZABETH SIDDONS - 5
21 JUL 1840 MARY KING - 59
26 AUG 1840 MATTHEW WHITE - 1
05 MAR 1841 ELIZABETH MATCHET - 45
08 APR 1841 MARY PEARSON of Gelsmoor in pa. of Worthington 86
28 JUL 1841 JOHN YOUNG - infant
28 JUL 1841 THOMAS YOUNG - infant
22 AUG 1841 MARY KING - 36
01 MAR 1842 MARY MOORE - 50
02 MAR 1842 JOHN WARRIS GREEN Ashby Union Workhouse 1
05 APR 1842 SARAH KING - 80
02 AUG 1842 MARY ANN KING - infant
30 AUG 1842 ELIZABETH CLARKE - 27
02 SEP 1842 SARAH HALL - infant
29 SEP 1842 WILLIAM CLARKE - infant
17 OCT 1842 THOMAS MATON HARRIS - 70
20 OCT 1842 HENRY MOSELEY of Belton 23

---

[1] Llanbadric = Llanbadrig a parish in the hundred of Talybolion, Anglesey.

27	NOV	1842	LOT	QUENBY		infant
01	FEB	1843	ELIZABETH	MOSELEY	of Belton	60
08	APR	1843	WILLIAM	MATCHETT	-	54
30	APR	1843	SAMUEL GILBERT	WALDROM	-	1
11	JUN	1843	JOSEPH	WALDROM	-	35
17	AUG	1843	THOMAS	HURST	of Griffy Dam	16
01	SEP	1843	JOHN	OSBOURNE	-	3
10	SEP	1843	ANN	BAILEY	-	70

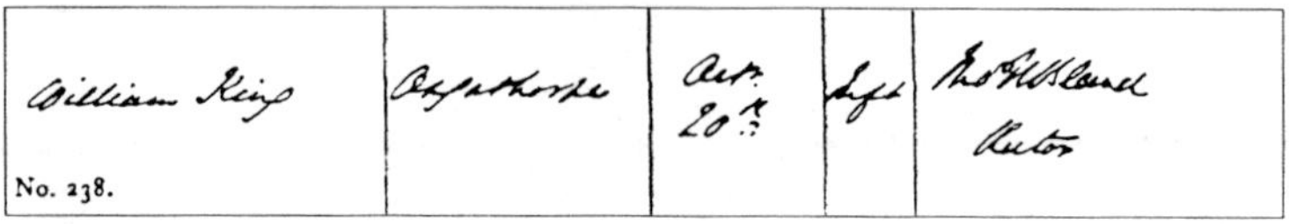
No. 238.
William King | Osgathorpe | Octr 20th | Inft | Rector

20	OCT	1843	WILLIAM	KING	-	infant
28	FEB	1844	HANNAH	MEAKIN	-	50
16	JUN	1844	GEORGE	BARRETT	-	73
06	OCT	1844	SARAH	MEAKIN	-	63
07	FEB	1845	JAMES	HARRIS	-	68
23	FEB	1845	MARY ANN	HURST	Burnt to death / coroners cert	18
06	MAY	1845	EMMA	WOOD	-	1
01	JUN	1845	MARY	SAUDERS[1]	clergymans widow	59
11	JUN	1845	JOSEPH	KING	-	79
15	JUL	1845	GEORGE	PERRY	of Leicester	45
17	JUL	1845	JOHN	HEROD	-	infant
17	NOV	1845	SAMUEL	SMALLWOOD	-	96
27	NOV	1845	SARAH SOPHIA	GIBBON	'came to Osga' a year ago in ill health'	71
02	DEC	1845	ALEXANDER	TABBENER	of Leicester	55
12	DEC	1845	SOPHIA MARY	BRANSON	-	22
25	DEC	1845	GEORGE	MOORE	-	infant
02	FEB	1846	EMMA ELIZABETH	TABBERER	of Leicester	26
24	MAR	1846	HANNAH	BLACK	-	5
03	MAR	1847	JAMES	DEXTER	Ashby Union	86
11	JUN	1847	GEORGE DAWKINS	WALE	-	24
21	JUN	1847	ISABELLA SUSANNA	KELK	of Worthington	16
13	OCT	1847	ELIZABETH	SMITH	of Chellastone, Derbys	67
09	DEC	1847	MARTHA	MORGAN	-	infant
05	JAN	1848	SAMUEL	MATCHETT	-	70
07	JAN	1848	LUCY	TABBERER	of Leicester	29
09	FEB	1848	MARY	MEDLEY	clergymans widow	56
06	APR	1848	MATILDA REBECCA	WALE	-	13
21	MAY	1848	ANN	HOLLOWAY	-	67
24	MAY	1848	SARAH	WALDROM	-	48
23	JUL	1848	WILLIAM	MOORE	Railway Labourer	32
19	OCT	1848	HENRY	ROE	-	infant

[1] Possibly SANDERS. Register also gave 'Came to Osgathorpe in a dying state lived a fortnight'.

08	NOV	1848	CHRISTOPHER	YOUNG	-	59
21	FEB	1849	MARY	KING	-	85
27	FEB	1849	JOSEPH	POPE	-	infant
17	MAR	1849	BENJAMIN	JOHNSON*	-	44
28	AUG	1849	WILLIAM	BRADLEY	-	85
15	OCT	1849	JOHN DELAP HASTINGS	KELK	-	22
22	OCT	1849	GEORGE	ROE	-	74
05	NOV	1849	EMMA	ALLT	-	18
04	APR	1850	THOMAS	MEAKIN	-	72
14	APR	1850	MARY ANN	BRANSON	-	26
02	MAY	1850	ELIZABETH	JEFFCOAT	-	infant
26	JUN	1850	WILLIAM	YOUNG	Ashby Union Workhouse, late of Tring, Herts	18
02	JAN	1851	MARY	SHARPE[MI]	-	32
21	JUN	1851	THOMAS	HARRIS	-	76
01	OCT	1851	SAMUEL	ALLT	junr	45
07	NOV	1851	SUSANNAH	PERRY	-	1
17	NOV	1851	SAMUEL	ALLT	senr	78
24	NOV	1851	ANN	BULL	-	83
05	DEC	1851	WILLIAM	GADSBY	-	24
16	DEC	1851	CHARLES	PERRY	-	26
29	DEC	1851	SARAH	CLARKE	-	34
12	JAN	1852	JOHN WILLIAM	CLARKE	-	infant
17	FEB	1852	HANNAH	BRADLEY[MI]*	of Belton	77
10	MAR	1852	FANNY	SCATTERGOOD	-	70
15	APR	1852	THOMAS	BULL	-	83
06	OCT	1852	ANN	GILBERT[MI]	-	77
27	DEC	1852	MARY	BURTON	-	7
10	JAN	1853	SARAH	WALDRAM	-	34
15	MAR	1853	WILLIAM	BRADLEY[MI]	of Belton	80
18	APR	1853	THERESA	WALDROM	-	infant
11	JUN	1853	MARY	MEAKIN	of Leicester	25
14	AUG	1853	JOHN	WALDROM	coroners cert	28
07	SEP	1853	THOMAS	GILBERT[MI]*	coroners cert	80
11	OCT	1853	SARAH	ASHER	-	19
13	NOV	1853	CLARA	BURTON	-	1
03	DEC	1853	THOMAS	WALE*	-	61
03	DEC	1853	ANN	ROE	-	37
17	DEC	1853	HANNAH	BRANSON	-	68
12	JAN	1854	MARY	JAMES	-	67
12	JAN	1854	JOHN CLIFFORD	HAYWOOD	-	infant
01	JAN	1854	JOHN	GREEN	-[1]	infant
07	MAR	1854	JAMES	WALDROM	-	85
29	APR	1854	GEORGE	HUTCHINSON	-	53
30	APR	1854	MARY	ROE	-	72

[1] BT & register both gave 'not inserted in regular order the incumbent absent'.

04	MAY	1854	MARY	WALDROM	-	84
18	MAY	1854	JULIA	ASHER	-	14
21	OCT	1854	SARAH ANN	SHEARYN	-	infant
08	NOV	1854	HANNAH	MEE	-	infant
01	DEC	1854	SAMUEL	JEFFCOAT	-	15 months
11	JAN	1855	JAMES	MACKIE*	-	74
13	FEB	1855	MARY ISABELLA	KELK	-	56
26	FEB	1855	MARY	QUENBY	-	42
05	MAR	1855	THOMAS	GADSBY	-	3
25	MAY	1855	FRANCIS	WRIGHT	-	1
20	JUN	1855	HENRY	MILES	-	82
27	AUG	1855	MARY ANN	HOROBIN	-	infant
31	DEC	1855	JOHN	WALDROM	-	infant
27	MAR	1856	SUSAN ANNE	LEES[MI]	-	22
28	MAR	1856	WILLIAM	PICKARD	-	82
25	SEP	1856	ANNE JESSE	PUTSEY	clergymans widow	74
31	DEC	1856	URSULA	HUTCHINSON	-	53
		1857	No Burials			
12	MAR	1858	SARAH	DARBY	of Belton	47
17	MAR	1858	JOHN THORPE	BRANSON	-	71
08	APR	1858	GEORGE	MEAKIN	-	79
09	APR	1858	WILLIAM HYDE	KELK	-	59
18	JUN	1858	ANN ELIZABETH	GILBERT	-	infant
31	OCT	1858	SARAH	HURST	-	61
01	NOV	1858	ELIZABETH	DARBY	-	29
06	NOV	1858	ELIZA	POXON	the Union	2
19	JAN	1859	JOHN	MEAKIN	-	76
12	MAR	1859	GEORGE	WRIGHT	-	3
06	APR	1859	WILLIAM	WRIGHT	-	7
09	APR	1859	SAMUEL	JEFFCOAT	-	2
30	APR	1859	WILLIAM	JEFFCOAT	-	infant
01	JUL	1859	HANNAH	HURST	-	88
17	JUL	1859	SARAH	MILLWOOD	-	35
18	JUL	1859	HARRIET	HURST	-	infant
31	JUL	1859	HANNAH	HARTSHORNE	-	infant
13	AUG	1859	ELIZA ANNIE	WARNER[MI]	-	1
14	SEP	1859	SARAH	HURST	-	27
05	DEC	1859	THOMAS	JOHNSON	-	2
03	FEB	1860	SAMUEL	HARRIS	Ashby Union Workhouse	78
17	FEB	1860	WILLIAM	BAILEY*	-	69
09	MAY	1860	MARY	WOLSEY	-	28
15	MAY	1860	THOMAS	JOHNSON*	-	73
25	MAY	1860	ELIZABETH	MOSELEY	from Leicester Infirmary	53
30	MAY	1860	THOMAS	JAMES	of Belton	79
09	JUN	1860	THERESA	WOLSEY	-	infant
18	JUN	1860	CHARLES JAMES FOX	YOUNGHUSBAND	-	63

17	JUL	1860	CHARLES	WRIGHT	-	infant
28	AUG	1860	MARY	ROE	Ashby Union Workhouse	26
08	SEP	1860	THOMAS	JOHNSON*	-	30
02	APR	1861	JOSEPH	BENNETT	-	21
24	MAY	1861	JOHN FOXTON	PATSEY	of Derby	25
07	JUN	1861	ADA	BURTON	-	infant
16	JUL	1861	ROBERT	WALDROM	'committed suicide being insane'	50
02	DEC	1861	SAMUEL	BLACK	-	67

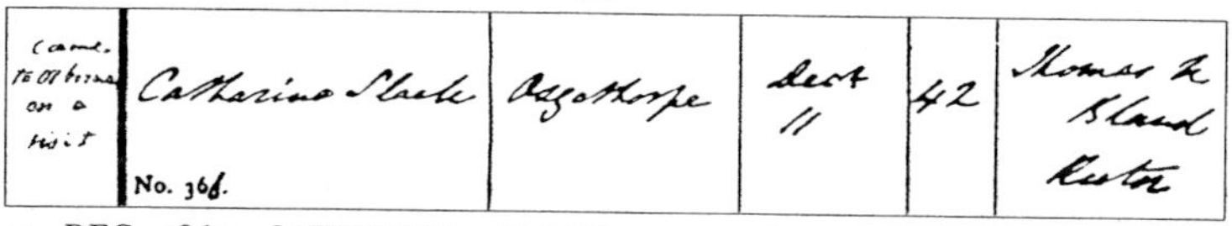

came to Osbornes on a visit	Catharine Slack No. 366.	Osgathorpe	Decr 11	42	Thomas N Bland Rector

11	DEC	1861	CATHARINE	SLACK	'came to Osbornes on a visit'	42
19	FEB	1862	GEORGE	TAYOR	-	infant
28	APR	1862	BENJAMIN	MORGAN[MI]	-	24
06	SEP	1862	WILLIAM	MOSELEY	-	81
12	NOV	1862	JOSIAH	PERRY	-	infant
15	JAN	1863	JOSEPH THOMAS	DARBY	-	5
02	MAR	1863	ELIZABETH	BLACK	-	10
06	APR	1863	LETITIA	HARRIS	Ashby de la Zouch Union Workhouse	61
15	MAY	1863	MARY	MILES[MI]	-	42
18	MAY	1863	BENJAMIN	WALDROM	Ashby de la Zouch Union Workhouse	59
27	MAY	1863	MARY	HICKINBOTTOM	-	48
02	JUN	1863	JOSEPH	BURTON	-	infant
27	JUN	1863	ELIZABETH	OSBORNE	-	72
27	JUN	1863	MARY	ROE	of Gelsmoor	84
20	NOV	1863	SARAH ANN	HORROBIN	Typhoid	7
25	NOV	1863	SARAH	BRANSON	sudden death	69
27	NOV	1863	GEORGE	PEAT*	sudden death	76
25	JAN	1864	GEORGE	OSBORNE	of Heather	75
05	FEB	1864	JOSEPH	MOORE	-	78
09	APR	1864	THOMAS	ROE	-	infant
30	APR	1864	HANNAH	BLACK	-	71
04	JUN	1864	JOHN	ASHER*	coroners order for burial	58
14	JUL	1864	HENRY	BAKER	-	2
12	OCT	1864	JAMES	SCATTERGOOD	-	74
06	DEC	1864	MARY	MILES*	-	79
20	JAN	1865	SARAH	MORGAN	-	33
12	APR	1865	SAMUEL	BRADLEY*	of Belton	85
05	AUG	1865	SARAH	ALDRIDGE	-	36
18	AUG	1865	MARY	PERRY	-	72
20	MAR	1866	JANE	GILBERT	-	44
24	MAR	1866	THOMAS NAYLOR	BLAND	Rector of this parish	59
12	APR	1866	FANNY	WARNER	-	9 months
04	AUG	1866	ELIJAH	HORROBIN	-	infant

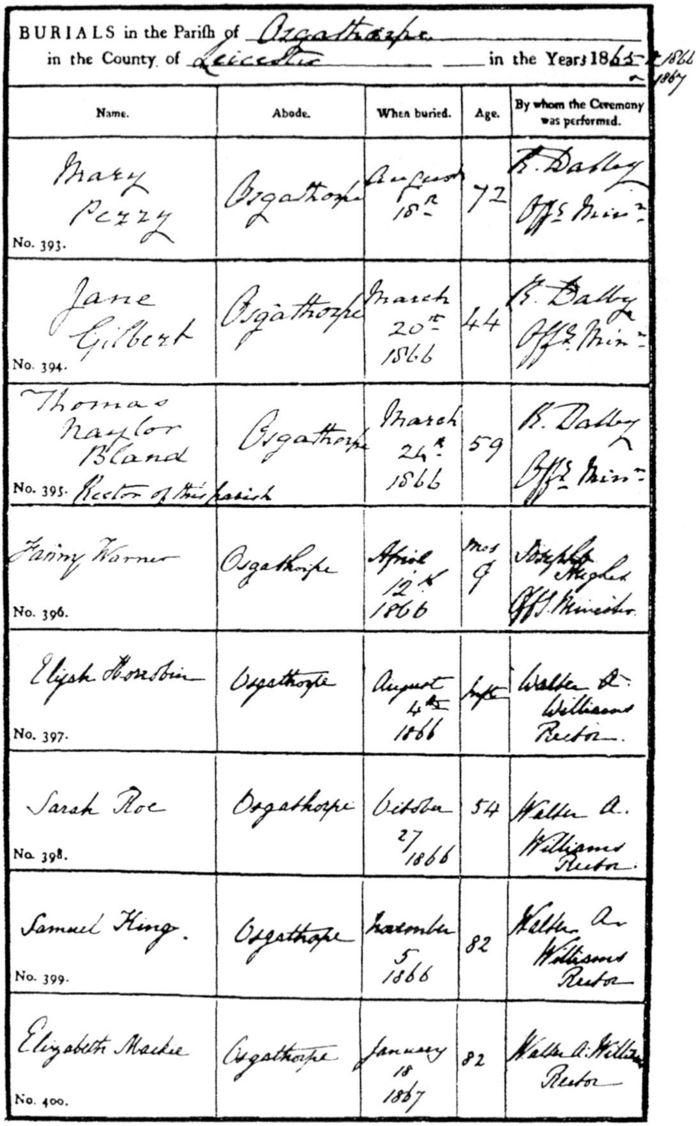

BURIALS in the Parish of Osgathorpe in the County of Leicester in the Years 1865 – 1866 – 1867

Name.	Abode.	When buried.	Age.	By whom the Ceremony was performed.
Mary Perry No. 393.	Osgathorpe	August 18th	72	R. Dalby Offg Minr
Jane Gilbert No. 394.	Osgathorpe	March 20th 1866	44	R. Dalby Offg Minr
Thomas Naylor Bland No. 395. Rector of this parish	Osgathorpe	March 24th 1866	59	R. Dalby Offg Minr
Fanny Warner No. 396.	Osgathorpe	April 12th 1866	mos 9	Joseph Hughes Offg Minister
Elijah Horsbin No. 397.	Osgathorpe	August 4th 1866	Infte	Walter A. Williams Rector
Sarah Roe No. 398.	Osgathorpe	October 27/1866	54	Walter A. Williams Rector
Samuel King. No. 399.	Osgathorpe	December 5 1866	82	Walter A. Williams Rector
Elizabeth Mackee No. 400.	Osgathorpe	January 18 1867	82	Walter A. Williams Rector

The 1813 Burial Register (1865-67)

27	OCT	1866	SARAH	ROE	-	54
05	NOV	1866	SAMUEL	KING	-	82
18	JAN	1867	ELIZABETH	MACKIE	-	82
01	APR	1867	HELEN	KING	-	22
27	AUG	1867	CATHARINE	BLACK	-	48
12	SEP	1867	JACOB	MATCHETT	Union Workhouse Ashby de la Zouch	82
11	OCT	1867	STEPHEN	BAILEY*	of Thringstone	69
12	JAN	1868	BERTHA MARY	QUENBY	-	infant
15	JAN	1868	WILLIAM	HOLLOWAY*	-	100
30	JAN	1868	MARY ELIZABETH	JOHNSON[MI]*	-	66
21	MAY	1868	SARAH	DAVENPORT	-	83
19	SEP	1868	ROBERT	YOUNG	Union Workhouse Ashby de la Zouch	62
11	JAN	1869	HENRY	RENNOCKS	-	66
08	FEB	1869	ELIZABETH	FRETTER	-	65
04	MAR	1869	SARAH	BAKER	-	32
14	MAR	1869	SARAH ANN	BAKER	-	3
09	JUN	1869	GEORGE	HICKINBOTTOM	-	54
16	OCT	1869	ELLEN	WALKER	-	4 months
24	OCT	1869	HERBERT	SMITH	-	9 months
18	NOV	1869	THEOPHILUS HENRY HASTINGS	KELK	of Newbold Worthington	72
24	NOV	1869	ESTHER	JOHNSON	-	78
29	NOV	1869	SARAH	JOHNSON	of Leicester	36
26	JAN	1870	MARY	JARVIS	-	72
02	FEB	1870	ANN	BULL	-	63
23	MAR	1870	WILLIAM	SMITH	-	72
30	APR	1870	EMILY	SMITH	-	2 weeks
24	JUL	1870	JOSEPH	DARBY	-	4 months
08	NOV	1870	GEORGE	MILES[MI]	-	58
18	APR	1871	WILLIAM MORRIS	WILLIAMS	-	3 weeks
04	AUG	1871	HARRIETT	WALKER	-	1
16	NOV	1871	JOSEPH	MEAKIN	-	57
26	NOV	1871	JAMES	WALDROM	Union Workhouse Ashby de la Zouch	74
07	JAN	1872	ELIZABETH	WHITE	-	70
11	JAN	1872	EMILY	GADSBY	-	[Blank] months
21	FEB	1872	JASON	BARNES	-	6 weeks
21	FEB	1872	MARGARET	KING	-	10 weeks
23	FEB	1872	ANN	DARBY	-	92
19	OCT	1872	CHARLES ELIJAH	BILLING	-	1 year 10 months
18	APR	1873	SAMUEL	HARTSHORNE	-	21
14	OCT	1873	SAMUEL	JARVIS	-	77
07	APR	1874	WILLIAM	KING	-	21
17	DEC[1]	1873	WILLIAM	UPTON	-	infant
30	JUN	1874	MARY	BLACK	-	18
06	JUL	1874	MARY	AULT*	-	77

[1] Out of chronological order in register.

17	AUG	1874	JOHN WILLIAM	ROWE	-	10 months
30	SEP	1874	WILLIAM WILSON	STATHAM	-	5 weeks
30	OCT	1874	JANE ELIZABETH	HALLAM	-	5 weeks
15	DEC	1874	MARY ANN	RENNOCKS	of Breedon	73
24	DEC	1874	HANNAH	DARBY	-	1 day
25	JAN	1875	HANNAH	PEAT	-	86
18	FEB	1875	JOHN	KING	-	82
19	FEB	1875	WILLIAM	BRADLEY	-	81
26	MAR	1875	WILLIAM	BAXTER	-	2 yrs 5 months
15	APR	1875	ELIZABETH	WALE	-	83
15	MAY	1875	WILLIAM	DAVENPORT	-	83
14	JUN	1875	HENRY	BURTON	-	9 months
14	JUN	1875	HARRIETT	BURTON	-	2
22	JUN	1875	GEORGE	KING	-	1
17	JUL	1875	WILLIAM	MEDLEY[MI]	of Derby	[Blank] years [49[MI]]
18	AUG	1875	GEORGE	JOHNSON[MI]*	-	23
22	DEC	1875	ELLEN	DARBY	-	28
17	JAN	1876	JANE	YOUNGHUSBAND[MI]*	-	68
21	FEB	1876	LYDIA	SMITH	-	83
19	APR	1876	JOSEPH	MOSELEY[MI]*	-	70
09	MAY	1876	BENJAMIN	MORGAN	-	66
17	JUN	1876	THOMAS	UPTON	-	infant
03	JAN	1877	HARRIETT	DARBY	Union Workhouse Ashby de la Zouch	69
04	JAN	1877	LOT	QUENBY	-	64
11	APR	1877	JOSIAH	BRANSON	-	83
30	JUN	1877	JOHN WRIGHT	BRANSON[MI]*	-	68
04	JUL	1877	ELIZABETH	HANDFORD	of Loughborough	77
11	FEB	1878	JOSEPH	KING	-	80
04	DEC	1878	CHARLES EDWIN	WARNER*	-	55
08	JAN	1879	ANNE	HUTCHINSON*	-	77
05	FEB	1879	WILLIAM	BAKER	-	26
25	FEB	1879	KATE	RICHARDS	-	7 months
05	MAR	1879	JOSEPH	HARTSHORN	-	2
28	AUG	1879	WILLIAM	ROE	-	72
05	NOV	1879	ISABELLA	BARNES	of Whitwick	5 weeks
10	DEC	1879	MARY	KING	-	66
05	JUN	1880	ADALINE	SMITH[MI]	-	22
03	NOV	1880	ANN	BENNETT	-	72
12	JAN	1881	HANNAH	GILBERT	-	46
01	JUN	1881	JOHN	JARVIS	Union Workhouse Ashby de la Zouch	58
27	AUG	1881	SELINA MORSE	WILLIAMS*	-	45
29	SEP	1881	FAITH	RICHARDS	-	10 hours
22	DEC	1881	MARY	BROOKS	-	7 months
05	JAN	1882	ELIZABETH	DEXTER	-	82
17	FEB	1882	AMOS	BILLING	-	16 months
11	JUL	1882	FANNY	GRIMLEY	-	5 months

23	OCT	1882	ANN	GADSBY	-	55
29	AUG	1883	CHARLES WILLIAM	RICHARDS	-	11 months
26	OCT	1883	EDWARD	KING	-	84
15	DEC	1883	EDWARD	MATCHETT	-	10 weeks
23	DEC	1883	WILLIAM	STATHAM	-	76
26	DEC	1883	MARY	MOSELEY*	-	73
13	FEB	1884	JAMES	ROE	-	80
29	MAR	1884	THOMAS	GILBERT*	of Merrill Grange, Belton	78
03	APR	1884	ALBERT	JARVIS	-	12 weeks
14	JUN	1884	LOUISA	RICHARDS	-	1 day
04	SEP	1884	ELIJAH	DARBY	-	3 months
20	OCT	1884	ELIZABETH	KING	-	63
29	OCT	1884	THOMAS JAMES	JOHNSON*	-	23
10	DEC	1884	JOHN	MATCHETT	-	64
27	DEC	1884	HARRIETT	GILBERT	of Breedon on the Hill	81
08	JAN	1885	JOHN	SMITH	-	56
24	JAN	1885	ANGELUS	BARNES	of Whitwick	4½ months
30	APR	1885	WILLIAM	WARDLE	-	77
01	MAY	1885	MATILDA	KING[MI]	-	65
29	MAY	1885	JOHN HENRY	PERRY	-	7 days
21	JUL	1885	MARY ANN	JARVIS	-	29
30	JUL	1885	JOSEPH	HURST	of Coalville	88
18	AUG	1885	ELLEN	GILBERT	of Breedon on the Hill	45
11	JUN	1886	ADA	PARKER	-	9
16	JUN	1886	WILLIAM	EDWARDS	-	63
04	AUG	1886	THOMAS	DARBY	of Belton	38
30	NOV	1886	FANNY	DAVENPORT	-	52
18	APR	1887	WILLIAM	TANSER*	-	68
11	OCT	1887	MARY	STATHAM	-	80
15	OCT	1887	GEORGE	DARBY	-	5 hours
07	JAN	1888	CHARLOTTE	BURTON	-	66
20	JUN	1888	SAMUEL	DEXTER	Union Workhouse Ashby de la Zouch	77
09	JUL	1888	JOHN THOMAS	BAKER	-	1 day
16	NOV	1888	JOSEPH	SIDDONS[MI]	-	78
15	JAN	1889	JOSEPH	MACKIE[MI]*	-	76
16	FEB	1889	FLORENCE	BARNES	of Whitwick	2
18	FEB	1889	JOHN	ROE[MI]*	-	75
06	JUN	1889	MARY	KING	Union Workhouse Ashby de la Zouch	89
28	AUG	1889	JOHN	DARBY	Union Workhouse Ashby de la Zouch	81
17	NOV	1889	RUDOLPH	ALLARD		31 days
02	DEC	1889	JOSEPH	BURTON	-	69
25	APR	1890	JOHN	BENNETT	Union Workhouse Ashby de la Zouch	85
27	SEP	1890	JOHN	SMITH[MI]	-	61
11	MAR	1891	ELIZABETH	WARDLE	-	78
14	MAR	1891	ELIZA	YOUNG[MI]*	-	71

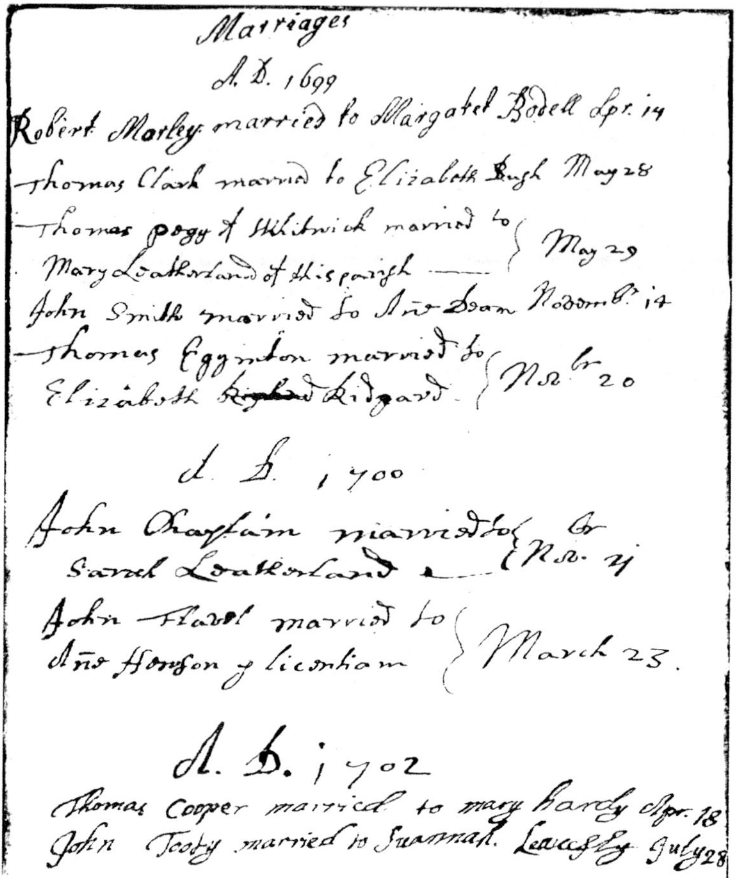

Marriages

A. D. 1699

Robert Morley married to Margaret Bodell Apr. 14

Thomas Clark married to Elizabeth Hugh May 28

Thomas Pogy of Whitwick married to
Mary Leatherland of this parish } May 29

John Smith married to Ane Dean Novemb. 14

Thomas Eggington married to
Elizabeth Ridgard } Nov. 20

A. D. 1700

John Chapman married to
Sarah Leatherland } Nov. 4

John Flavel married to
Ane Howson p licentiam } March 23.

A. D. 1702

Thomas Cooper married to mary hardy Apr. 18

John Tooty married to Susannah Leavesley July 28

The Marriage Section of the Parish Register 1699–1702

Note the marriage of John Flavel & Ane Hewson [Howson] on the 23 March 1700 was by *licentiam* [licence]. The records relating to licence marriages, which frequently gave information not recorded in either the parish registers or bishop's transcripts have been incorporated into this book.

7. MARRIAGES 1583 – 1891

The method by which a marriage took place was often recorded in the registers and these have been abbreviated to (Bs) = Banns, (Lic) = Licence and where no indication was given than a dash (-) has been inserted. These latter marriages were almost certainly by banns, as no licence allegations appear to exist.[1] If a licence allegation exists but was *not* indicated in the register or bishop's transcript, then (-Lic) has been used. The reader should note that information has been incorporated from all known allegations and their accompanying bonds, which frequently gave details not recorded in either the registers or bishop's transcripts. (See chapter 3 Marriage at Osgathorpe)

[1583–1679]	[This period has been transcribed from the surviving bishop's transcripts]		
1583–1584	No Marriages		
1585–1603	[No BTs]		
1604	No Marriages		
1605	[No BT]		
15 JUN 1606	RICHARD	BARTON	-
(-)	ISABELL	ADCOCKE	-
24 NOV 1606	WILLM	POULSON	-
(-)	ELEN	ROBYNS	-
1607	No Marriages		
23 NOV 1608	THOMAS	HALL	-
(-)	ELIZABETH	COOPER	-
06 FEB 1608	WILLIAM	HEELE	-
(-)	JUDITH	ROBYNS	-
1609	No Marriages		
1610–1611	[No BTs]		
1611	[WILLIAM]	[SHEPPARD]	[of Whitweeke. Blacksmith]
(-Lic) [2]	[SUSANNA]	[STEWARD]	[of Osgathorpe]
1612	No Marriages		

[1] Licence allegations were given by the groom, on oath, that there was no just impediment or other lawful hindrance to prevent a marriage by licence taking place.

[2] The BT for 1611 has not survived, however, a marriage licence was recorded in the licence index register (L.R.O.) dated 6 August 1611. Although a designated place of marriage was not stated, it is possible that the marriage took place at Osgathorpe, as it was *not* recorded in Whitwick's surviving parish register. Bond surety – Peter Sare, Sheppard of Glenfield.

		1613	[No BT]		
		1614	No Marriages		
		1615–1616	[No BTs]		
10	NOV	1617	WILLIAM	?GLEESE	-
(-)			MARGERIE	TOMLINSON	-
11	NOV	1617	WILLIAM	PICKERIN	-
(-)			ANNE	PARSONS	-
		1618–1620	[No BTs]		
		1621	No Marriages		
		1622–1624	[No BTs]		
20	FEB	1625	WILLIAM	ROBINS	-
(-)			JANE	ROSELL	-
02	OCT	1626	WILLIAM	BANCROFT	-
(-)			REBECCA	ERRINGTON	-
		1627–1630	No Marriages		
		1631	[No BT]		
		1632	No Marriages		
17	FEB	1633	HAMLET	DAKINS	-
(-)			ANNA	MARSHALL	-
14	OCT	1634	JOHN	GIBSON	of Bagworth
(-)			ELIZABETH	PARSONS	-
18	NOV	1634	PETER	SEALE	of Norton
(-)			ELIZABETH	ADCOCKE	-
		1635	[No BT]		
09	FEB	1636	ROBERT	ARME	Weaver
(-)			MILLICENT	TOE	of Belton
13	FEB	1636	WILLIAM	BROWNE	Yeoman
(-)			SARAH	SMITH	of Whatton
		1637–1639	No Marriages		
		[1640–1668]	[No BTs for the Civil War & Commonwealth period]		
		1669–1672	No Marriages		
23	NOV	1673	ABRAHAM	ADCOCK	-
(-)			ELIZABETH	GREENE	-
		1674–1675	No Marriages		
02	FEB	+1676	JOHN	FULGIUM	-
(-)		[1]	MARY	HATHAWAY	-
19	JAN	+1677	GEORGE RIDYARD alias JARUAS		-
(-)			ELIZABETH	JOYNES	widow
22	MAY	1676	EDWARD	BELTON	s./ Alice Belton. widow
(-)		[2]	ANNE	DOEL	-

[1] This & the following entry, marked with a plus sign+, appear to be dated using the 1 January as the beginning of the year and not Lady Day (25 March). This undoubtedly persisted from the Commonwealth period, when 1 January was the official start of the year.
[2] Out of chronological order on BT.

02 OCT 1676	WILLIAM	BELTON	s./ Alice Belton. widow
(-) [1]	widow	WOOD	-
20 NOV 1677	JAMES	WILLOWES	-
(-)	ELIZABETH	NORTH	-
28 MAY 1678	HENRY	PRESBURY	-
(-)	MARY	WRIGHTMAN	-
23 OCT 1678	THOMAS	GREENE	-
(-)	ANNE	JACKSON	-

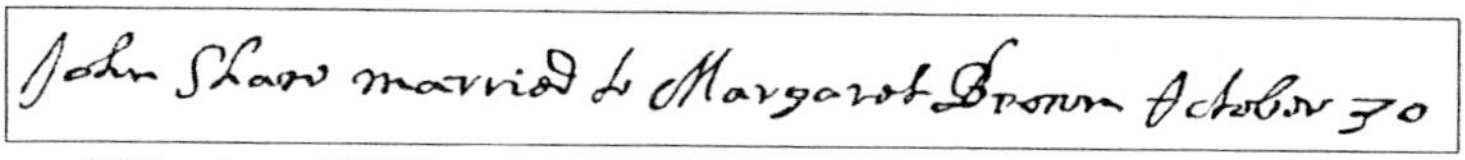
John Shaw married to Margaret Brown October 30

30 OCT 1679	JOHN	SHAW	-
(-Lic)	MARGARET	BROWN	-
	[The oldest surviving register starts in 1680]		
1680–1682	No Marriages		
12 AUG 1683	JAMES	RIDGEWAY	of Shepshead
(Lic)	MARY	BETTES	of same parish
08 NOV 1683	JOHN Esq.	BAINBRIGGE	of Lockington
(Lic) [2]	MARY	HARLEY	of this parish
12 DEC 1683	WILLM	ROE	of Ansty
(Lic)	ELIZABETH	COULTON	of Osgathorpe
12 DEC 1683	JOSEPH	WHITE	of Syston
(Lic)	DOROTHY	KIDDGER	of Osgathorpe
1684	No Marriages		
09 NOV 1685	JOHN	LOWE	of Barleston
(-)	ELLEN	BAILY	of this parish
17 JAN 1685	WILLIAM	DAKIN	of Belton
(Lic)	ANE	ABOTT	of Hemington
10 APR 1686	WILLIAM	MONTENEY	of Newbold
(Lic)	ANE	COULTON	of this parish
15 APR 1686	ABRAHAM	BATES	of Thringston
(Lic)	SUSANA	SLEATH	of this parish
29 JUN 1687	THOMAS	HOGKINS	of East Leeke, Notts
(-)	SARAH	MILNES	of this parish
03 JUL 1688	THOMAS	GREEN	of this parish
(-)	ANE	LACY	of Worthington
06 NOV 1689	WILLIAM	HEATHERLEY	-
(-)	ANE	ORTON	-
07 OCT 1690	WILLIAM	SMITH	of Thringstone
(-)	MARY	CLARKE	of this town
09 FEB 1691	JOHN	KNIGHT	of Whitwick
(-)	MARY	GOODMAN	of same parish

---

[1] Out of chronological order on BT.

[2] Register also gave 'only daur & heires of Thomas Harley citizon of London & founder of ye free school & hospital new built'.

21 APR	1692	THOMAS	AVERY	of Picwell
(-Lic)	[1]	DOROTHY	ROBINS	of pa. [torn], Leics
02 JUN	1692	CHARNELL	MEADE	of Narborough. widdower. Gent
(-Lic)	[2]	MARGARET	PALMER	of Osgathorp
02 DEC	1693	THOMAS	ORTON	-
(-)		MARY	NORTH	-
	1694	No Marriages		
06 JUN	1695	EDWARD	WILLSON	-
(-)		ELIZABETH	MEAD	-
06 JUN	1695	GEORGE	COULTON	-
(-)		MARY	SHIPLING	-
02 SEP	1695	THOMAS	SIMPKIN	-
(-)		MARY	STORER	-
01 NOV	1696	JOHN	SWAINE	-
(-)	[3]	BRIDGETT	LEATHERLAND	-
14 JAN	1696	WILLIAM	KIDDYER	-
(Lic)	[4]	DOROTHY	HENINGHAM	-
18 APR	1697	THOMAS	SHAW	-
(-)		ELLEN	HALL	-
	1698	No Marriages		
17 APR	1699	ROBERT	MORLEY (35)	of Osgathorpe
(-Lic)	[5]	MARGARET	BODELL (25)	-
28 MAY	1699	THOMAS	CLARK	-
(-)		ELIZABETH	BUSH	-
29 MAY	1699	THOMAS	PEGG	of Whitwick
(-)		MARY	LEATHERLAND	of this parish
14 NOV	1699	JOHN	SMITH	-
(-)		ANE	DEAN	-
20 NOV	1699	THOMAS	EGGINGTON	-
(-)		ELIZABETH	RIDGARD	-
11 NOV	1700	JOHN	CHAPLAIN	-
(-)		SARAH	LEATHERLAND	-
23 MAR	1700	JOHN	FLAVEL (27)	of Leicester. Blacksmith
(Lic)	[6]	ANE	HEWSON (-)	of Charley, Loughborough
	1701	No Marriages		
18 APR	1702	THOMAS	COOPER	-
(-)		MARY	HARDY	-
28 JUL	1702	JOHN	TOOTY	-
(-)		SUSANNA	LEAVESLY	-

[1] Bond surety – Samuel Martin, Woolin Draper of Leicester. Torn part probably - Osgathorpe.
[2] Bond surety – John Unwin, Clerk of Cosby.
[3] Register also gave 'married by Mr. S.' [probably Mr Cornelius Smedley, Schoolmaster & Clergyman]
[4] Licence was missing in the few that have survived for 1696.
[5] Bond surety – Thomas Mellowes, Gardener of Stanton, Leics.
[6] Bond surety – Thomas Howson, ?Basket maker of Charley. Licence gave ANE HOWSON.

Day	Month	Year	Forename	Surname	Remarks
07	SEP	1703	THOMAS	WOOTTON	-
(-)			MARY	SORES	-
03	DEC	1703	RICHARD	NORTON	-
(-)			FRANCES	WIGHTMAN	-
08	OCT	1704	THOMAS	TUGBY	-
(-)			MARGARET	SHAW	-
06	JUL	1705	JOSHUA	BAILY	-
(-)			CATHERINE	GREEN	-

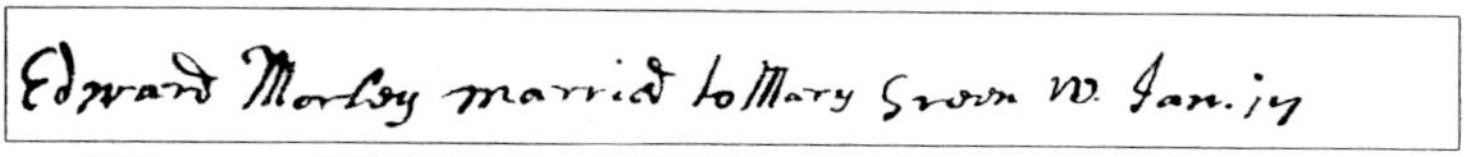
Edward Morley married to Mary Green W. Jan. 17

Day	Month	Year	Forename	Surname	Remarks
17	JAN	1705	EDWARD	MORLEY	-
(-)			MARY	GREEN	wid
01	APR	1706	THOMAS	GILBERT	-
(-)			ELIZABETH	MEE	-
14	APR	1707	JOHN	HUSKINSON (25)	of Osgathorpe
(-Lic)		[1]	MARY	WHITELOCKES (25)	of Osgathorpe
24	NOV	1707	THOMAS	HAYFIELD	-
(-)			MARY	BELTON	-
13	APR	1708	HENRY	TOWNSEND	-
(-)			DOROTHY	POXEN	-
04	MAY	1708	JOHN	HOW	-
(-)			ELIZABETH	GODARD	-
		1709	No Marriages		
13	MAY	1710	THOMAS	ALLESTREE (23)	of Alveston, Derbys. Gen[tleman]
(-Lic)		[2]	MARY	HARLEY (24)	of Osgathorpe
07	OCT	1710	THOMAS	GIBSON	of Groby in ye pa. of Ratby
(-)			MARY	BOYER	of the parish
30	APR	1711	THOMAS	BELTON	-
(-)			MARY	MUGLESTON	-
01	MAY	1711	GEORGE	HALL	-
(-)			MARY	GILBERT	-
14	OCT	1711	THOMAS	GILBERT	-
(-)			ANN	ALLWOOD	-
26	JAN	1712	WILLIAM	HAYS	-
(-)			ELIZABETH	HALL	-
13	APR	1713	MATTHEW	BRUGESS	-
(-)			ANNE	WOOTTON	-
		1714	No Marriages		
13	JAN	1715	HENRY	SHARP	-
( )			MARTHA	AUWOOD	-
24	JAN	1715	THOMAS	PEIRSON	-
(-)			SARAH	BELTON	-

1 Bond surety – George Coulton of Evington & Edrw. Biddle, Blacksmith of Leicester.

2 Bond surety – [Groom; only named surety].

22 APR	1716	HENRY	PALMER	-
(-)		ELIZ	ENDSOR	-
05 NOV	1716	JOHN	TOWNSEND	-
(-)		REBECKAH	LEAVESLY	-
05 MAR	1716	GEORGE	ROE	-
(-)		ANE	NORTH	-
	1717	No Marriages		
09 JUN	1718	CHARLES	GILBERT	of Castle Donington
(-Lic)	[1]	MARY	WALTON	of same
03 SEP	1718	WILLIAM	SIMPSON	of Loughborough
(-Lic)	[2]	DOROTHY	KILBURN	of same
08 SEP	1718	JOHN	BRACE	of St Martins, Leicester
(-Lic)	[3]	ELIZABETH	SHUNBURGH	of Loughborough
06 OCT	1718	ROBERT	BRADFORD	-
(-)		MARY	HALL	-
25 NOV	1718	THOMAS	GRIFFIN	-
(-)		ELIZABETH	SMITH	-
26 NOV	1718	JOHN	MOOR	of Thringston
(-Lic)	[4]	MARY	GRUNDY	of same
30 DEC	1718	JOHN	BRADLEY	-
(-)		CATHARINE	NORTH	-
02 JAN	1718	ROBERT	ROBINSON	of Whittwick
(-Lic)		JANE	PHEASANT	of Bredon
16 FEB	1718	RICHARD	WARD	of Burbidge
(-Lic)	[5]	ALICE	BROWN	of Swadlincote, Derbys
26 MAY	1719	WILLIAM	BABINGTON	of Rodeley. Clerk
(-Lic)	[6]	ELIZABETH	PORT	of Cussington
29 JUN	1719	EDWARD	RAGG	-
(-)		ELIZABETH	WHITWORTH	-
30 JUL	1719	WILLIAM	HURST	of Loughborough
(-Lic)	[7]	ALATHEA	ACKOLOM	of Holwell
07 OCT	1719	THOMAS	PIERCEFULL	of Worthington
(-Lic)	[8]	MARY	WRIGHT	of Worthington
19 APR	1720	JOHN	MARTIN	of Hemington
(-Lic)	[9]	ELIZABETH	ABBOT	of same

[1] Bond surety – William Rose of Castle Donington & John Stinson of Osgathorp.
[2] Bond surety – Thomas Foster & William Kilburn, both of Loughborough.
[3] Bond surety – John Burrows of Loughborough & John Farrow.
[4] Bond surety – William Avines of Thringston.
[5] Bond surety – William Dalby of Worthington.
[6] Bond surety – John Port of Cussington.
[7] Bond surety – William Cant of Loughborough.
[8] Bond surety – Daniel Wright of Worthington & Thomas Shaw of Osgathorpe.
[9] Bond surety – Thomas Martin & Thomas Bramley of Castle Donington.

24 APR 1720		WILLIAM	WRIGHT	of Appleby
(-Lic)	[1]	SUSANNAH	BURROWS	of Coleorton
12 JUN 1720		NICHOLAS	KIDDIER	-
(-)		MARY	BOULTBEE	-
21 JUL 1720		JOHN	MARTIN	of Ashby de la Zouch
(-Lic)	[2]	SARAH	TOON	of Ashby de la Zouch
08 AUG 1720		WILLIAM	NORTH	of Alfreton, Derbys
(-Lic)	[3]	JANE	PEGG	of Osgathorp

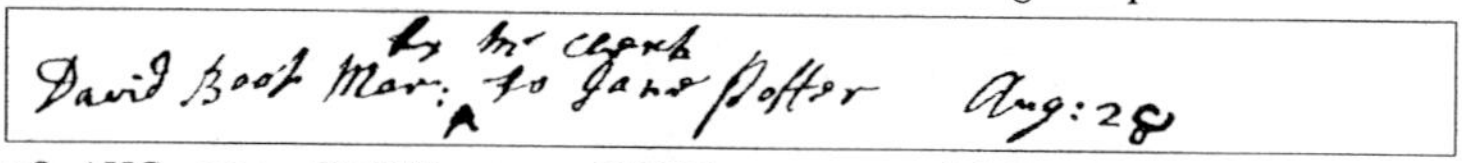
David Boot Mar: by Mr Clerk to Jane Potter Aug: 28

28 AUG 1720		DAVID	BOOT	of Coleorton
(-Lic)	[4]	JANE	POTTER	of ye same
25 NOV 1720		GEORGE	HICKINBOTTOM	of Diesworth. Carpenter
(-Lic)	[5]	MARTHA	SPARKS	of Breedon
19 FEB 1720		WILLIAM	ELVISON	of Thringston
(Lic)	[6]	JONE	ENDSWORTH	of Bredon
03 MAR 1720		RICHARD	NEWTON	of Ashby de la Zouch
(-Lic)	[7]	ELIZABETH	PRINSOP	of same
14 APR 1721		WILLIAM	GREGORY	of Whitwick
(-Lic)	[8]	ELLEN	HOOD	of Whitwick
15 APR 1721		THOMAS	UPTON	of Diesworth
(-Lic)	[9]	MARY	HICKINBOTTOM	of same
22 APR 1721		THOMAS	SIMNETT	of Ashby Old Parks
(-Lic)	[10]	ELIZABETH	MARSHALL	of Blackforby
24 APR 1721		JOSEPH	OLDERSHAW	of Diesworth
(-Lic)	[11]	ANNE	UNDERWOOD	of same
15 MAY 1721		NICHOLAS	PALMER	of Swepston. Shoemaker
(-Lic)	[12]	LYDDIA	LUDFORD	of Twicross

[1] Bond surety – Richard Wright of Osgathorpe.
[2] Bond surety – Nathanil Roberts of Smisby, Derbys.
[3] Bond surety – William Mugleston.
[4] Bond surety – James Toon of Thringston. Register also gave 'married by Mr [Charles] Clerk'.
[5] Bond surety – John Steward of Diseworth & Hugh Brooks of Breedon.
[6] Bond surety – John Cox of Thringston.
[7] Bond surety – Joseph Robinson of Ashby de la Zouch.
[8] Bond surety – Edmund Gregory of Saxilby. Register also gave 'married by Mr [Charles] Clerke'. The marriage was also recorded in the Whitwick register, the couples 'home' parish. A practice that was not uncommon, as parish registers were legal documents and could be produced in legitimacy & inheritance cases. The licence, which was issued at Osgathorpe the probable place of the ceremony, stated that the marriage could be performed at either church.
[9] Bond surety – Thomas Belton of Osgathorp.
[10] Bond surety – John Baily of Blackforby.
[11] Bond surety – Joseph Darby of Donnington Grange.
[12] Bond surety – Thomas Belton of Osgathorp.

30 MAY 1721	THOMAS	PIERCESON	of Osgathorp
(-Lic) [1]	ANNE	BLOCKLEY	of Whitwick
16 NOV 1721	JOHN	BOSWORTH	of Diesworth
(-Lic) [2]	FRANCES	WALKER	of Swannington
31 MAR 1722	JOHN	GARNER	-
(-)	MARY	WALKER	-
03 MAY 1722	THOMAS	BALL	of Norton
(-Lic) [3]	ALICE	WALLPLATE	of Norton

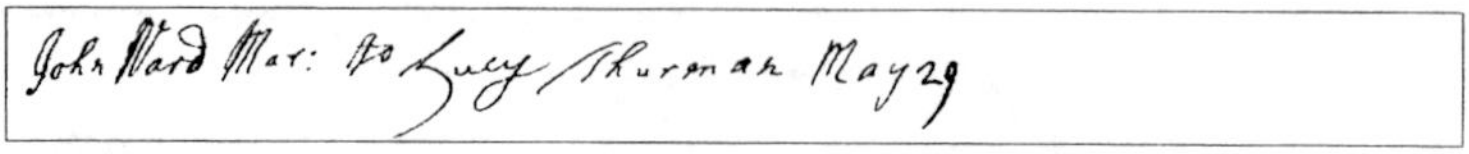
John Ward Mar: to Lucy Thurman May 29

29 MAY 1722	JOHN	WARD	of Markfield
(-Lic) [4]	LUCY	THURMAN	of Belton
12 AUG 1722	WILLIAM	RATFORD	-
(-) [5]	SARAH	POKER	-
26 NOV 1722	EDWARD	PEAT	-
(-)	KATHARINE	RAGG	-
26 FEB 1722	ISAAC	HENTON	-
(-)	MARY	SWAINE	-
07 MAY 1723	RICHARD	FOULKS	of Rodely
(-Lic) [6]	DOROTHY	FUKES	of same
02 JUN 1723	ROBERT	NEWBOLD	of Isley Walton
(-Lic) [7]	ELIZABETH	WRIGHT	of same
10 JUN 1723	THOMAS	FUKES	of Worthington
(-Lic) [8]	MARY	SIMS	of Loughborough
30 OCT 1723	CHARLES	VARNHAM	of Coleorton
(-Lic) [9]	ELIZABETH	RICHARDS	of Bredon
03 NOV 1723	THOMAS	PARSONS	-
(-)	ELIZABETH	CORBET	-
29 NOV 1723	EDWARD	PARSONS	of Hatherne
(-Lic) [10]	CHRISTIANA	ALLESTREE	of Belton
06 JAN 1723	GEORGE	BARKER	of Castle Donnington
(-Lic) [11]	MARY	BUCKNAL	of same

[1] Bond surety – George Hall of Osgathorpe. BT gave 20 January, but licence was dated 30 January.
[2] Bond surety – William Bosworth of Hemmington.
[3] Bond surety – John Hutchinson of Ashby de la Zouch.
[4] Bond surety – John Thurman of Belton.
[5] Register also gave '*?pso* Mr Clerk' [?performed [by] Mr Clerk].
[6] Bond surety – John Horton of ?Rodely.
[7] Bond surety – Joseph ?Belby of Isley Walton.
[8] Bond surety – Edward Fuekes of Quardon.
[9] Bond surety – George Hall of Osgathorp.
[10] Bond surety – John Leaersly of Belton.
[11] Bond surety – Thomas Shaw of Osgathorp.

05 JUL	1724	JOHN	KELLAM	of Ratby
(-Lic)	[1]	ANNE	PARKER	of Markfield
28 JUL	1724	JOHN	WARD	of Markfield
(-Lic)	[2]	ESTHER	HOLT	of same
31 DEC	1724	JOHN	LUDFORD	-
(-)		MARY	FOUKES	-
31 DEC	1724	BRIAN	STEEL	of Battle Flat in pa. of Thorneton
(-Lic)	[3]	ANNE	HICKLIN	of Bredon Lodge
30 JAN	1724	JOHN	CUMBERLAND	of Hatherne
(-Lic)	[4]	MARY	TWELVES	of same
01 JUN	1725	WILLIAM	MANSFIELD	of Coleorton
(-Lic)	[5]	CATHARINE	ARNOLD	of Thringston
10 JUN	1725	JAMES	WILKINS	of Ashby de la Zouch. Husbandman
(-Lic)	[6]	ELIZABETH	UNWIN	of Osgathorpe
24 OCT	1725	JOHN	WITE	-
(-)		ANNE	TOMLINSON	-
13 DEC	1725	EMMANUEL	JOHNSON	of Leicester
(-Lic)	[7]	ELIZABETH	TATE	of Loughborough
18 JAN	1725	FRANCIS	HARDEY	-
(-)		ELIZABETH	HACKET	-
19 MAY	1726	THOMAS	GOFF	of Kegworth
(-Lic)	[8]	ANNE	WILNER	of same
30 MAY	1726	THOMAS	WALLET	of Coleorton
(-Lic)	[9]	ANNE	TAYLOR	of same
27 JUN	1726	JOHN	TEBBUTT	of Kingston, Notts
(-Lic)	[10]	MARY	STANFORD	of Lockington
31 JUL	1726	WILLIAM	LESTER	of Long Whatton
(-Lic)	[11]	GRACE	MARSHALL	of same
30 DEC	1726	RICHARD	SIPLES	of Ratcliff, Notts
(-Lic)	[12]	HANNAH	JAQUES	of Isley Walton
01 FEB	1726	JOHN	BODLE	of Ashby de le Zouch
(-Lic)	[13]	HANNAH	BAILY	of same

[1] Bond surety – Thomas Hart of Markfield.
[2] Bond surety – Thomas Shaw of Osgathorpe.
[3] Bond surety – John Hemsley of Osgathorpe.
[4] Bond surety – John Twellves of Hatherne.
[5] Bond surety – William Cooper of Thringston.
[6] Bond surety – Richard Bannister of Ashby de la Zouch.
[7] Bond surety – William Tate of Loughborough.
[8] Bond surety – John Ramsdon of Kegworth.
[9] Bond surety – Henry Baily of Coleorton.
[10] Bond surety – Thomas Selvester of Osgathrop.
[11] Bond surety – William Kirk of Long Whatton.
[12] Bond surety – John Jaques of Isley Walton.
[13] Bond surety – John Pye of Repton, Derbys. Licence gave BODELL.

12 FEB	1726	PETER	WRIGHT	of Ashby de la Zouch	
(-Lic)	[1]	MARY	KEY	of same	
27 FEB	1726	JOSEPH	SHARMAN	of Swepston	
(-Lic)	[2]	MARY	PYE	of Ashby	
26 MAR	1727	JOHN	ASPERY	of Osgathorp	
(-Lic)	[3]	MARY	TOMLINSON	of Whitwick	
06 MAY	1727	JAMES	HALL	-	
(-)		ANNE	PLATS	-	
16 MAY	1727	THOMAS	THORNTON	of Anstrey, Warks	
(-Lic)	[4]	ELIZABETH	GREEN	of Norton	
09 OCT	1727	JOHN	BAILY	-	
(-)		MARY	FERBINS	-	
05 NOV	1727	WILLIAM	GIBSON	-	
(-)		SUSANNAH	HALL	-	
16 NOV	1727	ANTHONY	PLOWRIGHT	of Long Whatton	
(-Lic)	[5]	MARY	KILBOURNE	of Osgathorp	
14 MAY	1728	JOHN	FARMER	of Ashby de la Zouch	
(-Lic)	[6]	ELIZABETH	BLINCON	of same	
21 MAY	1728	BARTHOLOMEW	FIELDING	of Shepeshead	
(-Lic)	[7]	ANNE	SPENCER	of Normanton, Derby	
09 JUN	1728	RICHARD	BAILY	of Worthington	
(-Lic)	[8]	BENEMIAH	SHARP	of same	
13 JUN	1728	EDWARD	ORRILL	of Burton Hastings, Warks	
(-Lic)	[9]	ANNE	CHOICE	of Packington	
26 AUG	1728	JOHN	CARVER	of Cork, Derbys	
(-Lic)	[10]	SUSANNAH	HOWITT	of Ashby de la Zouch	
21 SEP	1728	GEORGE	CHAPMAN	of Ulscroft	
(-Lic)	[11]	MARY	WATKIN	of same	
01 OCT	1729	NICOLAS	BUCKERFIELD	-	
(Bs)		ELIZABETH	BOSS	-	
21 OCT	1729	WILLIAM	FOSTER	of Dyseworth	Husbandman
(Lic)	[12]	SARAH	PRAT	of Coleorton	

[1] Bond surety – Richard Ridgeway of Ashby de la Zouch.
[2] Bond surety – John Pye of Repton, Derbys.
[3] Bond surety – John Garner of Diesworth.
[4] Bond surety – Joseph Sharman of Swepston. Anstrey = Austrey, where their first child was baptised.
[5] Bond surety – John Hemsley of Osgathrop.
[6] Bond surety – John Tatenell of Osgathorp. Licence gave BLINCORN.
[7] Bond surety – John Hemsley of Osgathrope.
[8] Bond surety – John Boultbee of Swanington.
[9] Bond surety – Robert Bostock of Packington.
[10] Bond surety – Thomas Shaw of Osgathorpe.
[11] Bond surety – Dimmack Gee of Osgathorp.
[12] Bond surety – Joseph Foster of Dyseworth. Register gave FORSTER; BT FOSTER; Licence & signature gave FISHER.

20 NOV	1729	JOHN	NORTH	of Thrinkstone in pa. Whitwick	Husbandman
(Lic)	[1]	SARAH	MUCKLESTONE	of Osgathorp	
01 SEP	1730	RICHARD	CHISWELL	of Swepson. widower	Gentleman
(Lic)	[2]	MARTHA	POUGHFER	of Leicester	
14 NOV	1730	JOHN	JENNINGS	of Staunton in pa. Breedon	Servant
(Lic)	[3]	MARY	SUTTON	of Donnington	
01 APR	1731	THOMAS	SLEATH	of Dunton Basset	-
(Lic)	[4]	ELIZABETH	BOULTBEE	of Osgathorp	
15 JUL	1731	JOHN	EAMES	of Osbaldistone	Servant
(Lic)	[5]	ALICE	GERY	of Markeaton, Derbys	
21 SEP	1731	SIMON	RICHARDS	-	-
(Bs)		MARY	BADHAM	of ye parish	
09 NOV	1731	WILLIAM	PAGE (29)	of Whitwyck	-
(Lic)	[6]	MARY	BULL (28)	of Whitwyck	
26 DEC	1731	JOS	BANCROFT	of Ashby de la Zouch	-
(Bs)		ELIZ	MORLY	of Osg	
17 FEB	1731	JOHN	HITCHINS (30)	of Appleby	Weaver
(Lic)	[7]	SUSANNAH	KING (22)	of Appleby	
29 MAY	1732	NICOLAS	ORT	of Coleorton	-
(Bs)		ELIZ	WRIGHT	of Osgathorp	
22 SEP	1732	EDMUND	BROOKES (28)	of Belton	Gentleman
(Lic)	[8]	ELIZABETH	PRAT (34)	of Belton. wid[ow]	
08 MAY	1733	THO	GODDARD	-	-
(Bs)	[9]	JANE	MINION	of Osgathorp	
09 MAY	1733	JOHN	VICARS	of Breedon	-
(Bs)		DOROTHY	ROPER	of Osgathorp	
13 MAY	1733	JOHN	HUDSON	of Whitick	-
(Bs)		MARY	MACHET	of Osgathorp	
17 MAY	1733	THOMAS	MILLER (40)	of Repton, Derbys. widower	[torn]
(Lic)	[10]	SUSANNAH	GROVES (29)	of Ibstock	
10 SEP	1733	DAN[IEL]	LUDFORD	of Packington	-
(Lic)	[11]	MARY	MORLY	of Osgathorp	

[1] Bond surety – William Boultbee, junior, Yeoman of Osgathorp.
[2] Bond surety – John Presbury, Yeoman of Packington.
[3] Bond surety – Thomas Sutton, Tentor of Donnington.
[4] Bond surety – William Boultbee, jun, of Osgathorp.
[5] Bond surety – Thomas Shaw, Tailor of Osgathorpe.
[6] Bond surety – Thom. Mitchell of Shepeshead.
[7] Bond surety – John Hear, Carpenter of Appleby.
[8] Bond surety – [Groom; only named surety].
[9] BT gave 5 May.
[10] Bond surety – William Tetley, Shoemaker of Repton, Derbys.
[11] Licence could not be found in the index of Leicestershire marriage licences. Daniel's full name comes from their daughter's baptism, at Packington, in October 1734.

06 MAY	1734	JOHN	BISSELL (53)	of Burton Extra, Staffs. widower	Woodman
(Lic)	[1]	ANN	PAYNE (53)	of Osgathorpe. widow	
07 MAY	1734	WILLIAM	CHISWELL (31)	of Whitwick. widower	Coke Carrier
(Lic)	[2]	ELIZABETH	ROBY (21)	of Donnington	
28 MAY	1734	JOHN	BAKEWELL (30)	of Coleorton. widower	Cokeman
(Lic)	[3]	SARAH	CARTWRIGHT (30)	of Hugglescote Grange, Ibstock	
02 JUN	1734	JOHN	ROSE	of Belton	-
(Bs)		BARBARA	ALLEN	of Osgathorp	
04 MAR	1734	THOMAS	BODEL (21)	of Ashby de la Zouch	Cloath Worker
(Lic)	[4]	MARY	FLETCHER (24)	of Ashby de la Zouch	
12 JUN	1735	HENRY	CHURCHILL (24)	of Osgathorpe	Brass Founder
(Lic)	[5]	SARAH	GRACE (22)	of Birmingham, Warks	
26 JUN	1735	JOHN	WEBSTAR (27)	of Stanton under Bardon	Husbandman
(Lic)	[6]	ELIZABETH	SMITH (21)	of Swannington, pa. of Whitwick	
10 JUL	1735	THOMAS	SANDERS (22)	of Breedon	Husbandman
(Lic)	[7]	DOROTHY	TAYLOR (21)	of Breedon	
16 SEP	1735	THOMAS	PATRICK (28)	of Nethersail	Blacksmith
(Lic)	[8]	ELIZABETH	SHAW (24)	of Nethersail	
30 OCT	1735	JOS	SMITH	of Osgathorp	-
(Bs)		JANE	HEMSLEY	ditto	
02 NOV	1735	GEORGE	ATKIN (24)	of Dyseworth	Husbandman
(Lic)	[9]	RACHEL	ANNABLE (26)	of Dyseworth	
10 NOV	1735	WILLIAM	ADCOCK (27)	of Ashby de la Zouch	Stocken Weever
(Lic)	[10]	ANN	YELL (30)	of Ashby de la Zouch. widow	
17 DEC	1735	JOHN	TOON (22)	of Coleorton	Labourer
(Lic)	[11]	ELIZABETH	MANSFIELD (26)	of Coleorton	
11 FEB	1735	SAM	SMALLY	-	-
(Bs)		ELIZABETH	HUFFEN	of Whitwick	
15 JUL	1736	JOHN	HALL	of Moutsorrel	-
(Bs)	[12]	MARTHA	THATCHER	of Whitick	

[1] Bond surety – Joseph Paine of Osgathorp.
[2] Bond surety – Michel Hubbard, Labourer of Whitwick.
[3] Bond surety – John Berrsford of Coleorton.
[4] Bond surety – John Bodell, Butcher of Ashby de la Zouch.
[5] Bond surety – Tim Churchill, Grocer of Osgathorpe.
[6] Bond surety – John Smith (signed George Smith), Shoemaker of Swannington.
[7] Bond surety – James Taylor, Husbandman of Stanton, Derbys. BT gave SAUNDERS.
[8] Bond surety – Ralph Fallows, Stocken maker of Ashby de la Zouch.
[9] Bond surety – Thomas Shaw, Weaver of Osgathorp.
[10] Bond surety – Henry Ford, Carpenter of Osgathorp.
[11] Bond surety – Rich. Bodel, Coak Carrier of Coleorton.
[12] The marriage was also recorded in the Whitwick register, Martha's home parish; but dated the 14 July. A practice that was not uncommon, as parish registers were legal documents and could be produced in legitimacy & inheritance cases. As a precaution, some families made sure that a record of the event was kept in their 'home' parish register.

07 OCT	1736	RICH	PHILLIPS	-	-
(Bs)		ELIZ	ENSOR	of Whitwick	
02 FEB	1736	THO	SHAW	-	-
(Bs)		RACHEL	BOLLY	of Osgathorp	
02 MAR	1736	SAMUEL	JOHNSON (35)	of Barwell	-
(Lic)	[1]	SARAH	CHURCHILL (25)	of Osgathorp	
31 JUL	1737	THOMAS	SIBSON (26)	of Rodely	Farmer
(Lic)	[2]	ANN	HUNT (23)	of Rodely	

Will: Cochran of Smithsby & Deborah Barlow of Osga Aug. 5. Lic.

05 AUG	1737	WILLIAM	COCKRAN (35)	of Smithsby, Derbys	Framework Knitter
(Lic)	[3]	DEBORAH	BARLOW (19)	of Osgathorp	
23 DEC	1737	WILLIAM	BLENKARN (23)	of Ashby de la Zouch	Butcher
(Lic)	[4]	SARAH	BRIGGS (20)	of Coleorton	
31 DEC	1737	GEORGE	KINSY	of Melborn	-
(Bs)		ELIZ	DAWSON	of Osgathorp	
31 DEC	1737	WILLIAM	NEWARK (30)	of Whitwick. widower	Cole Master
(Lic)	[5]	SARAH	GETLY (33)	of Swannington, Whitwick. widow	
17 JUL	1738	HOSEA	WARDEL (23)	of Breedon	Taylor
(Lic)	[6]	MARY	GOUGH (18)	of Coleorton	
27 AUG	1738	JOHN	ENSER (27)	of Breedon	Collier
(Lic)	[7]	MARY	BOOT (23)	of Radcliff, Notts	
10 SEP	1738	GEORGE	MUCKLESTON (30)	of Caulk, Derbys	Husbandman
(Lic)	[8]	ELIZABETH	SMITH (28)	of Blackfordby in pa. Ashby de la Zouch	
28 NOV	1738	JOHN Revrd Mr	BOULTBEE (28)	of Donnington	Vicar of Donnington/Clerk
(Lic)	[9]	FRANCES	BOULTBEE (21)	of Stordon Grange, Thrinkstone	
10 DEC	1738	JOHN	GODFREY (30)	of Appleby	Bricklayer
(Lic)	[10]	SARAH	BAGNAL (30)	of Worthington, Breedon	
19 JAN	1738	JOHN	TUGBY (22)	of Breedon	Shoemaker
(Lic)	[11]	ANN	KNIGHT (20)	of Breedon	
24 APR	1739	WILLIAM	LITHERLAND (21)	of Appleby	Blacksmith
(Lic)	[12]	ELIZABETH	SMITH (22)	of Appleby	

[1] Bond surety – Joseph Goodwin of Leicester.
[2] Bond surety – Isaac Preston, Webster of Rodely
[3] Bond surety – George Boswell, the elder, of Smithsby.
[4] Bond surety – Thomas Sabin, Chandler of Ashby de la Zouch.
[5] Bond surety – Henry Ford, Joyner of Osgathorpe.
[6] Bond surety – Tho. Price, Taylor of Coleorton.
[7] Bond surety – Will. Knight, Collier of Breedon. Licence gave ENSOR.
[8] Bond surety – John Smith of Caulk, Derbys.
[9] Bond surety – [Groom; only named surety]. Licence witness Thos. Boultbee. Register gave CLERK.
[10] Bond surety – George Bagnall, of Breedon.
[11] Bond surety – John Shaw of Breedon. BT gave 17 January; Register & Licence both gave 19.
[12] Bond surety – William Bull, Farmer of Appleby.

29 APR	1739	GEORGE	CLARK (25)	of Loughborough	-
(Lic)	[1]	ELIZABETH	BANCROFT (25)	of Osgathorpe. widow	
19 MAY	1739	JOB	GERROM (23)	of Kegworth	Husbandman
(Lic)	[2]	SARAH	STARKEY (25)	of Kegworth	
03 JUN	1739	EDWARD	BEDFORD (34)	of Ashby de la Zouch. widower	Feltmaker
(Lic)	[3]	ALICE	BLADEN (31)	of Ashby de la Zouch	
10 JUN	1739	ROBERT	RICHARDS (21)	of Breedon	Carpenter
(Lic)	[4]	REBECCA	GIBSON (23)	of Breedon	

Tho: Sabin & Ann. Radford of Ashby de la Zouch July 26. Lic

26 JUL	1739	THOMAS	SABIN (28)	of Ashby de la Zouch	Chandler
(Lic)	[5]	ANN	RADFORD (26)	of Ashby de la Zouch	
29 SEP	1739	JOHN	MORRIS (39)	of Caulk, Derbys. widower	Taylor
(Lic)	[6]	HANNAH	MARTIN (30)	of Stordon Grange, Whitwick	
04 OCT	1739	GERVISE	YARWOOD (55)	of Breedon. widower	Husbandman
(Lic)	[7]	ELIZABETH	BOULTBEE (30)	of Stordon Grange, Whitwick	
14 OCT	1739	DAVID	SPENCER (27)	of Ashby de la Zouch	Husbandman
(Lic)	[8]	ELIZABETH	ORTON (30)	of Ashby de la Zouch	
26 NOV	1739	WILL	MATCHET	-	-
(Bs)		CATHERINE	DICKIN	of Osgathorp	
25 DEC	1739	WILL	WATTS	of Osgathorp	-
(Bs)		ELEONER	NORROD	of Belton	
02 FEB	1739	WILL	POUNDER	-	-
(Bs)		RUTH	MORLY	of Osgathorp	
08 JUN	1740	THOMAS	JESSEN (23)	of Snibston	Husbandman
(Lic)	[9]	SARAH	ENSOR (21)	of Ravenstone	
17 OCT	1740	JOHN	SMITH	-	-
(Bs)		ELIZ	BURROWS	of Osgathorp	
30 DEC	1740	EDWARD	SHARP (30)	of Coleorton	Butcher
(Lic)	[10]	ALICE	COATS (30)	of Whitwick. widow	
07 FEB	1740	JOHN	GILMAN (40)	of Sheepshead. widower	Husbandman
(Lic)	[11]	ANN	HEATELY (40)	of Sheepshead. widow	

---

1 Bond surety – Joseph Moseley of Osgathorpe.
2 Bond surety – Thomas Gerram, of Diseworth. Licence gave GERRAM.
3 Bond surety – James Hall, Husbandman of Osgathorp.
4 Bond surety – John Ought, Collier of Coleorton.
5 Bond surety – John Dobson, Blacksmith of Ashby de la Zouch.
6 Bond surety – John Bates, Maltstar of Stordon Grange.
7 Bond surety – [Groom; only named surety].
8 Bond surety – Sam. Orton of Ashby de la Zouch. Licence witness Thomas Spencer.
9 Bond surety – Henry Bonsar of Breedon.
10 Bond surety – Will. Sharp, Butcher of Coleorton.
11 Bond surety – Richard Yarwood, Weever of Sheepshead.

14 FEB 1740	WILLIAM	STANLY (30)	of Oversail	Farmer
(Lic) [1]	ELIZABETH	SALT (27)	of Oversail	
17 NOV 1741	JOHN	KENDAL (30)	of Sileby	Farmer
(Lic) [2]	SARAH	EXON (20)	of Ravenstone, Derbys. widow	
13 FEB 1741	WILLIAM	MILLER (26)	of Nethersail	Farmer
(Lic) [3]	ANN	SHAW (22)	of Oversail, Nethersail	
20 JUN 1742	GEORGE	HICKLING (30)	of Loughborough	Servant
(Lic) [4]	ELIZABETH	MASSY (23)	of Loughborough	
09 DEC 1742	CHARLES	BERRISFORD	-	-
(Bs)	RACHEL	WYTTOL	of Osgathorp	
13 FEB 1742	JOS	EVERARD	of Markfield	-
(Bs)	ELIZ	BELTON	of Osgathorp	
03 MAR 1742	RICHARD	JOYCE (28)	of Boothorpe, Ashby de la Zouch	Hatter
(Lic) [5]	ELIZABETH	FARMER (35)	of Ashby de la Zouch. widow	
22 MAR 1742	JOHN	STUART (26)	of Desford	Malster
(Lic) [6]	MARY	WILSON (23)	of Desford	
01 AUG 1743	THO	ORGIL	of Coleorton	-
(Bs)	SARAH	WARDEL	of Osgathorp	
03 AUG 1743	ROBERT	HATTON (25)	of Desford	Servant
(Lic) [7]	SARAH	MEASURES (23)	of Desford	
13 SEP 1743	JOB	WHITNAL (25)	of Boothorp, Ashby de la Zouch	Farmer
(Lic) [8]	MARY	RADFORD (27)	of the same. widow	
30 NOV 1743	THOMAS	RALPHIN (23)	of Walton	Labourer
(Lic) [9]	ELIZABETH	DEWICK (21)	of Loughborough	
05 FEB 1743	WILLIAM	FITCHET (45)	of Ashby de la Zouch. widower	Inn Holder
(Lic) [10]	ELIZABETH	CROWDER (40)	of Ashby de la Zouch. widow	
13 FEB 1743	HENRY	THORNTON (23)	of Breedon	-
(Lic) [11]	REBECCA	NEEDHAM (25)	of Breedon. widow	
21 MAY 1744	THOMAS	STEVENSON (24)	of Glenfield	Tailor
(Lic) [12]	SARAH	PARKER (26)	of Quarndon	

[1] Bond surety – Samuel Salt, Farmer of Rolleston, Staffs.
[2] Bond surety – John Bonsar, Grazier of Cotes, Leics.
[3] Bond surety – Tho. Needham, Farmer of Nethersail.
[4] Bond surety – William Massy of Griffy Dam.
[5] Bond surety – Abraham Clarson, Husbandman of Ashby de la Zouch.
[6] Bond surety – John Dobson, Blacksmith of Ashby de la Zouch.
[7] Bond surety – John Bakewell, Collier of Coleorton.
[8] Bond surety – Geo. Jervis, Stocken maker of Boothorp, Ashby de la Zouch. Licence gave Job's abode as BLACKFORDBY, ASHBY DE LA ZOUCH & Mary's as NETHERSEAL.
[9] Bond surety – Wm. Newberry, Butcher of Loughboro.
[10] Bond surety – Nicholas Farmer of Ashby de la Zouch. Register gave THO for WILLIAM, which appears to be an error as the licence allegation, bond and signature all gave WILLIAM.
[11] Bond surety – John Shakespear of Breedon.
[12] Bond surety – William Davison, Shoemaker of Loughboro. Register gave Glenvill.

15 JUL	1744	JOSEPH	DIMOX (29)	of Stretton	Servant
(Lic)	[1]	JANE	CRAGG (30)	of Stretton	
24 JUL	1744	THOMAS	CHOICE (36)	of Whitwick. widower	Collier
(Lic)	[2]	HANNAH	NEWTON (29)	of Ashby de la Zouch	
29 JUL	1744	THOMAS	RICHARDS (40)	of Normanton on Sore, Notts. widower	Farmer
(Lic)	[3]	ANN	JYMSON (40)	of Thorpe. widow	
27 SEP	1744	THO	SHAW	-	-
(Bs)		ANN	SMITH	of Osgathorp	

Tho: upton & mary upton of whitwick - Oct: 15 Bar:

15 OCT	1744	THO	UPTON	-	-
(Bs)		MARY	UPTON	of Whitwick	
03 NOV	1744	JOHN	HORE (45)	of Troye in Cornwall	-
(Lic)	[4]	ELENOR	SEAL (40)	of Long Whatton. widow	
09 NOV	1744	THOMAS	SUTTON (29)	of Donnington. widower	Husbandman
(Lic)	[5]	ELIZABETH	ALCOCK (24)	of same	
21 NOV	1744	NATHANIEL	ALLT (28)	of Sheepshead	Farmer
(Lic)	[6]	ANN	HADDON (20)	of Sheepshead	
09 JAN	1744	JOSHUA	WARDEL (22)	of Breedon	Collier
(Lic)	[7]	SARAH	MASSEY (21)	of Breedon	
14 MAR	1744	JAMES	BLENKARNE (25)	of Ashby de la Zouch	Sadler
(Lic)	[8]	ANN	STUART (22)	of Ashby de la Zouch	
23 APR	1745	THOMAS	BARNES (25)	of Austrey, Warks	Husbandman
(Lic)	[9]	MARY	ARNOLD (23)	of Packington	
27 MAY	1745	ROBERT	PLANT (25)	of Sheepshead	Stockener
(Lic)	[10]	SARAH	SHAW (18)	of Osgathorp	
17 JUN	1745	WILLIAM	SMEDLEY (23)	of Newton Slony, Derbys	Farmer
(Lic)	[11]	MARY	FALKONER (21)	of Ashby de la Zouch	
11 SEP	1745	NICOLAS	JOYCE (25)	of Donnington	Labourer
(Lic)	[12]	ALICE	ELSON (25)	of Donnington	

[1] Bond surety – William Parker, Husbandman of Stretton.

[2] Bond surety – Robert Palmer, Hatter of Ashby de la Zouch.

[3] Bond surety – Robert Tatenall, Farmer of Osgathorpe.

[4] Bond surety – Robert Smith, Labourer of Long Whatton.

[5] Bond surety – Thos. Parsons, Husbandman of Osgathorpe. Licence gave abodes as Hemmington in the pa. of Lockington, instead of Donnington.

[6] Bond surety – John Barradal, Stockener of Sheepshead.

[7] Bond surety – Hosea Wardel, Collier of Breedon.

[8] Bond surety – Edward Cotton, Husbandman of Breedon.

[9] Bond surety – Thomas Middleton, Taylor of Packington. Register gave Austria.

[10] Bond surety – John Hemsly, Husbandman of Osgathorp.

[11] Bond surety – Thomas Falkoner, Farmer of Repton, Derbys.

[12] Bond surety – William Joyce, Husbandman of Wharton, Warks.

30 NOV 1745		EDWARD	HALL	-	-
(Bs)		ALICE	FINCH	of Osgathorp	
26 DEC 1745		JOHN	GODFREY (28)	of All Saints Leicester	Servant
(Lic)	[1]	MARY	MARSHALL (28)	of All Saints Leicester	
05 JAN 1745		WILLIAM	LEE (26)	of Loughboro	Cooper
(Lic)	[2]	ANN	ICKLING (28)	of Loughboro	
13 JAN 1745		SAMUEL	PEACE (33)	of Ashby de la Zouch	Labourer
(Lic)	[3]	MARY	BAKER (38)	of Greasly, Derbys. widow	
20 MAR 1745		JOHN	BLENKARNE (22)	of Ashby de la Zouch	Sadler
(Lic)	[4]	MARY	DEWITT (20)	of Ashby de la Zouch	
03 APR 1746		SAM	ASHUR	of Osgathorpe	-
(Bs)		MARY	DEXTER	of Coleorton	
12 MAY 1746		JOSEPH	BROOKES (29)	of Loughborough	Husbandman
(Lic)	[5]	MARY	SORSE (29)	of Loughborough	
19 MAY 1746		JOHN	ROBY (25)	of Settington, Warks	Husbandman
(Lic)	[6]	ISABELLA	RICHARDS (20)	of Thorpe Acre	
20 MAY 1746		JAMES	WARD (21)	of Breedon	Carrier
(Lic)	[7]	SUSANNA	JAQUES (20)	of Breedon	
29 JUN 1746		EDWARD	BENNET (50)	of Ashby de la Zouch. widower	Feltmaker
(Lic)	[8]	MARY	ANDERTON (50)	of Ashby de la Zouch. widow	
10 AUG 1746		JOHN	WALLIS (25)	of Ashby de la Zouch	Chandler
(Lic)	[9]	ELIZABETH	ROBINSON (25)	of Ashby de la Zouch	
20 AUG 1746		THOMAS	GOUGH (27)	of Coleorton	Coke Carrier
(Lic)	[10]	MARY	GREEN (22)	of Swannington	
25 AUG 1746		THOMAS	ARNOLD (50)	of Whitwick. widower	Pot Carrier
(Lic)	[11]	SARAH	JOHNSON (30)	of Whitwick	
01 SEP 1746		BENJAMIN	WALKER (45)	of Coleorton. widower	Collier
(Lic)	[12]	DEBORAH	GAMBLE (45)	of Whitwick. widow	
13 SEP 1746		JOHN	PHILLIPS (26)	of Oversail	Husbandman
(Lic)	[13]	ELIZABETH	STANLY (29)	of Oversail. widow	

[1] Bond surety – Pates Owen, Husbandman of Newtown, Leics.
[2] Bond surety – Thomas Ickling, Servant of Loughboro.
[3] Bond surety – John Ford, Stock Taker of Melborn Furnace [Derbys].
[4] Bond surety – John Clifford, Barber of Ashby de la Zouch.
[5] Bond surety – Benjamin Brooks, of Loughborough.
[6] Bond surety – Thomas Richards, Husbandman of Thorpe Acre.
[7] Bond surety – Richard Potter of Whitwick.
[8] Bond surety – Stephen Frith of Ashby de la Zouch.
[9] Bond surety – William Choice, Joyner of Ashby de la Zouch.
[10] Bond surety – Samuel Heut, Blacksmith of Coleorton. Licence gave Worthington for Swannington.
[11] Bond surety – Thomas Parsons of Osgathorpe. BT gave MARY for SARAH, which appears to be an error as the register & licence both gave SARAH.
[12] Bond surety – Thomas Forster (signed Foster), Hatter of Whitwick.
[13] Bond surety – John Hodghskinson, Mason of Markfield, Staffs.

24 SEP	1746	WILLIAM	GLOVER (24)	of Loughborough	Husbandman
(Lic)	[1]	ABIA	HEMSLY (22)	of Osgathorpe	
28 SEP	1746	LEONARD	PALMER (25)	of Hether	Millar
(Lic)	[2]	ANN	FREEMAN (30)	of Hether. widow	
26 DEC	1746	WILL	FORD	of Ashby de la Zouch	-
(Bs)		ANN	BRADFORD	of Osgathorp	
05 JAN	1746	GODFREY	FLETCHER (30)	of Burton upon Trent, Staffs	Farmer
(Lic)	[3]	HANNAH	HARGRAVE (24)	of Coleorton	
26 JAN	1746	JOHN	INGLE (34)	of Ashby de la Zouch	Husbandman
(Lic)	[4]	ELIZABETH	JOYCE (22)	of Ashby de la Zouch	
11 FEB	1746	WILLIAM	TANSAR (26)	of Belton	Chandler
(Lic)	[5]	HANNAH	BROOKS (25)	of Osgathorpe	
04 MAY	1747	JOHN	FLAWELL (25)	of Norton	Shoemaker
(Lic)	[6]	JANE	WILLIAMSON (27)	of Shenton	
09 JUN	1747	WILLIAM	SAUNDERS (22)	of Desford	Farmer
(Lic)	[7]	MARY	KEMP (21)	of Brunson	
10 JUN	1747	SAMUEL	HEWITT (27)	of Breedon	Blacksmith
(Lic)	[8]	ELIZABETH	COLTMAN (28)	of Breedon	
18 JUN	1747	FRANCIS	ASHLEY (26)	of Hinckley	Hog Jobber
(Lic)	[9]	ANN	JERROMS (26)	of Kirkby Mallory	
27 JUL	1747	ROBERT	TIMPSON (30)	of Ibstock	Butcher
(Lic)	[10]	DOROTHY	BAKEWELL (23)	of Whitwick	
10 AUG	1747	TIMOTHY	BEIGHTON (32)	of Ticknall, Derbys	Farmer
(Lic)	[11]	ELIZABETH	ARCHER (29)	of Derby Hills, extra-parochial. widow	
01 SEP	1747	JOHN	TEXTON (26)	of Ashby de la Zouch	Flaxdresser
(Lic)	[12]	ALICE	POLEXTON (30)	of Ashby de la Zouch. widow	
03 SEP	1747	JOHN	PRINCEPS	of Norton	-
(Bs)		MARY	BARLOW	of Smithesby	
02 OCT	1747	WILLIAM	BAKEWELL (21)	of Coleorton	Collier
(Lic)	[13]	SARAH	DAVIES (21)	of Coleorton	

[1] Bond surety – John Hemsley, Innkeeper of Osgathorpe.
[2] Bond surety – John Heafield, Husbandman of Osgathorpe.
[3] Bond surety – Thomas Storer, Farmer of Coleorton.
[4] Bond surety – John Heathcoat, Husbandman of Packington.
[5] Bond surety – John Huskinson, Farmer of Osgathorpe.
[6] Bond surety – Melborn Williamson, Gardener of Breedon.
[7] Bond surety – William Smith, Innholder of Donnington on the Heath. Licence gave SANDERS. Register & Licence gave Branson; BT gave Brunson. Braunstone registers confirm Mary's baptism in 1720 and her burial; 'Mary Saunders buried 2 May 1748 wife of William & daughter of Michael Kemp'.
[8] Bond surety – Robert Coltman, Carpenter & Wheelwright of Breedon.
[9] Bond surety – John Jerroms, Labourer of Hinckley.
[10] Bond surety – John Prat, Farmer of Burbridge.
[11] Bond surety – John Newhouse of Kirby Hills, Derbys.
[12] Bond surety – Jas. Kerby, Stockener of Ashby de la Zouch.
[13] Bond surety – John Williamson, Collier of Coleorton.

27 OCT	1747	JOSEPH	SMITH (22)	of Lowth, Lincs	Servant
(Lic)	[1]	REBECCA	WATKINSON (27)	of Wonlip	
01 JAN	1747	SAM	GOODWIN	-	-
(Bs)		ANN	BLOWER	of Smithesby	
21 MAR	1747	WILLIAM	MARLER (21)	of Lullington, Derbys	Farmer
(Lic)	[2]	MARY	STORER (23)	of Coleorton	
17 APR	1748	SAMUEL	MATCHET	-	-
(Bs)		REBECCA	CORBET	of Osgathorpe	

Will: gough of Coleorton & Ann Barber of Ibstock may 30. Lic:

30 MAY	1748	WILLIAM	GOUGH (24)	of Coleorton	Cokeman
(Lic)	[3]	ANN	BARBER (21)	of Hugglescote in pa. of Ibstock	
13 JUN	1748	THOS	BLISS	-	-
(Bs)		ELIZTH	CHAPMAN	of Smitherby	
13 JUN	1748	JOHN	WOODFORD (30)	of Woodhouse. widower	Husbandman
(Lic)	[4]	ELIZABETH	PATCHET (25)	of Woodhouse	
14 AUG	1748	THOMAS	EAGLEFIELD (25)	of Snareson	Servant
(Lic)	[5]	ELIZABETH	LEAVELY (22)	of Snareson	
10 SEP	1748	FRANCIS	ALLEN (25)	of Burton upon Trent, Staffs	Husbandman
(Lic)	[6]	PATIENCE	POWIS (21)	of Packington	
11 OCT	1748	BENJAMIN	BROOKES (30)	of Loughborough. the younger	Husbandman
(Lic)	[7]	ELIZABETH	KENDALL (27)	of Loughborough	
13 OCT	1748	WILLIAM	WILKES (30)	of Overseal, Netherseal	Farmer
(Lic)	[8]	MARY	FARNEL (29)	of Overseal, Netherseal	
22 MAR	1749	JOHN	HALL	-	-
(-)		ELIZABETH	GADESBY	of Whitwick	
07 FEB	1750	WILLIAM	WHITTLEY	-	-
(-)		DOROTHY	WEST	both of Charley	
	1751	No Marriages			
		'NB. This year begins Jan ye 1st by act of Parliamt'[*sic*]			
11 FEB	1752	RICHARD	SLINGSBY	-	-
(-)		MARY	STEENSON	of Stordons	
14 SEP	1752	WILLIAM	COULTON (41)	of Belton	-
(Lic)	[9]	ELIZABETH	STEEL (29)	of Belton	

1 Bond surety – Benjamin Smith, Servant of Lowth, Lincs.
2 Bond surety – William Joyce, Hatter of Ashby de la Zouch.
3 Bond surety – William Smith, Vichialer of Swannington.
4 Bond surety – Thomas Parsons, Shoemaker of Osgathorpe.
5 Bond surety – John Leavesley, Taylor of Snareson. Licence gave LEAVESLEY.
6 Bond surety – Godfrey Fletcher, Husbandman of Burton on the Trent, Staffs.
7 Bond surety – Benjamin Brooks, the elder, of Loughborough.
8 Bond surety – John Blenkarn, Sadler of Ashby de la Zouch.
9 Bond surety – Thomas Loe of Belton. Licence bond & allegation both gave HICKLING instead of STEEL & Breedon for Elizabeth's abode. [Possibly connected with the 1724 - Steel/Hickling marriage].

26 OCT	1752	JOHN	WILSON	-	-
(-)		LYDIA	JOHNSON	of Whitwick	
19 FEB	1753	THOMAS	UNDERWOOD	-	-
(Bs)		MARY	CRESWELL	-	
23 SEP	1753	RICHARD	NEEDHAM (21)	of St Martins, Leicester	Grazier
(Lic)	[1]	MARY	FOSSET (21)	of Worthington in pa. of Bredon	
05 JAN	1754	WILLIAM	HICKLING	-	-
(Bs)		MARY	SMITH	-	

'NB. the Act of Parliamt relating to Marriages which require a different sort of register for them takes place on Lady day next 1754'[*sic*]

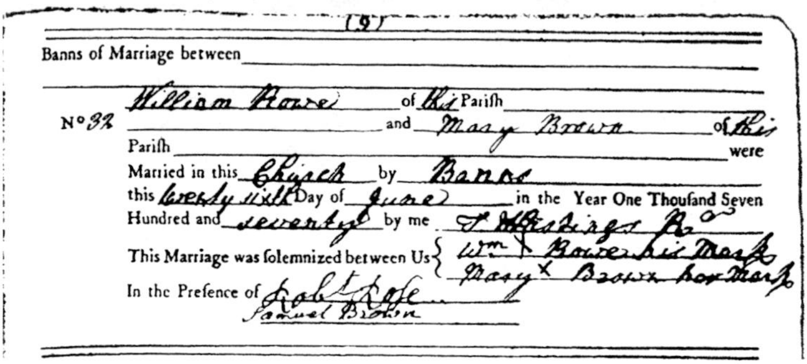
(9)
Banns of Marriage between
William Rowe of this Parish
N° 32 and Mary Brown of this
Parish were
Married in this Church by Banns
this twenty sixth Day of June in the Year One Thousand Seven
Hundred and seventy by me T. Hastings R^{r}
This Marriage was solemnized between Us { Wm. X Rowe his Mark, Mary X Brown her Mark
In the Presence of Robt Rose
Samuel Brown

The New 1754 Marriage Register - Osgathorpe (page 9)

Until Lord Hardwicke's Marriage Act of 1754, the law regarding marriage was lax & often abused by irregular & clandestine marriages. These marriages often took place without the reading of banns, the purchase of a licence or the consent of parents.

The Act required that a separate register be used to record marriages and that a precise form of wording be used. Entries also had to have the signatures or mark of the bride & groom and at least two witnesses.

№*32*. *William Roe* of *this* Parish and *Mary Brown* of *this* Parish were Married by *Banns* this *twenty sixth* Day of *June* in the Year One Thousand Seven Hundred and *Seventy* by me *T. Hastings* R^{r}. This Marriage was solemnized between us *Wm. X Rowe his mark*, *Mary X Brown her mark*. In the Presence of *Robt Rose*, *Samuel Brown*. [The dates the banns were read were not entered]

[1] Bond surety – Edward Buswell, Glazier of St Martins, Leicester.

From 1754, marriage witnesses were also recorded and these names have been included in brackets. Information has also been incorporated from the banns registers, which included details of marriages that were withdrawn at the last minute and those that took place elsewhere but had banns read at Osgathorpe. These are indicated as 'Bs only', with the month(s) of reading above.

– JUL	1754	SAMUEL	GILBERT	of this pa.	-
(Bs only)	[1]	ELIZABETH	ROBINSON	of Shepeshead	-
27 NOV	1754	THOMAS	SHAW	of this pa.	(William Wootton)
(Bs)		ELIZABETH	PALMER	of Shepeshead	(Joseph Smith)
20 JAN	1755	JOSEPH	PEGG	b./ this pa.	(Thos Parsons)
(Bs)		ANNE	MUGGLESTONE	-	(Thomas Belton)
– APR	1755	THOMAS	KENDRICK	of this pa.	-
(Bs only)	[2]	CATHARINE	ORTON	of Newton Lynford	-
15 JUL	1755	JOSEPH	HARDY	of Findon in pa. of Mickleover	(John Rose)
(Bs)		SARAH	WARD	of this pa.	(John Rose, junr)
23 JUN	1756	HENRY	DANIELS	b./ this pa.	(Charles Berisford)
(Bs)		JANE	WARD	-	(Joseph Hardy)
19 JUL	1756	JOHN	EARP	of this pa.	(William Earp)
(Bs)		MARY	FLETCHER	of Melbourne	(Joseph Morley)
06 DEC	1756	ROBERT	WILLOWS	b./ this pa.	(Thomas Huskisson)
(Bs)		HANNAH	MATCHET	-	(Samuel Brown)
31 MAY	1757	THOMAS	HEAP (22)	of Osgathorpe. Yeoman	(Sarah Chase)
(Lic)	[3]	ESTHER	CHASE (29)	of Osgathorpe	(Thomas Heap, ye elder)
26 DEC	1757	FRANCIS	EVERARD (28)	of Heather. Farmer	(Sam Benton)
(Lic)	[4]	HANNAH	EARP (24)	of Osgathorpe	(Thos Earp)
08 JAN	1758	JAMES	CHAPLAIN	b./ Stordon Grange,	(Thomas Parsons)
(Bs)		ELIZABETH	PARSONS	an extra-parochial place	(Samuel Brown)
28 MAR	1759	THOMAS	PEPERDY	of Normanton, Notts	(Sam Brown)
(Bs)		ELLEN	GODDARD	of Osgathorpe	(Mary Goddard)
OCT/NOV	1759	THOMAS	LAWKINS	of Long Whatton	-
(Bs only)	[5]	SARAH	JOYNES	of this pa.	-
	1760	No Marriages			
21 JAN	1761	JOHN	ROSE ye younger	of this pa.	(Robt Rose)
(Bs)		ELIZABETH	WILSON	of Worthington	(Kath'e Lakin)
25 MAR	1761	HENRY	WORTHINGTON (26)	of Breedon. Farmer	(Wm Earp)
(Lic)	[6]	MARY	EARP (30)	of Osgathorpe	(Joseph Morley)

[1] Married at Shepshed, 22 July 1754.
[2] Married at Newton Linford, 5 May 1755.
[3] Bond surety – Thos Heap, senr, Yeoman of Osgathorpe.
[4] Bond surety – Thos Earp, Farmer of Osgathorpe. BT gave 27 December.
[5] Married at Long Whatton, 12 November 1759, where register gave Lakins for Lawkins.
[6] Bond surety – Thomas Earp, Farmer of Osgathorpe, licence witness Wm Earp.

15 NOV	1761	WILLIAM	WALL	of Loughborough	(Richard Rapen)
(Bs)		REBECCA	BROWNE	of Osgathorpe	(Matthias Hope)
	1762	No Marriages			
29 SEP	1763	WILLIAM	BRADLEY	b./ Stordon Grange,	(Samuel Brown)
(Bs)		DEBORAH	MORRIS	an extra-parochial place	(James Foord)
01 NOV	1763	MATTHIAS	HOPE	of Whitwick	(Samuel Gilbert)
(Bs)		SARAH	ROE	of Osgathorpe	(James Foord)
30 NOV	1763	GEORGE	INSLEY	b./ this pa.	(Robt Tatnell)
(Bs)		MARY	ASHER	-	(Samuel Brown)
14 OCT	1764	THOMAS	GODDARD	b./ this pa.	(James Hall)
(Bs)		ELIZ	HALL	-	(Edward Bayley)
16 OCT	1764	JAMES	FORD	b./ this pa.	(John Ragg)
(Bs)		JANE	ROE	-	(Matthias Hope)
12 SEP	1765	JOSEPH	MATCHET	b./ this pa.	(Robt Rose)
(Bs)		ANN	BERRISFORD	-	(Eliz Asher)
29 OCT	1765	WILLIAM	STINSON	b./ this pa.	(Joseph Jaques Huskisson)
(Bs)		ANN	HUCKNELL	-	(John Huskisson)
14 OCT	1766	JOHN	MASON	of Stordon Grange	(Wm Lacey)
(Bs)		ELIZABETH	HILLS	of Stordon Grange	(Samuel Massey)
17 NOV	1766	WILLIAM	HARRIS	b./ this pa.	(Hannah Huskisson)
(Bs)		MARY	WRIGHT	-	(Rachel Pickilsford)
08 JUN	1767	DANIEL	ROSE	b./ this pa.	(Samuel Massey)
(Bs)		MARY	HATTON	-	(Sam Brown)
19 APR	1768	THOMAS	FORD	b./ this pa.	(Samuel Massey)
(Bs)		ELIZ	VERNON	-	(Ann Ward)
14 OCT	1768	EDWARD	QUEAIL (29)	of Stordon Grange. Yeoman	(James Foord)
(Lic)	[1]	ELIZABETH	BREWIN (21)	of Stordon Grange	(Samuel Massey)
13 DEC	1768	THOMAS	DEXTER	of Belton	(William Harris)
(Bs)		JANE	ASHER	of this pa.	(Edward Bailey)
26 MAR	1769	GEORGE	DEXTER	of Breedon	(Wm Ford)
(Bs)		ELIZ	ASHER	of this pa.	(John Dexter)
21 APR	1769	THOMAS	WOODWARD	b./ this pa.	(John Ward)
(Bs)		SARAH	EARP	-	(Elizabeth Earp)
17 APR	1770	WILLIAM	TAYLOR	of Netherseal	(James Foord)
(Bs)		ELIZABETH	ELTON	of Stordons Grange	(Thos ?Whileram)
26 JUN	1770	WILLIAM	ROE	b./ this pa.	(Robt Rose)
(Bs)		MARY	BROWN	-	(Samuel Brown)
01 APR	1771	JOSEPH	RAGG	of Diseworth	(Thos Brewin)
(Bs)		HANNAH	HARRIS	of this pa.	(Saml Brown)
17 OCT	1771	JOSEPH	WEBSTER (27)	of Loughborough. Steelmaker	(John Rose)
(Lic)	[2]	ELIZABETH	DALBY (21)	of Osgathorpe	(Mary Rose)
10 DEC	1771	WILLIAM	BLADON	b./ this pa.	(Samuel Brown)
(Bs)		ANN	ABEL	-	(William Harris)

[1] Bond surety – John Ingle, Farmer of Ashby de la Zouch.

[2] Bond surety – Daniel Green, Victualler of Leicester.

16 NOV	1772	JOHN	DENT	of Breedon	(Robert Rose)
(Bs)		MARY	WOOTTON	of this pa.	(Samuel Brown)
25 OCT	1773	JOHN	GIBSON	b./ this pa.	(James Foord)
(Bs)		HANNAH	STURGUS	-	(Samuel Brown)
12 JAN	1774	WILLIAM	ASHER (21)	of Osgathorpe. Potter	(Charles Robines)
(Lic)	[1]	MARY	ROPER (21)	of Osgathorpe	(Saml Brown)
18 JAN	1774	JOHN	PALMER	of Breedon	(Saml Brown)
(Bs)		ELIZABETH	HUSKISSON	-	(Thomas Swan)
01 SEP	1774	THOMAS	HUSKISSON	b./ this pa.	(John Farmer)
(Bs)		JANE	DANIELS	-	(Saml Brown)
29 NOV	1774	JAMES	YOUNG	b./ this pa.	(Thomas Swan)
(Bs)		ANN	WARDLE	-	(Sarah Huskisson)
26 DEC	1774	SAMUEL	BAGNALL	of Diseworth	(Thos Huskisson)
(Bs)		ANN	WARD	of this pa.	(Saml Brown)
13 FEB	1775	WILLIAM	BOWLEY	of Long Whatton	(Tho Bowley)
(Bs)		ANN	GLOVER	of this pa.	(Ann Bowley)
09 MAY	1775	WILLIAM	MEEKIN	b./ this pa.	(Thos Nadin)
(Bs)		HANNAH	ILLSLEY	-	(Sarah Smith)
14 MAY	1775	JOHN	ELVASTON (21)	b./ Stordon Grange. Husbandman	(James Foord)
(Lic)	[2]	DOROTHY	MORLEY (21)	an extra-parochial place	(Samuel Brown)
07 JUL	1776	ROBERT	YOUNG	b./ this pa.	(Ann Matchet)
(Bs)		SARAH	BERRISFORD	-	(Saml Brown) (Richard Roper)
— AUG	1776	JOHN	BAKEWELL	- [of Coleorton]	-
(Bs only)	[3]	ELIZABETH	PARSONS	of this pa.	-
13 OCT	1776	JOSEPH	CROSON	of Hartshorn	(William Crosan)
(Bs)		JANE	DARBY	of this pa.	(Saml Brown)
24 OCT	1776	JOHN	BARRATT (21)	of Low Toynton, Lincs. Grazier. widow	
(Lic)	[4]	CHRISTIAN	ROSE (21)	of Osgathorpe	(Mary Rose) (Mary Farrow)
26 DEC	1776	THOMAS	STINSON	of Breedon	(John Gostelow)
(Bs)		SARAH	HUSKISSON	of this pa.	(Ann Stinson)
26 DEC	1776	WILLIAM	KEMPSON (21)	of St Martins, Birmingham. Button-maker	
(Lic)	[5]	ELIZABETH	BOULTBEE (21)	of Stordons	(Tho Boultbee) (Mary Kempson)
15 JUL	1777	JOHN	FARMER	b./ this pa.	(Sarah Asher)
(Bs)		ANN	STINSON	-	(James Gilbert)
— NOV	1777	JOHN	MATCHET	of this pa.	-
(Bs only)	[6]	ELIZABETH	KING	of Whitwick	-
19 JAN	1778	WILLIAM	USHERWOOD	of St Mary's, Leicester	(Tho Bretley)
(Bs)		ELIZABETH	BOWLEY	of this pa.	(Jane Bowley)

[1] Bond surety – Richard Roper, Weaver of Osgathorpe.

[2] Bond surety – James Ford of Osgathorpe. Register stated that Stordon Grange was 'an extra-parochial place which adjoins this parish'.

[3] Married at Coleorton, 3 September 1776, where John appears to have been baptised in 1751.

[4] Bond surety – Robert Rose, Farmer of Osgathorpe.

[5] Bond surety – Thomas Boultbee, Gent. Licence stated Stordons was 'extra-parochial'.

[6] Married at Whitwick, 17 November 1777.

07 JUL	1778	ROBERT	ROSE (21)	of Osgathorpe. Farmer	(Mary Newbound)
(Lic)	[1]	JANE	ILLSLEY (21)	of Osgathorpe	(George Illsley)
23 SEP	1778	THOMAS	BALL	of Sheepshead	(John Matchet)
(Bs)		JANE	BOWLEY	of this pa.	(Saml Brown)
08 APR	1779	THOMAS	STARBUCK	of Merevale	(William Asher)
(Bs)	[2]	SARAH	ASHER	of this pa.	(Saml Brown)
16 OCT	1780	THOMAS	BRADLEY	b./ this pa.	(Thos Earp)
(Bs)		ELLEN	BROWN	-	(Saml Brown)
07 DEC	1781	THOMAS	KING	of Whitwick	(Ben Johnson)
(Bs)		SARAH	BROWN	of this pa.	(Saml Brown)
	1782	No Marriages			
18 MAR	1783	SAMUEL	GILBERT	b./ this pa.	(Geo Illsley)
(Bs)		MARGARET	JOHNSON	-	(Ellen Gilbert)
11 MAY	1783	WILLIAM	GLOVER	b./ this pa.	(Thos Bradley)
(Bs)		FANNY	BOWLEY	-	(Saml Brown)
03 JUN	1783	JAMES	GILBERT	of Breedon	(Ellen Gilbert)
(Bs)		ANN	HOOD	of this pa.	(Thomas Nadin)
01 DEC	1783	RICHARD	CHAPLAIN	of Lockington	(Abraham Mee)
(Bs)		ELIZABETH	CHAPLAIN	of this pa.	(Saml Brown)
28 JAN	1784	SAMUEL	PAGET	of Rothley	(Mary Asher)
(Bs)		JANE	ROPER	of this pa.	(Thomas Nadin)
11 MAR	1784	THOMAS	NADIN	b./ this pa.	(Dorothy Kelk)
(Bs)		ALICE	NEEDHAM	-	(Robert Boultbee)
06 JUL	1784	BENJAMIN	JOHNSON	b./ this pa.	(Eliz Rose)
(Bs)		MARY	ROSE	-	(Wm Toone)
25 JUL	1785	JOSEPH	NEWBOLD (21)	of Melbourne, Derbys. Woolcomber	
(Lic)	[3]	ELIZABETH	BAILEY (21)	of this pa.	(Ben Johnson) (Robert Mountney)
07 FEB	1786	RICHARD	BAKEWELL	b./ this pa.	(Jane Ford)
(Bs)		ANN	HORSLEY	-	(Thomas Nadin)
27 NOV	1786	JACOB	JOHNSON	b./ this pa.	(William Wilson Rose)
(Bs)		MARY	WILKINS	-	(Saml Brown)
	1787–1788	No Marriages			
31 AUG	1789	SAMUEL	BRIERLY	of Hathern	(Elizabeth Hutchinson)
(Bs)	[4]	CATHERINE	SPENCER	of this pa.	(Thos Gamble)
20 SEP	1789	FRANCIS	FARMER	b./ this pa.	(Thomas Stinson)
(Bs)		ANN	STINSON	-	(Saml Brown)
23 SEP	1789	WILLIAM	BROWN	b./ this pa.	(Robt Mountney)
(Bs)		URSULA	MOUNTNEY	-	(Sarah Swan)
18 MAR	1790	JOSEPH	MARTIN	b./ this pa.	(William Wilson Rose)
(Bs)		ELIZABETH	BRADLEY	-	(William Bailey)

[1] Bond surety – George Illsley of Osgathorpe, witnesses Mary Newbound & Hannah Meakin.

[2] Merevale, parts in Leics. & Warks., near Orton on the Hill.

[3] Bond surety – Benjamin Johnson, Worsted Maker of Osgathorpe.

[4] Register gave BIEARLEY. Hathern registers contain many references to BRIERLY, where a Samuel Brierly was baptised in 1763.

20 SEP 1790		GEORGE SAMUEL TETTLEY		of Ashby de la Zouch	(Joseph Wilkins)
(Bs)		ANN	WILLOWS	of this pa.	(John Williows)
21 SEP 1790		THOMAS	HANDFORD	of Whitwick	(Eliz Rose)
(Bs)		SARAH	ROSE	of this pa.	(Thos Johnson)
21 SEP 1790		THOMAS	BRADLEY (21)	of Osgathorpe. Victualler	(Thos Fearson)
(Lic)	[1]	ANN	BOWLEY (21)	of Osgathorpe	(Tho Nadin)
01 DEC 1790		WILLIAM	BAILEY	b./ this pa.	(Jos Sharp)
(Bs)		ANN	ROE	-	(Rebecca Bayley)
07 MAR 1791		THOMAS	STINSON	-	(Francis Farmer)
(Bs)		MARY	GODDARD	-	(Ann Gregory)
24 MAY 1791		FRANCIS	HARVEY	of this pa. widower	(George Insley)
(Bs)		CATHERINE	SIDDONS	of this pa. widow	(Thomas Nadin)
21 SEP 1791		JOHN	WOODWARD	b./ this pa.	(Thos Stinson)
(Bs)		ANN	CORBETT	-	(Mary Corbett)
30 JUL 1792		JOSEPH	WOODCOCK	b./ this pa.	(Mary Rose)
(Bs)		SARAH	HANDFORD	widow	(Ann Woodcock)
24 DEC 1792		SAMUEL	BAGGERLEY	of this pa. widower	(Ellen Gilbert)
(Bs)		ANN	PALMER	of this pa.	(Benj Johnson)
– JUN 1793		THOMAS MATON HARRIS		of this pa.	-
(Bs only)	[2]	SARAH	BURTON	of Breedon	-
28 MAY 1794		THOMAS	HURST (30)	of Osgathorpe. Servant	(Thos Johnson)
(Lic)	[3]	HANNAH	WILLOWS (23)	of Osgathorpe	(Matthew White)
21 SEP 1794		WILLIAM	DARRENTON	b./ this pa.	(Thomas Stinson)
(Bs)		ELIZABETH	GODDARD	-	(Matthew White)
09 FEB 1795		THOMAS	BULL	of Sheepshead	(William Roe)
(Bs)		ANN	FORD	of this pa.	(Ann Hope)
08 SEP 1795		THOMAS	GILBERT	b./ this pa.	(William Woodcock)
(Bs)		ANN	WOODCOCK	-	(Susanna Woodcock)
23 NOV 1795		THOMAS	NORMAN	b./ this pa.	(George Barratt)
(Bs)		HANNAH	BIRD	-	(Matthew White)
25 JAN 1796		WILLIAM	HARDY	b./ this pa.	(William Brown)
(Bs)		SARAH	BAGGERLEY	-	(Matthew White)
09 FEB 1796		WILLIAM	STINSON	of this pa.	(Thos Bull)
(Bs)		MILLICENT	BULL	of Whitwick	(Matthew White)
16 FEB 1796		WILLIAM	HUTCHINSON	of Whitwick	(William Rose)
(Bs)		MARY	ROSE	of this pa.	(Thos Potter)
16 FEB 1796		WILLIAM	WOODWARD	b./ this pa.	(Dawson Young)
(Bs)		ANN	MATCHET	-	(Matthew White)
06 SEP 1796		THOMAS	SWAN	of this pa.	(Wilm Smith)
(Bs)		CATHARINE	SMITH	of Whitwick	(Elizabeth Smith)
05 MAR 1797		FRANCIS	FARMER	b./ this pa.	(Matthew White)
(Bs)		RACHEL	YOUNG	-	(George Roe)

[1] Bond surety – Thos Freerson, junr, of Breedon on the Hill.

[2] Banns read 2, 9 & 16 June. Married (6 months later) at Breedon on the Hill, 15 December 1793.

[3] Bond surety – Thomas Johnson, Hosier of Osgathorpe.

28 MAR 1797	JOSEPH	KING	b./ this pa.	(Thomas Gilbert)
(Bs)	ELLEN	GILBERT	-	(Matthew White)
09 MAR 1798	WILLIAM MEEKIN WILLIAMSON (21) Farmers Servant			(Jno Branson)
(Lic) [1]	ALICE	BRADLEY (21)	both of Osgathorpe	(Matthew White)
01 JUL 1798	THOMAS	BLACK (40)	of Snibston in pa. of Packington. Husbandman	
(Lic) [2]	SARAH	LEE (30)	of Osgathorpe (Thos Lovett) (Matthew White)	
14 APR 1799	GEORGE	MOUNTANY	b./ this pa.	(Willm Brown)
(Bs)	ELIZABETH	YOUNG	-	(Matthew White)
09 DEC 1799	JAMES	HICKINGBOTTOM	b./ this pa.	(James Mackie)
(Bs)	SARAH	MILLNER	-	(Mary Everard)
13 OCT 1800	THOMAS	JINKS	b./ this pa.	(Matthew White)
(Bs)	MARY	GOODALL	-	(George Blunt)
16 DEC 1800	WILLIAM	DARBY	b./ this pa.	(William Hutchinson)
(Bs)	ELIZABETH	SMITH	-	(Matthew White)
09 APR 1801	JOSEPH	TREWMAN (40)	of Odstone in pa. Shackerstone. Farmer	
(Lic) [3]	MARY	STARBUCK (21)	of Osgathorpe (Thos Starbuck) (Jane ?Riate)	
20 OCT 1801	JOSEPH	SHEPHERD	b./ this pa.	(William Moseley)
(Bs)	ELIZABETH	DARBY	-	(William Shephard)
12 JUL 1802	WILLIAM	DEXTER	b./ this pa.	(Elizabeth Willamott)
(Bs)	REBECCA	WILLAMOTT	-	(Matthew White)
11 OCT 1802	JAMES	RAGG	of Ashby de la Zouch	(Wm Bailey)
(Bs)	JANE	PERRY	of this pa.	(Matthew White)
14 AUG 1803	FRANCIS	FARMER	b./ this pa.	(Ann Pepper)
(Bs)	MARY	SMITH	-	(George Meakin)
20 SEP 1803	WILLIAM	VARNAM	b./ this pa.	(Jno ?Annerall)
(Bs)	ANN	YOUNG	-	(Sarah Matchett)
13 AUG 1804	WILLIAM	ROE	b./ this pa.	(Robt Bancraft)
(Bs)	MARY	MACKIE	-	(Hannah Pallfreman)
28 MAR 1805	WILLIAM	MOSELEY (21)	of Osgathorpe. Farmer	(James Asher)
(Lic) [4]	ELIZABETH	PEAT (21)	of same	(Mary Cooper)
18 JUN 1805	JOHN	SMEDLEY	of Lockington	(Sarrah Harris)
(Bs)	ANN	BLADON	of this pa.	(Oney Parkins)
22 JUL 1805	JOHN	BRAMLEY	of Hoton	(Ann Slumber)
(Bs)	SARAH	COLLINGTON	of this pa.	(Wm Bailey)
20 AUG 1805	SAMUEL	KING	b./ this pa.	(Francis Swann)
(Bs)	MARY	SMITH	-	(Sarrah Harris)
09 JUN 1806	WILLIAM	HICKLING	of Belton	(John Higgett)
(Bs)	HANNAH	GLOVER	of this pa.	(Wm Bailey)
19 OCT 1806	JOHN	JORDIN	b./ this pa.	(Willi Darby)
(Bs)	ALICE	COOPSTAKES	-	(Matthew White)

[1] Bond surety – John Bradley, Farmer in liberty of Grace Dieu in parish of Belton.

[2] Bond surety – Thomas Lovatt, Blacksmith of Ibstock.

[3] Bond surety – Thomas Starbuck, Farmer of Barlston in parish of Market Bosworth.

[4] Bond surety – James Asher, Farmer of Osgathorpe.

21 SEP	1807	THOMAS	KING	b./ Osgathorpe	(Thomas Maton Harres)
(Bs)	[1]	ANN	BRADLEY	-	(Sarah Harres)
08 MAR	1808	WILLIAM	DEXTER	of Belton	(Mary King)
(Bs)		JANE	BAGGERLY	of Osgathorpe	(Thomas Maton Harres)
19 JUN	1808	WILLIAM	DARBY	b./ this pa.	(Hannah Price)
(Bs)		ANN	BONSOR	-	(Matthew Wite)
27 SEP	1808	JOHN	WEBSTER	of Belton	(Pheby Devenport)
(Bs)		HANNAH	DARBY	of Osgathorpe	(Abram Wallis)
03 OCT	1808	JOSEPH	MOORE	b./ this pa.	(Elizabeth Mooer)
(Bs)		SARAH	FARMER	-	(William Smith)
24 APR	1809	WILLIAM	PICKARD	b./ this pa.	(Ann Vernam)
(Bs)		ANN	CAROLINE	-	(Wm Vernam)
11 FEB	1810	WILLIAM	MILES	b./ this pa.	(Mary Johnson)
(Bs)		ANN	MOUSLEY	-	(Benj Johnson)
20 FEB	1810	ABRAM	WALLIS	of Worthington	(Hannah Peat)
(Bs)		ELIZABETH	HANFORD	of Osgathorpe	(Thomas Massey)
27 NOV	1810	GEORGE	HACKETT (21)	of Breedon on' Hill. Farmer	(Jane Hackett)
(Lic)	[2]	SARAH	BOSTOCK (21)	of Osgathorpe	(Joseph Bostock)
24 DEC	1811	CHRISTOPHER	YOUNG	b./ this pa.	(Ann Vernam)
(Bs)		HANNAH	REAVES	-	(William Devenport)
24 FEB	1812	THOS	SMALLWOOD	of Breedon	(Mary Underwood)
(Bs)		PHEBE	DAVENPORT	of this pa.	(Joseph Hicklin)
19 MAY	1812	JOSEPH	WINFIELD	b./ this pa.	(Wm Harvey)
(Bs)		ELIZABETH	WOOD	-	(Ann Harris)
19 MAY	1812	WILLIAM	HARVEY	b./ this pa.	(Joseph Winfield)
(Bs)		ANN	HARRIS	-	(Eliza'th Wood)
18 NOV	1812	JOSEPH	FARMER (21)	of Osgathorpe. Farmer	(Eliz'th Dexter)
(Lic)	[3]	MARY	DEXTER (21)	of Breedon	(John Dexter)
15 AUG	1813	JOSEPH	MOORE	b./ Osgathorpe	(Eliz'th Brown)
(Bs)		MARY	BROWN	c./ p.	(Francis Swann)
07 AUG	1814	JOHN	CROSS	b./ this pa.	(Mary Brown)
(Bs)		MARY	KING	c./ p.	(Thos King)
03 JAN	1815	WILLIAM	PARKER	of Thorny, Cambs. Farmer	(M A Fell)
(Bs)		JANE	FELL	of this pa. c./ p.	(Thos Fell)
24 OCT	1815	JOHN	WORLLIDGE	b./ this pa. Bricklayer	(Mary Whirledg)
(Bs)		ELIZTH	DEXTER	c./ p.	(Charles Hall)
	1816	No Marriages			
06 FEB	1817	ALEXANDER	TABBERER (25)	of Ash in pa. Sutton on' Hill, Derbys. Farmer	
(Lic)	[4]	SARAH	BOULTBEE (25)	of this pa. c./ p. (Sophia Gamble)	(John Branson)

---

[1] Banns published 8, 15 & 22 February 1807, 7 months before the marriage took place.

[2] Bond surety – Joseph Bostock, Farmer of Osgathorpe. BT incorrectly gave 7 November, as the marriage licence was not obtained until 26 November.

[3] Bond surety – Thomas Dexter, Grocer of Ashby de la Zouch. BT gave bride as ELIZTH, register & licence gave MARY. Register gave 'both of this parish', but licence gave Breedon for Mary's abode.

[4] Bond surety – William Clarke, Draper of Loughborough.

07 APR 1817	WILLIAM	FREEMAN	of Sheephead	(Elizth Matchett)
(Bs)	ANN	HURST	of this pa. c./ p.	(John Hurst)
01 NOV 1818	JAMES	SHARPE	of Breedon	(Elizabeth Gilbert)
(Bs)	ELLEN	GILBERT	of this pa. c./ p.	(James Gilbert)

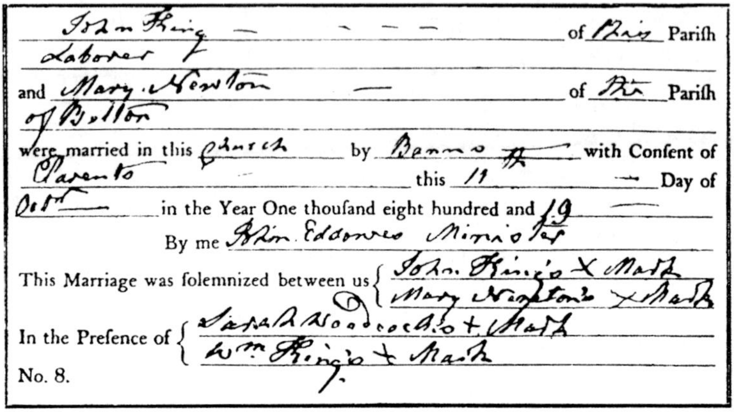

John King — — — of This Pariſh Laborer &

and Mary Newton — of the Pariſh of Belton

were married in this Church by Banns with Conſent of Parents this 11 Day of Octr in the Year One thouſand eight hundred and 19

By me Wm. Eddowes Minister

This Marriage was ſolemnized between us { John King's X Mark / Mary Newton's X Mark }

In the Preſence of { Sarah Woodcock's + Mark / Wm King's + Mark }

No. 8.

The New Register begun after the 1812 Marriage Act (marriage № 8)

11 OCT 1819	JOHN	KING	of this pa. Laborer	(Sarah Woodcock)
(Bs)	MARY	NEWTON	of Belton. c./ p.	(William King)
04 NOV 1819	WILLIAM	KING	of this pa. Labourer	(Sarah Rose)
(Bs)	SARAH	WOODCOCK	of this pa. c./ p.	(Thos King)
06 FEB 1820	JOSEPH	MEE	of Sheephead	(Ann Mee)
(Bs)	MARY	MATCHET	of this pa. c./ p.	(James Freer)
17 SEP 1820	THOS	WARD	of Whysall, Notts.	(Hannah White)
(Bs)	MARY	WHITE	of this pa. c./ p.	(John Dilks)
29 MAY 1821	THOS	BARRETT	of St Mary de Wigford, Lincoln	(Mary Slack)
(Bs)	SARAH	BURKIT	of this pa. c./ p.	(William Darby)
21 AUG 1821	JOHN	BRANSON (21) wid	of this pa. Schoolmaster	(Thomas Baker)
(Lic) [1]	MARY	UNDERWOOD (21)	of Osgathorpe c./ p.	(Elizabeth Browning)
09 DEC 1821	FRANCIS	HEWSON	of this pa. Laborer	(Ann Wakefield)
(Bs)	MARY	WAKEFIELD	of this pa. c./ p.	(William Marlow)
30 DEC 1821	THOMAS	BRADSHAW	of this pa. Currier	(Elizth Gilbert)
(Bs)	ELIZTH PARTRIGE SIMONDS		of this pa. c./ p.	(William Marlow)
21 APR 1822	THOS	HUTCHINSON	of Castle Donington	(Hursulah Brown)
(Bs)	ANN	BROWN	of this pa. c./ p.	(William Shaw)
30 JUN 1822	THOMAS	STINSON	of this pa. Stocking Maker	(Hannah Young)
(Bs)	ELIZABETH	HURST	of this pa. c./ p.	(William Devenport)

[1] Bond surety – Thomas Baker, Gent of Ashby de la Zouch. Licence gave Gentleman for schoolmaster.

	1823	No Marriages			
20 SEP	1824	JOSEPH	KING	of this pa. Laborer	(Martha Hays)
(Bs)		MARY	ALT	of this pa. c./ p.	(Edward King)
25 JUL	1825	FRANCIS	JAMES	of this pa. Laborer	(Mary King)
(Bs)		HANNAH	ALLT	of this pa. c./ p.	(Joseph King)
24 OCT	1825	JAMES	KING	of this pa. Laborer	(Hursulah Brown)
(Bs)		MARY	THOMPSON	of Breedon c./ p.	(George Thompson)
01 JUL	1826	GEORGE. I.	MEAKIN (19)	of Osgathorpe. Draper	(Mary Meakin)
(Lic)	[1]	M. C. C.	KELK (18)	of Osgathorpe. c./ p.	(W. Hyde Kelk)
10 JUN	1827	WILLIAM	WORTLEY	of Belton	(Elizabeth Devenport)
(Bs)		ANN	WALDRAM	of this pa. c./ p.	(Wm Devenport)
07 OCT	1827	GEORGE	HUTCHINSON	of Long Whatton	(John Fox)
(Bs)		HERSILID	BROWN	of this pa. c./ p.	(Rachel Brown)
24 DEC	1827	JOSEPH	BAKER	of Oakthorpe (William King)	(William Mackie)
(Bs)	[2]	ELIZABETH	DAVENPORT	of this pa. c./ p.	(Ann Woodcock)
05 FEB	1828	JOHN	BENNETT	of Kegworth. Servant	(Mary Woodcock)
(Bs)		ANN	KING	of this pa. c./ p.	(John Carter)
22 SEP	1828	CHRISTOPHER	YOUNG	of this pa. F.W.K.	(Elizabeth Hanford)
(Bs)		SARAH	HURST	of this pa. c./ p.	(William Davenport)
28 APR	1829	STEPHEN COX	WOOD	of Whitwick	(Mary Woodcock)
(Bs)		ANN	WOODCOCK	of this pa. c./ p.	(William Taylor)
14 JUL	1829	GEORGE	EARP	of Ocbrook	(Thomas Gilbert)
(Bs)	[3]	ELIZABETH	GILBERT	of Osgathorpe c./ p.	(Ann Gilbert)
23 NOV	1829	FRANCIS HASTINGS	NEEDHAM	of this pa.	(Mary Foster)
(Bs)		MARY	ROE	of this pa. c./ p.	(James Roe)
18 DEC	1829	JOHN	SHARP	of this pa.	(John Pegg)
(Bs)		MARY	PEGG	of this pa. c./ p.	(Sarah Mountney)
31 MAY	1830	FRANCIS	HADDEN	of this pa. Stocking Maker	(Mary Swann)
(Bs)		SARAH	SWAN	of this pa. c./ p.	(Robert Wheat)
24 JUN	1830	THOMAS	TRUMAN (21)	of Odstone in pa. Shackerstone. Farmer	
(Lic)	[4]	GEORGIANA JANE	HACKETT (19)	of this pa. c./ p. (Mary Meekin)	(Joseph Bostock)
29 NOV	1830	EDWARD	YOUMANS	of Long Whatton. Labourer	(Mary Robinson)
(Bs)		RACHEL	BROWN	of this pa. c./ p.	(Samuel Youmans)
26 MAY	1831	WILLIAM	STATHAM	of this pa. Servant	(Rebecca Hill)
(Bs)		MARY	WOODCOCK	of this pa. c./ p.	(John Roberts)
29 NOV	1831	GEORGE	ROE	of this pa. widower	(Ann Bull)
(Bs)		MARY	NEWTON	of Whitwick widow	(Wm Bailey)

[1] Licence gave Gentleman instead of Draper. It also gave '... he further made oath, that the consent of George Meakin the father of the said George Illsley Meakin, and of Elizabeth Catherine Kelk the mother of the said Mary Caroline Charlotte Kelk, her father being dead and she having no guardian of her person lawfully appointed and her mother being unmarried, hath been obtained to such marriage'.

[2] BT gave 'William MACKIE' instead of 'the mark of William KING'.

[3] OCBROOK = OCKBROOK, Derbys. where their banns were also recorded the 7, 14 & 21 June 1829.

[4] Licence gave, 'with consent of father George Hackett, Farmer of Breedon'.

01 MAR 1832	DANIEL	HUTCHINSON	of Stretton en le Field	(Mary Gilbert)
(Bs)	ANN	GILBERT	of this pa.	(Samuel Gilbert)
FEB/MAR1832	FRANCIS	HADDEN	of this pa. widower	-
(Bs only) [1]	MARY	MOORE	of this pa.	-
10 APR 1832	JOHN	DARBY	b./ this pa. Labourer	(Sarah Hancock)
(Bs)	SARAH	GREETE	-	(George Needham)
APR/MAY1833	EDWARD	KING	of this pa.	-
(Bs only) [2]	ELIZA	JEFFERSON	of this pa.	-
15 OCT 1833	THOMAS	PICKARD	of this pa. Brickmaker	(Sarah Perkins)
(Bs) [3]	CHARLOTTE	PERKINS	of Whitwick	(Joseph Pickard)
18 NOV 1833	THOMAS	BIRD	of Worthington	(Chris: Young)
(Bs)	MARY	HURST	of this pa.	(Elizabeth Waldram)
30 DEC 1833	JAMES	ROE	b./ this pa.	(Mary King)
(Bs)	SARAH	ALT	-	(Joseph King)
19 AUG 1834	GEORGE	STEVENSON	of Worthington	(William Bowler)
(Bs)	SARAH	WALLIS	of this pa.	(Ann Wallis)
— SEP 1834	JOSEPH	SIDDONS	of this pa.	-
(Bs only) [4]	ANN	MEAR	of Worthington	-
11 JUN 1835	THOMAS	KING	of this pa. widower	(John Darby)
(Bs)	ELIZABETH	BARNETT	of this pa.	(Mary King)
— NOV 1835	SAMUEL	WEBSTER	of this pa. widower	-
(Bs only) [5]	ELIZA	HARDING	of Sheepshead	-
25 DEC 1835	JOSEPH	MUSGROVE	of Hathern	(Elizabeth Smith)
(Bs)	SARAH	KINSEY	of this pa.	(William Moore)
1836	No Marriages			
09 FEB 1837	WILLIAM	MILES (21)	of Osgathorpe. Farmer	(Jane Stevens)
(Lic) [6]	HANNAH	STEVENS (21)	of Osgathorpe	(Thomas Wyatt Stevens)
— FEB 1837	JOHN	MEAKIN	of this pa.	-
(Bs only) [7]	HANNAH	ALT	of Breedon	-
04 APR 1837	JOSEPH	MOSELEY	of this pa. Farmer	(Stephen Bailey)
(Bs)	MARY	BAILEY	of the pa. of All Saints, Derby	(M. Moseley)
05 APR 1837	EDWARD	KING	of this pa. Labourer	(Wm King)
(Bs)	MARY	MUGGLESTON	of this pa.	(Elizabeth Mugglestone)
19 JUN 1837	BENJAMIN	HOLLOWAY	b./ this pa.	(Ann Hucthinson)
(Bs)	MARTHA	GILBERT	-	(Samuel Gilbert)

'See the new register of marriages'

1 Banns register entry was crossed through. [No evidence that marriage took place].
2 Banns register entry was crossed through. [No evidence that marriage took place].
3 Banns register gave Thringstone instead of Whitwick.
4 Married at Worthington, 6 October 1834.
5 Married at Shepshed, 1 December 1835.
6 The original licence can be found, within the marriage register (Leics. Record Office, DE 1668/5).
7 Married at Breedon on the Hill, 3 April 1837.

From 1837, the fathers of the groom & bride were also recorded and these appear in that order on the 3rd line of each marriage. Due to the limitations of space & for clarity, Osgathorpe has been omitted where it was given for either the groom or bride. All other places of abode have been included. In some cases it has been necessary to abbreviate 'Framework Knitter' to F.W.K.

25 DEC 1837	JAMES	MATCHETT (21)	Collier	(Ann Bruen)
(Bs) [1]	SARAH	YOUNG (22)	Framework Knitter	(Thomas Gibson)
	William Matchett - Potter		Christopher Young - F.W.K.	
— DEC 1837	JAMES	GILBERT	of this pa.	-
(Bs only)	SARAH	MORLEY	of Kegworth	-
	— [N.B. Married at Kegworth 25 Dec 1837]			
MAR/APR1838	LOT	QUENBY	b./ this pa.	-
(Bs only)	MARY	YOUNG	-	-
	— [N.B. Marriage not recorded at St Mary's, Osgathorpe]			
17 DEC 1838	HENRY	SMALLWOOD (wid/ofa)	of Griffy Dam, Worthington. Collier	
(Bs)	JANE	HAYWOOD (wid/ofa)	Lace Runner	(Thos Johnson)
	Geo Smallwood - Stocking Maker		Geo Bark - Labourer	(Sarah Glover)
19 DEC 1839	WILLIAM	KING (ofa)	Labourer	(William King)
(Bs) [2]	MATILIDA	PERRY (20)	Lace Worker	(Sarah King)
	Samuel King - F.W.K.		George Perry - Hawker	
16 NOV 1840	JOHN	ALLT (ofa)	Labourer	(Stephen Cox Wood)
(Bs) [3]	ELIZABETH	FREARSON (ofa)	of Worthington. Lace Runner	(William Mee)
	Samuel Allt - Labourer		Lovett Frearson - Labourer	
JUL/AUG 1841	JOHN	KING	b./ this pa.	-
(Bs only)	MARY	MARSHALL	-	-
	[Banns entry was crossed through. No evidence that marriage took place]			
13 SEP 1841	WILLIAM	MUGLESTON (wid/ofa)	Labourer	(Jane Stevens)
(Bs)	HANNAH	ROE (ofa)	Lace Runner	(Henry Stevens)
	Joseph Muglestone - Farmer		William Roe - Labourer	
17 APR 1842	JOHN HURST	BROWN (ofa)	Labourer	(Henry Stevens)
(Bs)	DINAH	CONER (ofa)	Lace Runner	(Steven Cox Wood)
	Joseph Hurst - Labourer		William Coner - Labourer	
24 JUL 1842	JOHN	HALL (minor)	of Belton. F.W.K.	(John King)
(Bs)	MARY	WARD (minor)	Lace Runner	(Mary Hallam)
	Charles Hall - F.W.K.		James Ward - Coal Carrier	
14 MAR 1843	GEORGE	BLACK (ofa)	Labourer	(John Revell)
(Bs)	ELIZABETH	KING (ofa)	Dress Maker	(?Mary King)
	Samuel Black - Carpenter		John King - Labourer	

[1] Same marriage was also recorded in previous register, but has only been entered here once. Banns originally published Aug/Sep 1837, but crossed through, republished Dec 1837.

[2] Banns originally published Nov/Dec 1838, but crossed through, republished Nov/Dec 1839.

[3] Same marriage was also recorded in previous register, but has only been entered here once.

29 MAY 1843	JAMES	CLARKE (wid/ofa)	Farmer	(John Black)
(Lic)	SARAH	MILES (21)	-	(Mary Miles)
	William Clarke - Farmer		Henry Miles - Farmer	
29 MAY 1843	GEORGE	PERRY (ofa)	Collier	(Samuel Gilbert)
(Bs)	CATHARINE	BLACK (minor)	Lace Runner	(Henry Swinfen)
	Joseph Perry - Potter		Samuel Black - Carpenter	
20 JUN 1843	THOMAS	COX (ofa)	of Thringstone. Shoemaker	(Sarah Cox)
(Lic) [1]	ANN	BAILEY (ofa)	-	(Stephen Bailey)
	Robert Cox - Publican		William Bailey - Blacksmith	
18 SEP 1843	JOSEPH	BURTON (ofa)	Labourer	(James Nelson)
(Bs)	CHARLOTTE	MOORE (ofa)	Framework Knitter	(Mary Hallam)
	John Burton - Labourer		Joseph Moore - F.W.K.	
30 OCT 1843	JOSEPH	MOORE (wid/ofa)	F.W.K.	(Hannah Pope)
(Bs)	HANNAH	HOWARD (wid/ofa)	of Worthington. Lacemaker	(Joseph King)
	William Moore - F.W.K.		Thos Whyman - Travaller	
21 DEC 1843	SAMUEL	EAGLEFIELD (ofa)	Labourer	(James Eaglefield)
(Bs)	SARAH ANN	ROE (ofa)	Domestic Servant	(Ann ?Enigon)
	James Eaglefield - Labourer		William Roe - Labourer	
04 MAR 1844	ESAU	PEMBERTON (ofa)	Coal Miner	(George Hickinbottom)
(Bs)	DINAH	BRADLEY (ofa)	Framework Knitter	(Stephen Cox Wood)
	Samuel Skirmer - Farmer		William Bradley - F.W.K.	
23 SEP 1844	JOSEPH	KING (wid/ofa)	Labourer	(Sarah Waldram)
(Bs)	ELIZABETH	WALDRAM (ofa)	Lace Runner	(Stephen Cox Wood)
	Joseph King - Labourer		James Waldram - Labourer	
04 JAN 1845	WILLIAM	WARD (ofa)	Labourer	(Mary Hale)
(Bs)	HANNAH	POXON (minor)	Lace Runner	(Stephen Cox Wood)
	James Ward - Labourer		Samuel Poxon - Labourer	
29 OCT 1845	JOHN	DARBY (wid/ofa)	Labourer	(Samuel Darby)
(Bs)	SARAH	BRADLEY (ofa)	Charwoman	(Elizabeth Darby)
	William Darby - Labourer		William Bradley - Labourer	
23 NOV 1846	THOMAS	KING (ofa)	Labourer	(John Ellis)
(Bs)	ELIZABETH	HARRISON (ofa)	Servant	(William Davenport)
	John King - Labourer		John Harrison - Labourer	
23 MAR 1847	THOMAS	JEFFCOAT (ofa)	of Whitwick. Sawyer	(Samuel Jeffcoat)
(Bs)	ELIZABETH	JOHNSON (ofa)	-	(Martha Johnson)
	Samuel Jeffcoat - Labourer		Thomas Johnson - Butcher	
20 SEP 1847	SAMUEL	DARBY (ofa)	Labourer	(William Pope)
(Bs)	ELIZABETH	POPE (ofa)	-	(William Davenport)
	William Darby - Labourer		Ralph Pope - Publican	
20 MAR 1848	THOMAS	HALLAM (ofa)	Framework Knitter	(George Hickinbottom)
(Bs)	ELIZABETH	BRADLEY (ofa)	Framework Knitter	(William Davenport)
	George Hallam - F.W.K.		William Bradley - F.W.K.	

[1] Licence gave 'Thomas Cox of the Hamlet of Thringstone in the pariah of Whitwick *Schoolmaster*'.

31 JUL 1848	JOHN	HOROBIN (-)	Labourer	(William Davenport)
(Bs)	HANNAH	HURST (minor)	Lace Runner	(William Davenport Junr)
	William Horobin - Labourer		Joseph Hurst - Labourer	
30 OCT 1848	WILLIAM	GADSBY (ofa)	Servant	(Thomas Hallam)
(Bs)	ANN	BRADLEY (ofa)	Framework Knitter	(William Davenport)
	William Gadsby - Labourer		William Bradley - F.W.K.	
19 FEB 1849	JAMES	MILLWOOD (ofa)	of Whitwick. Labourer	(Benjamin Adams)
(Bs)	CHARLOTTE	JARVIS (ofa)	Framework Knitter	(Elizabeth Millwood)
	James Millwood - Labourer		Samuel Jarvis - Labourer	
— APR 1849	GEORGE	HEYWOOD	b./ this pa.	-
(Bs only)	ANN	CHESTER	-	-
	— [N.B. Marriage not recorded at St Mary's, Osgathorpe]			
05 NOV 1849	JOSEPH	KING (ofa)	Labourer	(Thomas Soare)
(Bs)	DOROTHY	MASSEY (ofa)	of Breedon. Servant	(William Davenport)
	Samuel King - F.W.K.		John Massey - Labourer	
29 OCT 1850	GEORGE	FIELDING (ofa)	of Sheepy. Collector of Tolls	(Wm Platts)
(Bs)	HANNAH	JARVIS (ofa)	Servant	(William Davenport)
	George Fielding - Surveyor of roads		Samuel Jarvis - Labourer	
09 DEC 1850	FREDERICK	PERRY (ofa)	Collier	(Giles Morgan)
(Bs)	HANNAH	HALL (minor)	Seamstress	(William Davenport)
	George Perry – Potter		Charles Hall - F.W.K.	
22 JUL 1851	WILLIAM	BREWIN (ofa)	of Markfield. Labourer	(Joseph Welham)
(Bs)	HANNAH	OSBORNE (ofa)	Servant	(Mary Ann Goodrich)
	William Brewin - Farmer		George Osborne - Labourer	
04 NOV 1851	WILLIAM	POPE (ofa)	of Ashby de la Zouch. Tailor	(Joseph Platts)
(Cert) [1]	MARTHA	JOHNSON (ofa)	-	(Maria Johnson)
	Ralph Pope - Publican		Thomas Johnson - Farmer	
JAN/FEB 1852	JOHN	WALDRAM	b./ this pa. widower	-
(Bs only)	ELIZABETH	GREEN	-	-
	[Banns entry was crossed through. No evidence that marriage took place]			
25 OCT 1852	JOHN	FREEMAN (20)	of Belton. Tailor	(Edward Freeman)
(Bs)	SARAH	HICKLING (24)	of Belton. Seamstress	(Mary Freeman)
	Edward Freeman - Miller		Christopher Hickling - Labourer	
OCT/NOV1852	JOHN	MATCHET	b./ this pa.	-
(Bs only)	SARAH	YOUNG	widow	-
	[Banns register entry was crossed through, with note saying 'Not married']			
OCT/NOV1852	JOHN	JORDAN	of Breedon	-
(Bs only)	MARIA	YOUNG	of this pa.	-
	[Banns register entry was crossed through, with note saying 'Not married']			
15 NOV 1852	JOHN	WALDRAM (wid/28)	Collier	(John Jordan)
(Bs)	SOPHIA	YOUNG (21)	Seamstress	(Matilda Young)
	John Waldram - Labourer		Christopher Young - F.W.K.	

[1] Married by Registrar's certificate: From July 1837, it was possible to marry by obtaining a certificate from the local Superintendent Registrar.

24 NOV 1852	GEORGE	DARBY (30)	Labourer	(William Davenport)
(Bs) [1]	ANN	BAKER (21)	Seamstress	(Sarah Stanley)
	William Darby - Labourer		Joseph Baker - Labourer	
20 SEP 1853	JOHN	SMITH (24)	of Whitwick. F.W.K.	(Henry Stretton)
(Bs)	CAROLINE	PERRY (ofa)	Seamstress	(George Sowter)
	Thomas Smith - F.W.K.		George Perry - Potter	
28 NOV 1853	SAMUEL	BAILEY (22)	Servant	(John Smith)
(Bs)	CATHERINE	GREASLEY (23)	Servant	(James Leeson)
	Joseph Bailey - Labourer		Joseph Greasley - F.W.K.	
— DEC 1853	JAMES	SHARPE	of this pa. widower	-
(Bs only)	SARAH	NEAL	of Belton	-
	[Banns register had note saying 'Married at Belton']			
— DEC 1853	JAMES	WATTS	of Thringstone	-
(Bs only)	MARY ANN	MATCHET	of this pa.	-
	[Banns register had note saying 'Withdrawn']			
26 DEC 1853	JOSIAH	PERRY (ofa)	Miner	(Giles Morgan)
(Bs)	ANN	HARRISON (20)	Servant	(Sarah Hawkesworth)
	George Perry - Hawker		John Harrison - Gardener	
27 FEB 1854	CHARLES	WRIGHT (ofa)	of Coleorton. Miner	(George Hurst)
(Bs)	MARY	BENNETT (ofa)	Servant	William Davenport)
	William Wright - Labourer		John Bennett - Labourer	
24 APR 1854	JAMES	MANN (nearly 21)	of Woodhouse Eaves. Blacksmith	
(Bs)	JANE	BRADLEY (ofa)	Seamstress	(Sophia Hickinbottom)
	James Mann - Labourer		William Bradley - F.W.K.	(William Davenport)
18 SEP 1854	WILLIAM	WOLSEY (21)	Labourer	Samuel Jarvis)
(Bs)	MARY	JARVIS (22)	Glove Knitter	(Mary Matchett)
	Daniel Wolsey - Labourer		Samuel Jarvis - Labourer	
31 OCT 1854	WILLIAM	BAILEY (ofa)	Labourer	(Elizabeth Middleton)
(Bs)	ELIZABETH	WRIGHT (ofa)	Charwoman	(William Davenport)
	Thomas Bailey - Labourer		Thomas Wright - Labourer	
OCT/NOV1854	JOHN	SMITH	of this pa.	-
(Bs only)	MARY	PEPPER	of Belton	-
	— [N.B. Register still retained by Belton Church]			
14 NOV 1854	WILLIAM	GRIFFEN (22)	Miner	(John S Hill)
(Bs)	LOUISA	MATCHETT (ofa)	Servant	(William Davenport)
	Thomas Griffen - F.W.K.		Samuel Matchett - Labourer	
27 NOV 1854	GEORGE	HURST (ofa)	Miner	(Eliza Wood)
(Bs)	SARAH	HOWARD (ofa)	Servant	(William Davenport)
	Joseph Hurst - Labourer		William George Howard - Hawker	
12 DEC 1854	HENRY	ROBINSON (ofa)	of Whitwick. Miner	(Thomas Cooper)
(Bs)	ELIZABETH KING	MUGGLESTON	(ofa) Seamstress	(William Adams)
	James Robinson - Bricklayer		Edward King - Labourer	

[1] Banns originally published Mar/Apr 1852, but crossed through, republished Oct/Nov 1852, with note saying 'Married'.

— — 1854/5	JOHN	COWLEY	b./ this pa.	-
(Bs only)	MARY ANN	GREEN	-	-
	[Banns register had note saying 'Withdrawn']			
05 MAR 1855	SAMUEL	JARVIS (20)	Labourer	(William Wolsey)
(Bs)	MARY ANN	MATCHETT (19)	Servant	(Mary Wolsey)
	Samuel Jarvis - Labourer		Samuel Matchett - Labourer	
21 AUG 1855	DAVID CHARLES	HEYWOOD (21)	Labourer	(John Briggs)
(Bs)	ELIZABETH	GREEN (23)	Servant	(Mary Ann Green)
	Samuel Heywood - Labourer		John Green - Carrier	
04 MAR 1856	JAMES BRADLEY	STEVENSON (23)	of Belton. Labourer	(Sarah Hucthinson)
(Bs)	MARY	BRADLEY (25)	Servant. Spinster [Single]	(John Statham)
	William Stevenson - Labourer		William Mackie -Labourer	
24 JUN 1856	THOMAS	JOHNSON (21)	Farmer	(Maria Johnson)
(Lic)	SARAH	CLARKE (21)	Dress Maker	(Joseph Platts)
	Thomas Johnson - Farmer		James Clarke - Farmer	
16 DEC 1856	WILLIAM	TAYLOR (20)	Labourer	(Joseph Bird)
(Bs)	ELIZA	YOUNG (19)	Seamstress	(William Davenport)
	John Taylor - Labourer		Lot Quenby - F.W.K.	
23 MAR 1857	JOHN	MATCHETT (ofa)	Labourer	(Mary Ann Bird)
(Bs)	SARAH	YOUNG (wid/ofa)	Seamstress	(William Davenport)
	Samuel Matchett - Labourer		Thomas Hurst - Labourer	
30 NOV 1857	JOSEPH	HARRIS (24)	Labourer	(William Moore)
(Bs)	MARY ANN	COOPER (20)	Servant	(William Davenport)
	William Harris - Labourer		William Cooper - Hawker	
01 DEC 1857	JOHN	RENNOCKS (23)	Shoe Maker	(John Robinson)
(Bs)	MARY	BROOKS (22)	Servant	(Ann Harris)
	Henry Rennocks - Publican & Shoemaker		John Brooks - Labourer	
03 MAR 1858	EDWARD	MOORE (21)	of Whitwick. Butcher	(Thomas Johnson)
(Lic)	MARIA	JOHNSON (21)	-	(Catharine Platts)
	William Moore - Butcher		Thomas Johnson - Farmer	
06 JUL 1858	GEORGE	PARSONS (ofa)	of Feltham, M'sex. Gentleman	(Henry Parsons)
(Bs) [1]	ISABELLA BLYTHE	DODD (ofa)	-	(Annie Mary Dodd)
	Jonathan Parsons - Gentleman		John Dodd - Clerk in Holy Orders	
18 OCT 1859	GEORGE	WALKER (22)	Labourer	(Sarah Lager)
(Bs) [2]	SOPHIA	HICKINBOTTOM (19)	Seamstress	(William Davenport)
	Joseph Walker - Labourer		George Hickingbottom - F.W.K.	
01 DEC 1859	LEVI	BAKER (ofa)	Labourer	(Hezekiah Baker)
(Bs)	SARAH	KENT (ofa)	Servant	(William Davenport)
	Joseph Baker - Labourer		James Kent - Labourer	
31 DEC 1859	JOHN	EMMERSON (21)	of Belton. Shoemaker	(Paul Gibson)
(Bs)	ALICE	BRADLEY (17)	-	(Sarah Lager)
	Francis Emmerson - F.W.K.		James Bradley - Farmer	

[1] Register gave two further witnesses, Charles Warner & Thomas N. Bland.

[2] Banns originally published May 1858, but crossed through with note saying 'Not married', republished Sep/Oct 1859.

25 DEC 1860	LANCELOT	BENNETT (ofa)	of Sheepshed. Labourer	(Mary Bennett)
(Bs)	ELIZABETH	ROE (ofa)	Servant	(William Davenport)
	William Bennett - Labourer		James Roe - Labourer	
MAY/JUN1861	SAMUEL	DARBY	of this pa. widower	-
(Bs only)	ELIZA	WOODWARD	of Breedon on the Hill	-
	[Banns register entry had note saying 'Not married']			
17 MAR 1862	JACOB	SHAW (22)	of Burton on Trent. Labourer	(Ann White)
(Bs)	HANNAH	WHITE (17)	Servant	(William Davenport)
	John Shaw - Labourer		Mathew White - Labourer	
02 APR 1862	WILLIAM	BRADLEY (ofa)	Labourer	(James Bradley)
(Bs)	SARAH	HICKLING (ofa)	of Belton. Seamstress	(Ann Bradley)
	James Bradley - Farmer		John Hickling - Labourer	
21 OCT 1862	GEORGE	BANCROFT (21)	of Breedon on' Hill. Labourer	(John Smith)
(Bs)	ELIZABETH	POTTS (19)	-	(George Potts)
	Daniel Bancroft - Labourer		John Potts - Labourer	
28 OCT 1862	SAMUEL	SMITH (30)	of Draycott, Derbys. Butcher	(John Smith)
(Lic)	ANN REBECCA	MOSELEY (25)	-	(William Moseley)
	Philip Smith - Butcher		Joseph Moseley - Farmer	
29 DEC 1862	JOHN	STANYER (21)	of Whitwick. Collier	(Thomas Holloway)
(Bs) [1]	ANN	HAWKSWORTH (21)	Seamstress	(William Davenport)
	Joseph Stanyer - Blacksmith		John Williamson - Wheelwright	
31 JAN 1863	WILLIAM THOMAS	HENSON (ofa)	of Whitwick. Clerk at the Colliery	
(Bs)	HARRIET	HODGKINSON (ofa)	Servant	(William Hodgkinson)
	Thomas Henson - Yeoman		Thomas Hodkinson - Malster	(Sarah Hardy)
JAN/FEB 1863	SAMUEL	BENNET	of this pa.	-
(Bs only)	HARRIET	ROSE	of Belton	-
	— [N.B. Register still retained by Belton Church]			
13 FEB 1863	JOSEPH	HODGES (ofa)	Miner	(Catharine Siddons)
(Bs)	ELIZABETH	SIDDONS (ofa)	Servant	(William Davenport)
	John Hodges - Potter		Joseph Siddons - Labourer	
19 OCT 1863	SAMUEL	RICHARDS (24)	Miner	(George Hallam)
(Bs)	ALICE HALLAM	BRADLEY (21)	Framework Knitter	(William Davenport)
	John Richards - Miner		[Blank - Blank]	
22 OCT 1863	JOSEPH	JARVIS (ofa)	Miner	(Samuel Jarvis) (Charles Jarvis)
(Bs)	HANNAH	PICKERING (ofa)	of Normanton le Heath. Servant	
	Samuel Jarvis - Labourer		Henry Pickering - Labourer	
07 NOV 1863	EDWARD	MATCHETT (ofa)	Miner	(George King)
(Bs) [2]	GEORGINA	KING (18)	Seamstress	(William Davenport)
	Samuel Matchett - Labourer		Joseph King - Labourer	
30 NOV 1863	SAMUEL	ROE (ofa)	Labourer	(John Wood)
(Bs)	HANNAH	WOOD (ofa)	Servant	(Charlotte Baker)
	James Roe - Labourer		Francis Wood - Miner	

[1] The name Mary Hawksworth was crossed out in the fathers name section & John Williamson - Wheelwright was added.

[2] Georgina's age appears to have been entered as 19 and then altered to 18.

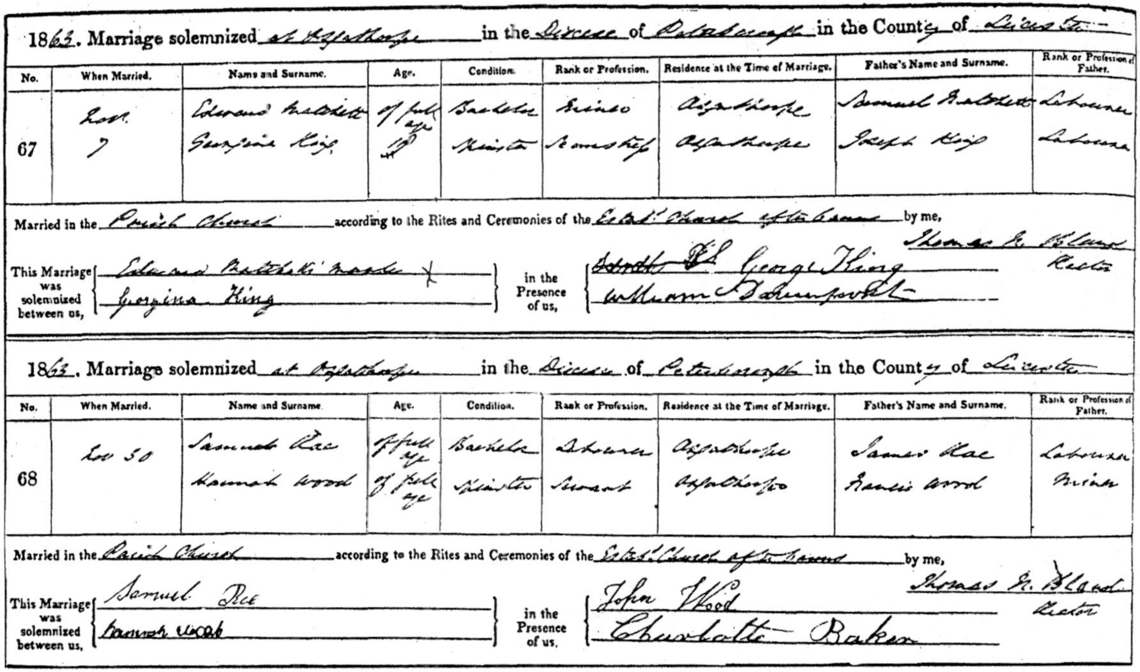

18*63*. Marriage solemnized *at* [illegible] in the *Diocese* of *Peterborough* in the County of *Leicester*

No.	When Married.	Name and Surname.	Age.	Condition.	Rank or Profession.	Residence at the Time of Marriage.	Father's Name and Surname.	Rank or Profession of Father.
67	*Nov. 7*	[illegible]	*of full age*	*Bachelor*	[illegible]	[illegible]	[illegible]	*Labourer*
		Georgina King	*of full age*	*Spinster*	[illegible]	[illegible]	*Joseph King*	*Labourer*

Married in the *Parish Church* according to the Rites and Ceremonies of the *Estabd Church after Banns* by me, *Thomas N. Bland Rector*

This Marriage was solemnized between us, *[illegible] mark X*, *Georgina King*; in the Presence of us, *George King*, *William [illegible]*

18*63*. Marriage solemnized *at* [illegible] in the *Diocese* of *Peterborough* in the County of *Leicester*

No.	When Married.	Name and Surname.	Age.	Condition.	Rank or Profession.	Residence at the Time of Marriage.	Father's Name and Surname.	Rank or Profession of Father.
68	*Nov. 30*	*Samuel Rae*	*of full age*	*Bachelor*	*Labourer*	[illegible]	*James Rae*	*Labourer*
		Hannah Wood	*of full age*	*Spinster*	*Servant*	[illegible]	*Francis Wood*	[illegible]

Married in the *Parish Church* according to the Rites and Ceremonies of the *Estabd Church after Banns* by me, *Thomas N. Bland Rector*

This Marriage was solemnized between us, *Samuel Rae*, *Hannah Wood*; in the Presence of us, *John Wood*, *Charlotte Baker*

The New Register started in 1837 (page 34)
See bottom of opposite page for a transcription
Note the ages given as 'of full age' (21 & over)

03 DEC 1863 JOHN WALL (23) of Castle Donington. Baker (Henry Parson)
(Bs) MARY ANN STATHAM (minor) Servant (Mary Ann Fretter)
James Wall - Shoemaker William Statham - Labourer

— DEC 1864 SAMUEL CHAPLIN of Markfield -
(Bs only) FANNY BROOKS of this pa. -
— [N.B. Married at Markfield 20 Dec 1864]

DEC/JAN 1865 JOSEPH BROOKS of this pa. -
(Bs only) [1] MARTHA HARTSHORN of Long Whatton -
— [N.B. Married at Long Whatton 3 Jan 1865]

04 APR 1865 STEPHEN DEAVILLE (ofa) Blacksmith (Caroline Clarke)
(Bs) MARY CLARKE (minor) - (William Deacon)
Jesse Deaville - Blacksmith James Clarke - Farmer

18 SEP 1865 THOMAS KING (22) Miner (Sarah Black)
(Bs) ELLEN JAMES (21) Servant (William Davenport)
Edward King - Labourer William James - Labourer

25 DEC 1865 THOMAS STOCKS (ofa) Labourer (Charlotte Baker)
(Bs) SARAH WARD (wid/ofa) Servant (William Davenport)
James Roe - Labourer Eli Moore - Labourer

— DEC 1865 GILES MORGAN of this pa. widower -
(Bs only) ELIZA HAMMOND of Belton -
— [N.B. Register still retained by Belton Church]

30 JAN 1866 JOHN SIDDONS (ofa) Collier (William Siddons)
(Bs) MARY ANN FRETTER (ofa) Semstress (Louisa Fretter)
Joseph Siddons - Labourer William Fretter - Labourer

09 FEB 1867 HENRY WEBSTER (23) of Breedon. Labourer (James Winfield)
(Bs) SARAH BLACK (23) Servant (Mary Elliott)
Samuel Webster - Labourer Samuel Black - Wheelwright

26 FEB 1867 WILLIAM BILLING (21) Miner (Joseph Hood)
(Bs) [2] CHARLOTTE BAKER (20) Semsstres (Mary Wright)
John Billing - Farmer [Blank - Blank] ~~William Baker - Labourer~~

23 SEP 1867 JOSEPH BRADLEY (22) Miner (William Tanser)
(Bs) FRANCES TANSER (24) - (Marther ?Peace)
James Bradley - Yeoman William James - Farmer

— SEP 1867 HEZEKIAH TAYLOR of this pa. -
(Bs only) HANNAH PARSONS of Market Bosworth -
— [N.B. Marriage not recorded at St Peter's, Market Bosworth]

15 JUN 1868 SAMUEL DARBY (wid/44) Labourer (Charles Everley)
(Bs) ELIZA EVERLEY (30) - (Sarah Everley)
William Darby - Labourer Thomas Everley - Labourer

18 AUG 1868 WILLIAM GILBERT (wid/48) Blacksmith (William Mason Brooks)
(Bs) ELIZABETH HODGKINSON (32) - (Harriett Henson)
Thomas Gilbert - Cordwainer Thomas Hodgkinson - Maltster

---

[1] Banns published 18, 25 Dec 1864 & 1 Jan 1865.

[2] The name of William Baker - Labourer, was crossed out and no other name entered.

Date	Forename	Surname	Details	Witness
22 SEP 1868	WILLIAM	SIDDONS (21)	Miner	(Catherine Siddons)
(Bs)	LOUISA	FRETTER (20)	-	(William Burton)
	Joseph Siddons - Labourer		William Fretter - Labourer	
08 DEC 1868	WILLIAM	BURTON (21)	Miner	(George King)
(Bs)	HARRIETT	HUDSON (23)	-	(Eliza Burton)
	Joseph Burton - Miner		Thomas Hudson - Blacksmith	
25 DEC 1868	THOMAS	GREEN (24)	of Sheepshed. Labourer	(John Green)
(Bs)	MATILDA	YOUNG (25)	-	(Eliza Richardson)
	George Hewitt Green - F.W.K.		Christopher Young - F.W.K.	
05 APR 1869	RICHARD	TRIGGER (21)	of Sheepshed. Labourer	(William Gadsby)
(Bs)	JANE	HALLAM (20)	-	(Ruth Hallam)
	Joseph Trigger - Labourer		Thomas Hallam - Miner	
22 JUN 1869	ENOCH	BARNES (22)	of Ratcliff on Soar. Labourer	(Josiah Perry)
(Bs)	SARAH ANN	KING (20)	-	(Fanny Ellis)
	William Barnes - Labourer		Thomas King - Carrier	
29 NOV 1869	JOHN WILLIAM KING (22)		Miner	(William King)
(Bs)	MARY JANE	GARNER (21)	-	(Fanny Harrison Ellis)
	Thomas King - Carrier		John Garner - Publizcan	
25 DEC 1869	JOHN	SMITH (20)	Miner	(Samuel Hartshorn)
(Bs)	MARY	HARTSHORN (16)	-	(Eliza Burton)
	Benjamin Smith - Labourer		John Hartshorn – Labourer	
08 FEB 1870	GEORGE	KING (23)	Shoe Maker	(Georgiana Matchett)
(Bs)	SARAH	QUENBY (25)	-, of Knight Thorpe in pa. All Saints, Loughb'	
	Joseph King - Labourer		William Quenby - Labourer	(Amos Quenby)
— — 1870	RANDAL JOSEPH UPTON		of this pa.	-
(Bs only)	SARAH ANN	HOLLINGHEAD	of Grinestone [Grimston]	-
	— [N.B. Register still retained by Grimston Church]			
19 SEP 1870	JOSEPH	ROOM (wid/52)	of St George's, Birmingham. Ironmonger	
(Bs)	LOUISA	BRANSON (40)	- (Samuel Branson)	(Caroline Cufflin)
	Richard Room - Wool Comber		William Branson - Farmer	
26 DEC 1870	JOSEPH	BILLING (21)	Labourer	(William Billing)
(Bs)	RUTH	HALLAM (20)	-	(Ruth Hallam)
	John Billing - Carrier		Thomas Hallam - Pit Labourer	
09 MAY 1871	WILLIAM	DARBY (21)	Miner	(William Quenby)
(Bs)	MARY ANN	QUENBY (16)	-	(Mary Ann Darby)
	Samuel Darby - Labourer		Lot Quenby - Stockinger	
— JUN 1871	WILLIAM	GADSBY	of this pa.	-
(Bs only)	ELIZA	PAULEY	of Sheepshead	-
	— [N.B. Married at Shepshed 4 July 1871]			
04 SEP 1871	FREDERICK	BAXTER (23)	of Kegworth. Wagoner	(Thomas King)
(Bs)	ELIZA	KING (22)	-	(Ann Ault)
	John Baxter - Labourer		Edward King - Labourer	
24 JAN 1872	WILLIAM	PARKES (23)	of St Peters, Derby. Bricklayer	(Clara Parkes)
(Bs)	MARY ANN	DARBY (20)	-	(Thomas Darby)
	Jesse Parkes - Labourer		Samuel Darby – Labourer	

15 APR 1872	WILLIAM	KING (23)	Miner	(Joseph King)
(Bs)	MARY	KING (20)	-	(Sarah King)
	Joseph King - Labourer		Thomas King - Carrier	
— AUG 1872	JOSEPH	DARBY	of this pa.	-
(Bs only)	MARY	FLAMSON	of Thringstone in the district of St George's	-
	— [N.B. Married at St George's, Swannington 15 Oct 1872]			
26 NOV 1872	JOSHUA SAMUEL GOUGH (26)		of Thringstone. Butcher	(Giles Morgan)
(Bs) [1]	HARRIETT	MORGAN (21)	-	(Hannah Quenby)
	William Gough - Butcher		Benjamin Morgan - Dealer in Earthenware	
29 JUL 1873	JOHN	BENNETT (26)	Labourer	(George Burton)
(Bs)	ELIZA	BURTON (22)	-	(Sarah Ann Bennett)
	John Bennett -Labourer		Joseph Burton - Miner	
26 AUG 1873	JASON HERRIOTT REEVES WHITE (22)		Civil Engineer	(John Puxley White)
(Bs)	LOUISA	KNIGHT (21)	-	(Edward Price Knight)
	John Puxley White - Accountant		John Knight - Farmer	
15 DEC 1873	GEORGE	HORROBIN (20)	Labourer	(Samuel Matchett)
(Bs)	EMILY	DARBY (19)	-	(Sarah Darby)
	[Blank - Blank]		William Darby - Labourer	
26 NOV 1874	THOMAS	DARBY (26)	Pit Labourer	Samuel Matchett
(Bs)	ELLEN	BURBIDGE (24)	Servant	(Ann Pepper)
	Samuel Darby - Labourer		Edward Burbidge - Labourer	
02 MAR 1875	JAMES	LAKIN (24)	of Hathern. Cordwainer	(William Siddons)
(Bs)	HANNAH	SIDDONS (24)	-	(Catherine Siddons)
	Joseph Lakin - Labourer		Joseph Siddons - Labourer	
07 JUN 1875	GEORGE	BURTON (26)	Miner	(Thomas Clifford Burton)
(Bs)	SARAH	JARVIS (21)	-	(Eliza Bennett)
	Joseph Burton - Miner		George Jarvis - Miner	
16 MAR 1876	CHARLES	JARVIS (20)	Collier	(W. Rowbotham)
(Bs)	MARY ANN	ROWBOTHAM (20)	-	(H. Rowbotham)
	Samuel Jarvis - Collier		Samuel Rowbotham - Labourer	
24 OCT 1876	WILLIAM	DAVENPORT (64)	Coal Carrier	(Joseph Darby)
(Bs)	FANNY	WARDLE (42)	of St Andrew's, Thringstone	(Mary Darby)
	William Davenport - F.W.K.		John Wardle - F.W.K.	
25 DEC 1876	THOMAS	DARBY (29)	Labourer	(Samuel Matchett)
(Bs)	HANNAH ELIZABETH QUENBY (28)		-	(Hannah Millward)
	Samuel Darby - Labourer		Lot Quenby - F.W.K.	
02 JUL 1877	JOHN	HAYWOOD (22)	Miner	(Thomas Platts)
(Bs)	HANNAH	MILWARD (22)	-	(Elizabeth Milward)
	Hosea Haywood - Miner		James Milward - Labourer	
03 SEP 1877	JOSEPH	WRIGHT (20)	of Sheepshed. F.W.K.	(John Haywood)
(Bs)	SELINA	MILWARD (17)	-	(Hannah Haywood)
	Thomas Wright - F.W.K.		James Milward – Labourer	

[1] Banns register gave JOSHUA'S abode as 'Thringstone in the district of St George's'.

23 DEC 1878 WILLIAM BROWN (22) of Belton. Tailor (Terringham Peberdy)
(Bs) SARAH KING (32) Servant (Mary Ann Brown)
William Brown - Labourer Edward King - Labourer

— SEP 1879 WILLIAM STEVENSON of this pa. -
(Bs only) HANNAH WILLIAMS of Morville, Shrops -
—

NOV/DEC1879 CHARLES SMITH of this pa. -
(Bs only) MARTHA HUDSON of Blackfordby -
— [N.B. Married at Blackfordby, 26 Dec 1879]

20 SEP 1880 JOSEPH WALKER (22) of All Saints, Loughborough. Carter
(Bs) HANNAH KING (20) Servant (Thomas King) (Eliza Barkby)
John Walker - Carter Thomas King - Carrier

17 MAR 1881 RICHARD HANLEY VESTY (24) of Castle Donington. Farmer (James Gilbert)
(Bs) MARY JANE GILBERT (28) - (Elizabeth Gilbert)
Samuel Vesty - Farmer William Gilbert - Farmer

13 JUL 1881 GEORGE BRYERS (27) of Lewknor, Oxfords. Coachman
(Bs) ELIZABETH KING (24) Servant (Charles Smith) (Emma Gadsby)
Andrew Bryers - Labourer Thomas King - Carrier

25 DEC 1882 THOMAS BURTON (28) Miner (James Burton)
(Bs) ANN DARBY (19) of St Andrew's, Whitwick (Mary Bancroft)
Joseph Burton - Labourer William Darby - Labourer

— FEB 1884 WILLIAM ROBINSON of Swannington -
(Bs only) FANNY EDWARDS of this pa. -
— [N.B. Married at St George's, Swannington 11 March 1884]

— DEC 1884 WILLIAM MOTT of All Saints, Loughborough -
(Bs only) SELINA KING of this pa. -
— [N.B. Married at All Saints, Loughborough 25 Dec 1884]

JUN/JUL 1885 EDWARD EDMUND SERRES of this pa. -
(Bs only) [1] BERTHA SAUNDERS of pa. of St Peters, Baywater -
—

— DEC 1885 SAM BENNETT of Midway in pa. of Hartshorne -
(Bs only) ELLEN BAKER of this pa. -
—

16 FEB 1886 JOSEPH KING (34) Farmer (John Smith)
(Bs) MARY JANE SMITH (29) - (Clara Perry)
Joseph King - Labourer John Smith - F.W.K.

13 NOV 1886 GEORGE HICKLING (25) of Breedon on the Hill. Labourer
(Bs) EMMA RICHARDS (17) - (Alice Richards) (Samuel Hargraves)
Isaac Hickling - Miner Samuel Richards - Labourer

11 APR 1887 JOHN ANDREW WOOD (21) of Great Wyrley, Staffs. Grocer
(Bs) EMMA GADSBY (24) - (Frederick William Wood) (Millicent Gadsby)
John Wood - Grocer Charles Gadsby - Labourer

[1] Bay[s]water is in the Paddington/Kensington area of London.

05 JUL 1888 GEORGE BAKER (23) Labourer (Walter Israel Bradley)
(Bs) SARAH SMITH (23) Servant (Harriett Baker)
Levi Baker - Labourer Isaac Smith - Labourer
17 SEP 1888 WILLIAM NORTH (19) of Rothby. Shoemaker (Charles Smith)
(Bs) ADA BURTON (19) Servant (Bertha Burton)
Charles North - Labourer William Burton – Miner
02 MAY 1889 FREDERIC DRAPER (26) of St Albans, Herts. Commissione Agent
(Bs) ANNIE SMITH (26) Servant (John Hill) (Clara Hill)
William Draper - Civil Servant Hugh Smith - Brewer
– SEP 1889 HENRY MEE of this pa. -
(Bs only) MARY NEWBOLD of St Martins, Leicester -
– [N.B. Marriage not recorded at St Martins, Leicester]
26 SEP 1889 JOHN JOHNSON COWLISHAW (29) of St Chads, Derby. Coast Guardsman
(Bs) PHOEBE DARBY (29) Servant (Elizabeth Ann Darby)
Joseph Cowlishaw - Printer George Darby - Labourer (Samuel Darby)
04 NOV 1889 WILLIAM SMITH (22) of Braunstone. Labourer (Charles Smith)
(Bs) MARY ANN BURTON (20) Servant (Sarah Smith)
William Smith - Labourer William Burton - Miner
25 DEC 1889 FRANK ARTHUR KELHAM (21) of Hathern. F.W.K. (Martha Caldwell)
(Bs) FLORENCE KING (20) Servant (John Edward Mitchell)
Samuel Kelham - F.W.K. John William King - Miner
15 FEB 1890 JOHN GREEN (20) of The Oaks. Labourer (William Green)
(Bs) MARY ANN BILLING (19) - (Emma Grimley)
Thomas Green - Labourer Joseph Billing - Blacksmith
FEB/MAR1890 JOHN HENRY HAYS of St Lukes, Derby -
(Bs only) ELEANOR MARY HINDS of this pa. -
—
27 SEP 1890 JOHN SPRINGTHORPE (22) of Worthington. Miner (Elias Darby)
(Bs) LOUISA DARBY (20) - (Ellen Darby)
John Springthorpe - Miner Samuel Darby - Labourer
01 JUN 1891 ALBERT HINDS (20) of St Barnabas, Derby. Coachman
(Bs) ANNIE LOUISA HOLT (20) - (Percy Austin Hinds) (Violet Ann Hinds)
George Hinds - Miner Edwin Holt - Green Grocer
29 JUN 1891 JARVIS MILWARD (26) Miner (John Andrew Wood)
(Bs) MILLICENT GADSBY (26) - (Bessie Milward)
James Milward - Labourer Charles Gadsby - Publican

8. INDEX

Surnames have been indexed as they were spelt in the original documents, which may differ significantly from the modern spelling and the reader is advised to look under all variants of a name. The index also includes the surnames of marriage witnesses, fathers of the bride & groom, marriage bonds-men and those names that appear in the footnotes. The index does *not* indicate the number of times a particular surname appears on a page.

C

D

E

F

G

H

I

N

O

P

Q

R

S

T

U

V

W

EACH SURNAME MAY APPEAR SEVERAL TIMES ON EACH PAGE

Y